D0326979

The Inventive Organization

Jill Janov

The Inventive Organization

HOPE
AND
DARING
AT
WORK

 Jossey-Bass Publishers
San Francisco

Copyright © 1994 by Jossey-Bass Inc., Publishers, 350 Sansome Street, San Francisco, California 94104. Copyright under International, Pan American, and Universal Copyright Conventions. All rights reserved. No part of this book may be reproduced in any form—except for brief quotation (not to exceed 1,000 words) in a review or professional work—without permission in writing from the publishers.

Excerpts from Kenneth Patchen, *Hallelujah Anyway*. Copyright © 1966 by Kenneth Patchen. Reprinted by permission of New Directions Pub. Co.

Excerpts from THE WISDOM OF THE SANDS by Antoine de Saint-Exupery, copyright 1950 and renewed 1978 by Harcourt Brace & Company, reprinted by permission of the publisher.

Substantial discounts on bulk quantities of Jossey-Bass books are available to corporations, professional associations, and other organizations. For details and discount information, contact the special sales department at Jossey-Bass Inc., Publishers. (415) 433-1740; Fax (415) 433-0499.

For international orders, please contact your local Paramount Publishing International office.

TCF Manufactured in the United States of America on Lyons Falls Pathfinder Tradebook. This paper is acid-free and 100 percent totally chlorine-free.

Library of Congress Cataloging-in-Publication Data

Janov, Jill, date.
 The inventive organization : hope and daring at work / Jill Janov. — 1st ed.
  p. cm. — (The Jossey-Bass management series)
 Includes bibliographical references and index.
 ISBN 1-55542-627-1
 1. Organizational change. 2. Organizational effectiveness.
I. Title. II. Series.
HD58.8.J36 1994
658.4'06—dc20   93-48661
                                                  CIP

FIRST EDITION
HB Printing   10 9 8 7 6 5 4 3 2   *Code 9439*

The Jossey-Bass
Management Series

*For Ted
and the next generation—
for whom leading and following
are in everyone's domain*

Contents

Preface

In recent years, organizations have been entangled in a plethora of programs, techniques, processes, and theories that beckoned because they held out *the promise of hope* — the hope that we could solve our organizational problems and realize our collective aspiration to achieve lasting success. Many people in organizations have implemented some or all of these programs and processes, often in the face of great resistance that infrequently is overcome and more often never abates. But the difficulties we experience are not in the programs we initiate; the difficulties are in our relationships. We cannot revitalize our organizations by implementing new initiatives. We can only revitalize them when we reframe how we think about the relationships required to get work done.

The Inventive Organization: Hope and Daring at Work is drawn from my own relationships with my work, with my clients whom I serve as a consultant, and with my colleagues with whom I consult. It is based on twenty-seven years of organizational experience, seeing what happens when people are fully engaged with their endeavors, and attending to those organizational relationships that make such engagement possible.

This book contains new frameworks that help us make new meaning from our organizational experiences. It is not a quick-fix book, nor is it full of recipes that can be applied regardless of organizational context, history, strategy, structure, or support mechanisms. If you take the time to read it, it will cause you to think about how you think and about what is required for people to work collaboratively to serve self and others.

This book contains practical applications from stories about the hardships, struggles, risks, dreams, and passions of those who go beyond what is expected, who focus on *potential* and not simply *what is*. It is about *hope — the possibilities of recreating our organizational relationships by daring to leave the comfort zone of our old perspectives and assumptions to find and use the power and richness inherent in those institutions we call organizations.*

Our current notions about organizational relationships developed during the Industrial Era — an era recently ended and characterized by mass production, centralized operations, steep hierarchies, and command-and-control environments where a few made decisions for the many who did the work. We are now in a transition, entering the Information Era. This new era is characterized by mass customization, global competition, and the need to continuously enhance organizational capacities to learn, imagine, and create. Our success in this era depends on our readiness to act — on consistently having the right people with the right skills and information at the right place at the right time. We are no longer served by rigid, steep hierarchies that constrict organizational relationships and, ultimately, organizational performance. What we need now are flexible, flatter structures based on organizational relationships of partnership, self-regulation, and interdependence.

The changes we need in our organizational relationships are more than cosmetic. Real change is not simply a matter of creating teams to replace individual contributors or renaming roles — changing manager to coach and employees to work associates. The change we need is more subtle and more complex. It is *a change in what we assume and how we think about work and, more importantly, the relationships needed to get work done.*

This book is about how to develop these relationships. It is about what we must *dare* in order to enrich the relationships between individuals and the means by which they produce, between work associates, and between the enterprise and its customers, stakeholders, and suppliers. It is about the potential for realizing our *hopes,* through something I call the *inventive organization.* Primarily it is about how we can rethink the stereotyped roles of leaders and followers and uncover the underlying acts of leading and following so that we can create *inventive* organizations — ones capable of consistently learning and improving.

We can create inventive organizations when we consistently seek to uncover and challenge our underlying assumptions about relationships, control, and power and when we commit ourselves to learning and understanding more about

- What creates success — for ourselves and others
- The wisdom in our "mistakes"
- The people who use our products and services
- The essential work that creates or exceeds our customers' satisfaction
- What it means to be self-regulating, whether we work in teams or are individual contributors
- Our relationships with ourselves and one another
- Our own processes of discovery

AUDIENCE

The Inventive Organization is for managers, organization development professionals, and other agents of change who are willing to consider organizational competence and long-term viability as outcomes of organizational relationships—relationships between those who follow and those who lead, between those who work directly together and those whose work is separate but allied, between those who produce and those who consume.

OVERVIEW OF THE CONTENTS

This book is organized in four parts. Part One covers the *problem* and the *promise*. In the first chapter, I write about the problem—why we are hurting in spite of all our efforts to implement new programs and techniques. Chapter 2 is about a *third path* I call *the inventive organization*. The inventive organization is one with the capacity to anticipate and lead change. It is differentiated from *fixed organizations*, which ignore change until their survival is threatened, and *adaptive organizations*, which respond to change but only in an effort to maintain the status quo.

Part Two is about *hope*. It covers the *six frameworks* that *underlie inventive organizations*. Chapter 3 focuses on *customer requirements* and our need to develop organizations in which everyone has "line of sight"—direct knowledge of how their endeavors contribute to end user satisfaction. Chapter 4 describes the importance of differentiating between *core work*, which is essential, and support work. It emphasizes our need to structure our organizations based on end user requirements and the core work that enables us to meet and exceed these requirements. Chapter 5 is about how our *values* create our organizational relationships. In particular it differentiates between words and deeds in how we relate to our customers, our work associates, and the work itself. Chapter 6 is about why we need to *think systemically*—to see an organization as a series of relationships and to understand that each of these relationships is a microcosm and a mirror image of all other organizational relationships. Chapter 7 covers *self-regulation* and how it relates to our needs for support and control regardless of the job we are in. Self-regulation is different from regulation by policies and hierarchy. It can only occur when each of us has the support and control we need to work collaboratively in pursuit of our common cause. It occurs when our organizational responsibilities are commensurate with our authority, which enables us to be accountable for the outcomes of our actions. Chapter 8 introduces *interdependence* as a mind set — a way of thinking and doing that creates partnership and enables us to act in service and support of the entire enterprise rather than in self-serving and ultimately self-defeating ways.

Part Three of this book is about *daring — the bold acts of leading and following that sustain inventive organizations.* It introduces the notion that organizational relationships are not based on the traditional roles we have identified as leader and follower. Rather, our organizational relationships are created out of our own internal dialogue — a dialogue that causes us to choose whether we will lead or follow, guide or pursue, in any given circumstance. These acts of leading and following are depicted in two models, each of which contains three dimensions — personal power, style, and expertise. Chapter 9 introduces the models. In Chapter 10, personal power is differentiated from role power. Personal power is based on trust and integrity, and it is the only power that is lasting in our organizational relationships. Chapter 11 differentiates styles of leading and following that reinforce old hierarchical structures of "one up, one down" — autocracy and dependency — from styles of leading and following that create partnerships. Chapter 12 covers the kind of leading and following expertise that supports inventive rather than fixed or adaptive organizations.

Part Four of this book is about how to manage the transition that occurs when our organizational relationships change from command and control to self-regulation and interdependence, and when our organizations move from fixed or adaptive to inventive. Chapter 13 is about how to support and sustain new acts of leading and following that reinvent organizational relationships. Chapter 14, the final chapter of this book, contains some of my *hopes* for the remainder of this decade and some musings on what we must *dare* if we are to remain inventive.

The Inventive Organization is about the world of work — a world of hopes and fears. I wrote this book partly to help heal the wounds inflicted by the fears that we experience in our workplaces. And mostly I wrote this book to understand more fully what I have learned about courage and hope — my own and others — in our quest to make work an enriching contribution to ourselves and humankind. This book may engage your defenses because it is not always easy to grasp new ways of thinking about what is already familiar. My hope is that it will open your eyes by helping you to see old things anew while it supports you in daring to achieve your deepest aspirations in those endeavors we call work and in that community we call organization.

San Francisco, California   Jill Janov
February 1994

Appreciation

This book is the result of twenty-seven years of corporate experience in which I have had the good fortune to learn from many outstanding individuals. To David Rees (First Interstate Bancorporation) and Carl Philipp (The Automobile Club of Southern California), my deep appreciation for your trust and confidence in me and for providing me with opportunities to learn and contribute simultaneously. To my mentor, the late Dr. Maurice Mann (The Federal Home Loan Bank of San Francisco), I am ever grateful for his inspired leadership and support, which led to the development of an organization where continuous improvement, learning, and service to the total system were, quite simply and profoundly, the only way to do business.

To my clients, with whom I am in a partnership of discovery, I am deeply indebted. Your willingness to "test the envelope" has provided the learning, inspiration, and experience from which this book is written. Many thanks to Eldon Arden, who coined the term "entrenched assumptions" and whose work at 3M Corporation is truly inspired. I am also indebted to Patrick Williams and the late David Peters, the cofounders of the Masters of Organization Development Program at Pepperdine University, who guided my journey through the theory and concepts of OD. As well, I am indebted to Edwin Nevis, Elaine Kempner, Claire Stratford, John Carter, Jeffrey Voorhees, and Gwendolyn Wade of the Gestalt Institute in Cleveland. My participation in GIC's Organization and System Development Program provided rich learning around many of the processes and theories contained in this book.

From the beginning of 1987 to the end of 1990, I had the good fortune to be a member of Block Petrella Weisbord, a firm that has a stellar reputation in organization development. I feel privileged to know and have worked with such remarkable colleagues, whose wisdom, vision, and support enriched and accelerated my learning. In particular, I wish to thank and commend my colleague, Kathleen Emery, whose recent and untimely death has created a great loss for me and the many hundreds of people whose lives she touched. Kathleen collaborated with me on the Xerox program for leaders of self-regulated teams. It was this program, which Xerox titled Manager as Work Group Developer, that led to the writing of this book. I am deeply indebted to Tony Petrella and Marvin Weisbord, who inspired me and facilitated my understanding of whole-systems work; to Peter Block for his active encouragement to develop my own vision of organizational greatness; to Jim Maselko for his enthusiastic support and tireless efforts to secure opportunities for me to test my ideas with organizations in the United States and internationally; to Davidson Jones, whose consulting skill, energy, and commitment enriched several projects on which we co-consulted; and to John Dupre and Dominick Volini, who have contributed greatly to BPWs work with whole-systems improvement. To Kay Callaghan, Lynda Caccitori, and Gloria Co, my gratitude for all your efforts at Block Petrella Weisbord—you made it not only possible but so much easier to do the challenging work of consulting during some of the writing of this book. To Kellie Nordby, my deep appreciation for all the hours, technical ingenuity, and creativity that resulted in the layout and endless revisions of the models in this book.

To the Organization Effectiveness Group at Xerox Corporation, which included Bob Mann, Bob Barstatis, Paul Robilliard, Rich Thier, Bob Barachevsky, Jim Vanderbeck, Dick Shermach, and Pam Klobucher, my great appreciation for your commitment to the process of developing the Manager as Work Group Developer program. And to Chuck Ray, Vice President for Customer Services at Xerox, my deep gratitude for supporting and enhancing the writing of this book by securing permission for me to tell the Xerox story and supplying the historical data contained in these chapters. I am also indebted to Jim McCown, Region Operations Manager; Pat Perry, District Manager; Mike Vigil, Field Manager; and Cathy Shuffield, Customer Service Specialist for their willingness to share their experiences from Manager as Work Group Developer in several national conferences in the United States and Canada. Their learnings about and understanding of self-regulating workforces has enriched others from many companies seeking to create more support and control at every level of their system.

I am extremely grateful to Judith Schuster, friend and colleague, who provided many valuable observations about the first draft of my manuscript as well as options for presenting my ideas. A big thank you goes to my father, who painstakingly combed the original manuscript and told me he had "caught all my mispelled (*sic*) words" and who provided extensive comments that enabled me to clarify my thinking. I also am indebted to Sybil Perlmutter and Rick Eigenbrod, whose willingness to engage in a continuing dialogue has added immeasurably to the development of this material. And to my family and friends, thank you for your enthusiasm for this project and for your patience with my long hours at the computer. Your support and encouragement helped me stick to my writing.

A book cannot be written without some conviction that it may be of use to others. John Hassett's abiding love, friendship, and belief in me encouraged me to dare to write. Pat Murray's insight, wisdom, counsel, supportive feedback, and unconditional regard for me reignited my commitment to complete this endeavor, which at times I wanted to abandon. And both of these men have supported my continued development in ways that may or may not be known to them.

Finally, my thanks to the wonderful people at Jossey-Bass. First to Cedric Crocker, whose support sustained my hope of getting this book published and who dared me to continue to sculpt my material when my energy waned for completing the process. His skill and perception guided the completion of the final manuscript and helped me find a clearer voice to state my convictions. I am very appreciative of Bill Hicks, who invited me to write this book and whose commitment to getting it published helped me to stay the course. To Mary Garrett, who managed the process that made a bound volume of my manuscript, I am enormously thankful—and particularly for her selection of Kate Fuller as my manuscript editor. Kate's editorial gifts grace this book, and for her enthusiasm, warmth, and care with my writing, I am forever grateful.

It is perhaps unusual to thank the pre-readers of a book, particularly because most often their names are not made known to an author. I was lucky enough to learn the names of some of the people who read my manuscript. I wish to thank Peter Block, Alan Briskin, Aubrey Cramer, Frank Basler, Jr., and Jeff Voorhees for so clearly delineating how I could pare down a 476-page tome into a more readable and flowing text.

J.J.

The Author

Jill Janov is a native of California and lives in San Francisco. She is the founder of Jill Janov Associates, a consulting firm that works internationally with a variety of Fortune 500 corporations, medium and small privately held companies, government agencies, educational institutions, and nonprofit organizations. Her firm works with people at all levels of the organization—from assembly line workers to CEOs.

During the first four years of her career, she earned her living as a writer, first as a copywriter, then as editor of a trade publication, and then as publications manager for a real estate development company. In 1970, a recession in California ended her work as a writer, but her communication skills brought her to the attention of The Automobile Club of Southern California, where she joined the management training and development staff. In 1976, she was named to head up Human Resources for The Federal Home Loan Bank of San Francisco, which was followed by a stint at Levi Strauss & Co. as manager of Human Resources Development. Jill received her master of science degree in organization development in 1982 from Pepperdine University and then headed

Human Resources for The Federal National Mortgage Association in Washington, D.C., before becoming an external consultant.

In 1987, Jill merged her consulting practice with Block Petrella Weisbord. In 1989, she completed an eighteen-month program in Organization and System Development at the Gestalt Institute in Cleveland and, after eight years on the East Coast, returned to California. In 1991 she founded Jill Janov Associates.

Her firm's focus is on developing organizations that lead change through employee and stakeholder involvement. Her primary work is in two areas. She consults on whole-systems improvement initiatives, in which those who do the work have responsibility for designing the technical and social systems in which they work, and on how to manage self-regulating workforces, whether people work in teams or are individual contributors.

She is affiliated with Design Learning, a Plainfield, New Jersey, training firm, whose programs develop the person at work and redistribute accountability and control in workplaces. Through DL, she is a frequent presenter on empowerment and how to manage self-regulating workplaces.

Although her primary office is in San Francisco, she is an avid skier and spends as much of the winter as possible in Park City, Utah, where she completed this book.

The Inventive Organization

PART ONE

THE PROBLEM
AND THE PROMISE

We in the United States have been very good at creating and producing. Ours is the nation that created the means for mass production and, in so doing, defined the standard for greatness in the Industrial Era. But the processes and assumptions that worked well then no longer serve us. We are now in the Information Era, and the standard for greatness has changed from "best in America" to "world class." The processes by which we compete are no longer based on our ability to achieve fixed standards; they are based on our capacity for continuous improvement. In judging effectiveness, we are no longer confined to the technology of production. Effectiveness today involves the creation and maintenance of relationships among customers and suppliers, among those who toil together, and between individuals and their places of work.

Our ability to achieve our highest potential at work now rests on the relationships we create. Until recently, our focus on these relationships has been ancillary to our focus on creating products and services. We will not be able to duplicate or surpass our previous organizational achievements until we understand more about organizational relationships as the

1

key to our individual and collective futures. If we can reframe our relationships, we can revitalize ourselves and reinvent our organizations.

To invent is to create the unexpected. It is to seek the unfamiliar, to go beyond what is customary, to leap to non-conformity. Invention is difficult because we are conditioned to conform and we are often constrained by how we think. To examine our conditioning and to break our constraints, we must think about how we think. We must uncover the assumptions that underlie our thoughts and that ultimately dictate the nature of our relationships, the scope of our actions, and the meaning we make of our experience.

It is rare to find people who want to continuously reinvent their organizations. There is challenge enough in steering a steady course through the myriad challenges of the status quo. To reinvent is to risk the status quo, even when it seems to be working. We all favor certainty over uncertainty, the familiar over the unfamiliar, the conventional over the unconventional. When we achieve what we believe is a degree of safety in our organizational lives, we often consciously and unconsciously rationalize the merits of "the way we do things around here." Such rationalization depletes the energy required to start anew, which is what invention is all about.

Many of us start out wanting to make a difference in our organizations by creating relationships in which work can be good for everyone, not just a few, and by developing workplaces where everyone is valued as an asset to be nurtured rather than treated as an extension of the means of production. What accounts for the erosion and eventual loss of our early aspiration? Somehow, in our need for safety, acceptance, a sense of belonging, and the affection and esteem of others, we endure the hardships that result when we conform to prescribed roles. Rather than seek emergent relationships, we choose not to confront outmoded processes and structures. This organizational phenomenon of perpetuating the status quo was vividly illustrated by my son, Ted, in his experience as an initiate and then leader of his high school boy's club.

Ted grew up in one of the small incorporated cities in the East Bay, near San Francisco. Most of the families in our community were in upper-income or upper-middle-income brackets. And although our city was small and had no train service, we still had the proverbial demarcations known as the "right side" and "wrong side" of the "tracks." We lived in what was called the "lower" section of the town. Both the lower and upper sections fed into one high school, which had two boy's clubs, each with thirty members. Invitations to join a club were coveted as signs that you were part of the "in" group—the elite. Invitations were rarely offered to boys from the "lower" section of town, but Ted was invited to join both clubs. These invitations meant he had been anointed.

Ted pledged the club called the Rigmas. As part of his initiation process, he had to make a long, thick wooden paddle, with several quarter-sized holes drilled through it. When he turned this weapon over to the leaders of the club, they told him he would be kidnapped and taken to an undisclosed place at an undisclosed time to be paddled with it. Ted and his friend, Mike Finn, another initiate, talked endlessly about their fears of this ceremony. To avoid kidnap, they hid every day after school. On weekends, they left the community to hide. Even so, after about four weeks, they were kidnapped and paddled. The paddlings were not as bad as they feared, but Ted vowed that one day he would have enough influence to change this ceremony so no one else would have to go through the awful weeks of fright that he and Mike had experienced. He had submitted to the rites of initiation as a price for inclusion. He had subordinated his fear of being paddled to the fear of not belonging. He had, at that moment in his young life, bartered his soul, just as so many followers barter their souls, for the presumed safety of being part of an organization.

Three years later, Ted became an officer of the club. When I asked if he was going to change the initiation ceremony, he replied, "Mom, I had to go through it and it wasn't so bad. It's just part of the process. No one really gets hurt."

I hear Ted's words echo in my head when I talk to executives who have gone through similar rites of passage. They, too, paid their dues in joining organizations and climbing corporate hierarchies. Early in their careers, many promised themselves that they would not create for others what they had experienced as subordinates—too little say about how their work should be done, a sense of being underutilized and overcontrolled, and little or no access to information they needed to do their best work and understand the big picture. Upon becoming executives, however, many find themselves doing to others what they disliked when it was done to them. What appears to be a loss of memory actually results from the gradual absorption of the assumptions underlying successive processes of initiation that accompany the climb up the corporate ladder.

Today more than ever before, we need to question our entrenched assumptions about organizational structures and practices that cause us to behave in ways that threaten our viability. Rapid changes are affecting every aspect of our operations. We need greater skills and everyone's participation in anticipating and addressing these changes. We need fluid organizations; yet, paradoxically, the impact of change creates a stultifying need for certainty—a need for control. Among our entrenched practices is the vesting of control in a few, who then have power over the many. The few, however, never feel completely in control, and the many stifle their impulses to contribute in order to play by the rules of the game—play it safe.

Today more than ever before, we need to discard our need to exalt the role of management—an exaltation based on both managers' and subordinates' expectation that management should have all the answers. When we believe that management has to have all the answers, we constrain the potential in our organization. We constrain the wisdom inherent in everyone in the entire organization in exchange for a false sense that a designated few—management—can control both resources and production. In truth, today's managers control only resources: subordinates control production. Worse yet, when we need to believe that some person or persons have all the answers, we fuel the need for someone to have all the answers.

Finally, today more than ever before, we must give up our wish for others to ensure the viability of our organizations. We can no longer afford the luxury of believing that others will be responsible for us if they are granted the power and perquisites associated with climbing the hierarchy and becoming "members of the management club." We all feel the need to preserve our position and livelihood, and that need can easily override the knowledge of how best to serve and support the entire organization, regardless of whether we are called managers or subordinates.

What we need most today are organizational structures and hierarchies that exist only to link diverse efforts, not to confer status. When our status is derived from our position in the hierarchy, we focus on preserving that status rather than on providing service to the entire system. When we seek to preserve status, we also wind up preserving the status quo. Ultimately we decrease our organizational value because hierarchies that confer status constrain those who are seen as not having status from contributing to the organization. When the opportunity to contribute is limited, the potential to create satisfaction — in relationships with customers, work associates, and the work itself — is limited.

It is now common to experience less and less job satisfaction at the same time that work is demanding more and more of our time and attention. How did we get here? And more important, how can we change things?

The first chapter of this book is about why we are hurting. While the reasons may sound familiar, it is more important to understand the underlying assumptions that once served us and that have led to our current struggles. The second chapter is about a way out of our current quandary. It introduces the idea of *inventive* organizations, differentiating these from the *fixed* and *adaptive* organizations that served us well in the Industrial Era but are too inflexible for the Information Era. These chapters set the stage for Part Two, which addresses our hopes that there are, indeed, new frameworks that will invigorate our willingness to risk and experiment, that work can become a creative act instead of a reaction, and that everyone who contributes to an enterprise — employees, customers, suppliers, and stakeholders — can experience deep levels of satisfaction and success.

1

Why Are We Confused and Hurting at Work?

Today, when I ask people to describe their work environments, most respond, "Chaotic." At every level of the corporate hierarchy people feel pushed and pulled in multiple directions. Stated simply, they report that "the harder we work, the faster we go, the more nothing seems to change." This stress is primarily attributable to three things. First, we made the uncomplicated complicated when we inadvertently traded the wisdom of basic principles—such as "Do unto others as you would have them do unto you"—for the wizardry of technology and techniques that track our ineffectiveness when we *do not* do unto others as we would have them do unto us. Second, we have seduced ourselves into thinking that we can adopt new methods and programs without changing our operating principles and beliefs. Third, we have confused activities and programs with results—means and ends.

WE CONFUSE MEANS AND ENDS

Activities and programs are addictive. If one is good for the organization, ten must be better. What is worse, activities and programs take on lives of their own. Too often, we find ourselves spending all our energies to sustain activities and programs rather than produce results.

The Nuclear Group of a large utility company provides an example of what usually happens when an organization implements multiple improvement initiatives simultaneously. In this case, these initiatives were undertaken in response to the Nuclear Regulatory Agency's shutdown of one of the company's power plants for a nontechnical reason. (A nontechnical reason means the fault lies in management practices, culture, communications, and/or organizational values.) As a result of the shutdown, the old chief executive officer retired and the utility named a new CEO to head the Nuclear Group. The new man was a seasoned professional who had a stellar reputation in the industry. He was seen as a visionary, charismatic leader who knew how to spearhead change.

The new CEO joined the Nuclear Group with two clear mandates: to get the plant restarted and to complete the building of two other reactors on time and within budget. During the next three years, he directed two major reorganizations of the Nuclear Group, which included some 2,900 employees. New people were hired for senior positions, some from within and some from outside the company. Multiple improvement initiatives were started, all in an effort to become a "world-class operation." In the midst of all this change, the CEO decided to try implementing work groups. He had visited nuclear plants in Sweden and other parts of the world. He had seen teams create enhanced efficiencies that he believed needed to be duplicated in the United States.

As a consultant to organizations, I am frequently asked to help companies create self-managed teams. Like the CEO of the utility company, many of those who call me have read numerous articles and books about companies that have snatched success from failure by empowering their workforces through the creation of autonomous work groups. Thus the group or team concept is seen as an end in itself, rather than as a means to an end.

In my initial conversation with the CEO, we decided to start with a feasibility study, rather than a pilot for a team concept. A feasibility study is a readiness assessment. It helps a client determine if the requisite leadership, energy, and business opportunity exist to support work redesign. Work redesign affects the whole system. It empowers the entire workforce to determine the best organizational structure, processes, work flows, and practices to achieve desired organizational results.

My colleague, Davidson Jones, and I interviewed 270 employees (almost 10 percent of the organization) who represented all levels and all functions within the Nuclear Group and included some individuals from the corporate level. In the process of this study, we discovered that twenty-seven major change efforts had been started during the past three years. These efforts included changes in technology, reporting, and accounting procedures, as well as supervisory initiatives, quality initiatives, training programs, work rule changes, and redrawn organizational boundaries, to name a few. A work redesign effort was the last thing the Nuclear Group needed at this time. Rather than reducing what interviewees had reported as chaos within the system, redesign would add to it. Not only would it be viewed as just another program, there simply was not enough energy in the system to undertake this total-system initiative at that particular time.

I called the CEO with a work-in-progress report. I told him we would recommend against work redesign at this time. However, we felt we could assist him in another way. There was a long pause. Then he said, "I am relieved and I am impressed." He, too, had begun to realize that there was no energy in the system to start anything new until the initiatives already under way were successfully implemented.

Our recommendation to the Nuclear Group was to have those who were spearheading each of the twenty-seven improvement initiatives meet with the CEO and members of the senior management team, who were his direct reports. Together they would determine the viability of each initiative as well as its sequence and relationship to other initiatives. Each change effort would be assessed against its impact on these factors:

- *Customer requirements*
- *The strategy developed to meet or exceed these requirements*
- *The essential work that meets or exceeds customer requirements*
- *The espoused values of the Nuclear Group*

It was our belief that some of these efforts needed to be better aligned, some needed to be sequenced differently, and some needed to be dropped. Our recommendation, which was a far cry from self-managed teams, called for the same systems framework used in work redesign.

Today, it is commonplace to find organizations in overdrive when it comes to improvement initiatives. One of my client's colleagues describes it this way: "We have a full-time job to begin with, and then they give us projects." Consider these examples:

- A plant with three hundred employees manufacturing silver halide film had created eighty teams in an effort to respond to changing environmental demands. The teams represented the newly appointed plant manager's effort to get everyone involved in improving operations and feeling ownership for the plant's success. People had no time to do their work because they were too tied up with team meetings.

- In another organization, a work group strategy was part of a collective bargaining agreement. Twenty-five hundred employees were launched into work groups over a three-year period. During the same time, the plant built and moved into a new facility, adopted all new technology, eliminated many existing products, introduced several new products, and implemented a new corporate manufacturing requirements planning system (MRP).

■   In yet another organization, the corporate head of Human Resources (HR) had benchmarked Xerox Corporation after it won the Malcolm Baldrige Award. He learned that Xerox had one HR person for every ninety-three employees. His corporation had one HR person for every fifty-seven employees. He announced a target of one HR person for every seventy-five employees, which was to be achieved in one year. Forty-seven decentralized HR functions began to search separately for ways to achieve this goal, which had been set without assessing the needs of the different sites served by each of them. The site that called me wanted to investigate self-managed teams as a way to reduce their current ratio, which resulted, in part, from a lack of technology. Paradoxically, the company, which manufactures computer technology, does not have an effective human resources information system.

Are these examples of Machiavellian madness? No! More often than not, undertakings like these are honest attempts to respond to perceived or actual opportunities and threats in an organization's external operating environment. Unfortunately, those who initiate multiple change efforts often are unaware of their effects further down the hierarchy. The first real need is to build awareness throughout the organization of current threats and opportunities, and to create a clear image of a desired future state out of everyone's perceptions and commitments. The need to build this foundation may be obscured by preoccupations with such things as self-managed teams, the plethora of programs known by three-letter acronyms, and the Malcolm Baldrige Award. These are means, not ends in and of themselves. When means become confused with ends, organizations get trapped into reacting to circumstances in their operating environments. Worse yet, the common focus shifts from results to activities. The result is frequently something I call the dried peas syndrome—a metaphor I learned in the world of advertising and one that has great applicability to organizations.

WE KEEP LOSING OUR FOCUS:
THE DRIED PEAS SYNDROME

I learned about the dried peas syndrome from a senior art director at a large West Coast advertising agency, where I worked early in my career as a junior copywriter. He gave a workshop for copywriters on how to write billboard slogans that could be grasped by people driving by at sixty miles an hour. He began his presentation by reaching under the podium and pulling out a volleyball. He threw the ball out to his surprised audience and yelled "catch." A man caught the ball. The art director then reached under the podium and grabbed two volleyballs and threw them out. They, too, were caught by two different people. Then he threw an orange, which was caught. Next, he threw two oranges, which were caught. Then he threw five oranges. Two were caught and three hit the floor. Finally, he threw out a handful of dried peas. They scattered everywhere. He told the copywriters that people driving sixty miles an hour could read billboards with one or two volleyballs or one or two oranges. Multiple oranges and dried peas got lost. He then showed us slides of billboards and we called out, "That one has one volleyball." "That one has two oranges." "Oops, that one is full of dried peas!"

I often think of the dried peas syndrome when I hear of multiple improvement programs thrown out by well-intentioned executives who are unaware that their initiatives are scattering all over the plant floor, much like that handful of dried peas. Simply stated, there are too many initiatives to be understood, much less implemented simultaneously. We no sooner gear up for one major change effort in our work processes, our technology, or the way we lead or follow, than we are hit with another major change initiative.

Through the miracles of technology, we can now generate more data than we can possibly use. Almost weekly, we find new buzzwords creeping into our vocabulary—such as "world class" and "total quality management"—and sometimes we adopt the words as if we have achieved the results they convey. We are deluged with invitations to conferences on quality and employee involvement. We are afflicted with a malady my friend Elaine Curran calls "management by best-seller": we purchase and distribute in quantity books that chronicle the lessons learned by others because they hold out the promise of shortcuts to success. And we are enticed by programs that go by three-letter acronyms—TEI, VAM, TPM, JIT, SPC, QIP, EIP, MRP, EAP, CAD, CAM, CIM, CIE, EDI, MBO, ZBB, TQI—which we try to implement with such fervor and rapidity that employees at one consumer products company call them "flavor of the month." (To me, they sound like alphabet soup.) All too often these initiatives turn our attention toward doing activities and away from achieving results.

WE TAKE ACTION
WITHOUT AWARENESS

Prior to World War II, the United States was the world's benchmark of success. We created the means for mass production. We formulated ways to manage large-scale production through unity of command and span of control. As we moved into the late Industrial Era, we perfected organizational structures that allowed for the control of many by a few. It was not until the late 1960s, when we were engaged in a debilitating war in Vietnam and all our social institutions were under attack, that we became aware of the possibilities for formidable international competition—not from Europe, but from Japan. Our awareness was not keen enough to make us question our entrenched assumptions about what creates organizational success. So we continued with "business as usual"—until some of our industrial giants began to lose significant market share and profitability. It was only when we were confronted by Japanese competitors, who were flooding many markets with goods superior in quality and lower in cost, that U.S. companies in the manufacturing sector were forced to review their operations. Their reviews uncovered problems like these:

- Underutilized and often wasted human resources
- Redundant jobs
- Fragmented operations
- Often complacent or apathetic employees who had learned only too well to leave their brains at the door and do as they were told

To regain their competitive advantage, U.S. companies began to undertake myriad initiatives aimed at matching the competition. These initiatives duplicated programs and processes that were credited with creating Japan's success— *kaizen*, statistical process control, problem solving and quality tools, and just-in-time inventory, to name a few. Too often these efforts resulted in the dried peas syndrome and missed the critical step necessary for sustainable improvement to occur; namely, to uncover our entrenched assumptions about (1) who really controls what, (2) what information will show which actions should be taken and who has this information, and (3) who needs to be involved for sustainable improvements to occur.

When we act too quickly, without considering who needs to be involved to bring about desired change, we most often do not achieve what we intended. Often nothing happens; hence the build-up of frustration that comes when people do as they are told and the problems stay the same or worsen. Sometimes something unintended happens. We may get some semblance of desired change, but at the cost of forcing others to comply. Forced compliance is malicious compliance, which shows up in the organization's inability to sustain desired improvement or to create enthusiasm for future change efforts.

When those "in charge" react to threats or opportunities by launching improvement initiatives without engaging those whose efforts are needed to create the desired change, the change does not occur. Worse, perceptions of these perceived opportunities or threats persist so another improvement initiative is launched. Attempts to implement program after program make it impossible to focus on any one effort. This creates the dried peas syndrome, which results in more stress for everyone. Rather than achieving intended results, these multiple initiatives build resistance, which thwarts future efforts to implement change.

In his book, *Well Made in America*, Peter Reid says it this way: "Too often companies trying to improve their manufacturing systems throw in a whole bunch of programs with no apparent interconnection — a work methods improvement program, a quality improvement program, an inventory reduction program, a cost reduction program, and so on and on. That can lead to disaster because your employees become confused, threatened and resentful" (1990, p. 162).

WE MISINTERPRET RESISTANCE

Resistance is a force for sameness. Resistance is often associated with fear of change. In actuality, resistance has more to do with fear of loss. It is our way of holding on. It is part of an ongoing internal dialogue: "should we or shouldn't we?" Resistance exists within us even when our dominant internal voice is urging change. Resistance persists if it is ignored by those who are trying to overcome it. To accomplish change, we need to understand resistance. We need to be curious about the need to hold on. We need to be willing to examine what should stay the same, what should change, and how. Another way to look at resistance is as stored energy or energy that is going in a different direction. When we see resistance as energy, we see the folly in trying to "overcome" it or "annihilate" it.

Still another way to understand resistance is as a means of protection against being overinfluenced by outside forces. When I teach at the Gestalt Institute in Cleveland, we ask people to assemble into groups according to causes they believe in, such as pro-life, pro-choice, the National Rifle Association, Mothers Against Drunk Drivers, and so on. Each group is asked to discuss and report on how it protects itself from being overly influenced by critics. All the tactics we see on the nightly news are presented; however, these tactics are seen in a new light. Rather than seen as screaming epithets or forming human barricades to communicate their point, people are seen using such tactics to protect themselves from being overly influenced. The act of resistance is the same. The interpretation of resistance is what changes.

Resistance is a universal phenomenon. It is experienced by everyone, regardless of role. Leaders can resist followers' requests to change "the way we operate," and followers can resist leaders' imperatives, coercions, or exhortations. Often there is agreement about the need for change, but this agreement is obscured by each side's view of how change can and should occur. What is resisted is not the need to change, but the way change is being conceived and implemented.

While conducting a feasibility study to determine whether a plant had the leadership, energy, and business opportunity to warrant undertaking a redesign of the way work was done, my colleague Marvin Weisbord and I were told that we were just "another flavor of the month." This was a euphemism for the plant's history of allocating people and time for corporate improvement initiatives, mainly training programs. The plant would gear up to train everyone, but before the training could be absorbed or applied, a new initiative would be announced and a new program would begin. The employees soon took the attitude that "this, too, shall pass." They experienced most of these efforts as fragmented, time-consuming, and exhausting. Most of them felt that the programs, which were intended to enhance production, actually interfered with achieving production goals.

As we toured the plant, we saw an example of what had created some of the frustration we heard expressed. Framed posters of Crosby's Quality Principles were hung all around the facility. These posters contained the four key principles taught in Crosby Quality Training workshops, which every employee had attended.

One principle is "Quality is prevention and not inspection after the fact." But although training had occurred, the organizational structure had not changed. Quality assurance (QA) was entirely separate from manufacturing. QA specialists inspected products after they were made but before they were shipped. Production employees were frustrated. They had been trained to do something the organizational structure did not enable them to do. In effect, an improvement initiative had been undertaken and training had occurred, but there had been no changes in the organization's structure and job roles that would allow the training to be used.

In this example, leaders were unaware that training alone would not change (improve) quality. Redesign of the organization's structure and job roles was required if the desired change was to be achieved. The frustration of being trained but prevented from using what they had learned made employees resistant to other improvement initiatives. When Marv and I showed up to talk about work redesign, employee resistance to yet another initiative was evident in their use of the epithet "flavor of the month." This expression indicated resistance to anything that sounded or felt like another dried pea.

Resistance is natural. When we understand it as a force for sameness, a means of protecting ourselves from being overly influenced, or as energy going in a different direction, we are more willing to explore and find ways to use the energy represented in the act of resisting. Joel Henning, an organization development (OD) consultant, says, "Passion, exuberance, and commitment are the key ingredients in employees"—meaning both leaders and followers. Jim Maselko, a valued colleague and friend, says, "You cannot buy these, coerce them, or bargain for them." But you can build them by listening to all the voices—those that persist, those that resist, those that insist, and all the other voices that exist.

Recently I worked with the Package Development Department of a consumer products company. This department includes the company's project managers, who are responsible for coordinating the launch of new products. For six months, the entire department had been grappling with redesigning its work, work processes, structure, and roles. I was asked to work with them for two days because they could not agree on how to move forward. They had collected and analyzed data—from each other and from their internal customers. And they were stuck. On the first day, we did a work design simulation called the Flying Starship Factory. The entire department worked through redesigning a traditional factory into a productive workplace.

On the morning of the second day, I asked the participants to do something they might consider high risk. I asked them to place themselves in whichever one of three categories best described them:

- *True believer*
- *Forced believer*
- *Nonbeliever*

True believers were those who thought a redesign of the department was the best way to create a future of their own choosing. Forced believers were those who thought that change was inevitable and, therefore, they should get involved with the change or not complain when the change occurred. Nonbelievers were those who saw no need to change. Two groups formed—believers and forced believers.

I asked each group to list on a flipchart all the reasons the department should stay the same and all the reasons it should change. When the groups presented their lists to each other, they found that their lists contained the same items. My intention had been to find a way for them to experience their own individual internal dialogues. Everyone had reasons to change and everyone had reasons to stay the same. In some, the voice for change was the dominant voice. In others, the voice for sameness was dominant. Looking at their own polarities allowed them to honor their own resistance. Later that day, they created three potential redesign plans for the department. Everyone was engaged in the process.

WE DICTATE RATHER
THAN BUILD COMMON CAUSE

When we view our organizations as hierarchies of roles, we necessarily assume that some of those who occupy organizational boxes can dictate to and control the work of others in the organization. In the Industrial Era, this assumption worked. In the Information Era different assumptions are required. The gist of these comes down to organizations—as assemblies of people—succeeding or failing on the nature of their relationships. The fall from grace experienced by many of our industrial giants can be directly attributed to poor relationships between the organization and its customers and suppliers, between "bosses" and "subordinates," between peers, and between internal customers and suppliers. Only when we understand the interdependencies among customers and suppliers, technology and workers, the external operating environment and the internal organizational environment, and the acts of leading or guiding and following can we overcome our current quandaries. To achieve the common organizational good in the Information Era, all organizational members—

whether we call them leaders and followers, managers and employees, or executives and subordinates—need to be aligned in the pursuit of common cause. To find out what it is possible for us to create, everyone in the organization needs to become aware of each other's corporate reality as well as the realities of the corporations' customers, suppliers, stakeholders, regulators, and shareholders.

When we acknowledge each other's needs and opinions and agree on our common cause, we are better able to determine, initiate, and implement what is required to achieve our organizational goals. We are also better able to avoid losing our focus, diffusing our efforts, and exhausting our resources—all of which lead us nowhere. When we involve those who are first to see the need for change and those who are impacted by change, we build awareness of what creates the need for change. When we listen to each other's opinions about what is going on, we create more options about how to improve what is going on. And when we measure our intended actions against our customer requirements, the essential work that meets or exceeds these requirements, and the values we want to live in our relationships with our customers, our work associates, and the work itself, we are more likely to choose the actions that will lead to our desired results.

Common cause must be built. It cannot be created by edict, announcement, or "proof by belligerent assertion." (A colleague, Elliott Green, coined this phrase. The rationale is that if the first edict does not work, we become belligerent and thereby prove what we assert.) When everyone affected participates in discussions about why and how to achieve change, awareness builds, a bigger picture of possibilities emerges, energy is mobilized, and resistance is avoided. In building common cause, we discover three important differences:

1. Seeing part of the picture as opposed to the whole picture: the whole is only visible when we understand the interdependent nature of organizational relationships and see the enriching possibilities that come from the

different vantage points and perspectives of organizational members

2. Reacting or adapting to the existing external operating environment as opposed to creating a future of everyone's choosing

3. Fragmenting our efforts and running ourselves ragged as opposed to mobilizing our energies in pursuit of a common goal

In his book, *The Fifth Discipline: The Art and Practice of the Learning Organization,* Peter Senge writes, "There are two fundamental sources of energy that can motivate organizations: fear and aspiration" (1990, p. 225). *Fear* motivates reaction or adaptation. *Aspiration* is the source of invention. The energy from aspirations — the energy of hope — encourages people to achieve goals, stimulates people to determine their mission, and inspires people to create a vision of their desired future state. To mobilize the energy inherent in aspirations, organizations develop planning processes to guide individual and group efforts. Often only a select few from the top of the organization's hierarchy are involved in these processes. When this occurs, the results are edicts that are imposed on others. When planning processes are properly designed, however, they can engage virtually everyone in creating meaningful and satisfying relationships — with customers, work associates, and the work itself. The best process is one in which, individually and collectively, organizational members (1) review the past and their learnings about themselves, the organization, and the world; (2) assess current reality, which includes the identification of major trends and developments that are affecting individuals, groups, the organization, the industry, and the world; and (3) develop alternative — likely and unlikely, desirable and undesirable — scenarios for the future; (4) honor in their actions the critical linkages between leaders and followers, people and technology, customers and suppliers, the company and the communities in which the company exists. (One of the best processes for visioning is a search conference, which has been written about extensively by my colleague, Marvin Weisbord, in his book, *Discovering Common Ground.*)

Jonas, Fry, and Srivastva (1990, p. 43) have captured the essence of the well-designed planning process: "When executives create a context for change, they are dealing with the interaction between novelty and transition, striving to translate new ideas into a plan that can be implemented. When concerned with building commitment and ownership, they are linking transition with continuity, so that those who must implement change feel less the sense of disruption and more that their contributions are valued. Finally, when executives strive to balance stability and innovation, they are concerned that respect for the old ways is not totally invalidated by a preoccupation with the new."

WE GO FROM ONE EXTREME TO ANOTHER

In seeking new ways to address perceived opportunities and threats, we are often too quick to adopt the latest business fads. Any urgency that leads us to try out quick fixes or to seek one-minute answers and surefire recipes (as if these exist), will likely cause us to move from one extreme to another. Consider these examples:

- Moving from a steep hierarchy to a flat organization
- Moving from individual contributors to "self-managed teams"
- Moving from concern for the external customer to a focus on the internal customer
- Moving from manual operations to automated operations—from low tech to high tech and from high touch to low touch

- Moving from centralized operations to decentralized operations, or vice versa
- Moving from a short-term focus to a long-term focus
- Moving from powerful staff functions to powerful line functions

And the list goes on.

When we create change out of urgency, the result is usually a new and more complex imbalance in the very system we are trying to improve. We may inadvertently let go of helpful mechanisms or neglect to secure in place aspects of the system, such as structure and roles, that are necessary to support the desired change. To avoid knee-jerk reactions to our sensations, we must pay attention to two things.

1. We can move only as quickly as the whole system can move, which means that all aspects of the system need to be considered if we are to create the *desired* change. Changes begin as alterations in our espoused values and philosophy. We are far more adept at adopting a slogan that captures our desired future state than we are at changing our implicit business assumptions and practices and processes they give rise to, which are part of our current reality. We are just beginning to learn how to design flexible organizations—ones in which it is possible to see the big picture as well as the parts and to easily align all aspects of the system so we achieve lasting, desired changes.

2. We need to beware of overcorrection. The most agile organizations are those that know how to maintain balance—to act on an awareness of the organization as multiple relationships in action.

WE DISCOUNT THE CONNECTION BETWEEN PROCESS AND RESULTS

Our world, our organizations, and we, as individuals and groups, are in the process of becoming. A process is not static;

rather, it is in motion. We reach milestones and plateaus, and our journey continues. We are at our best when we envision a destination and are willing to learn from our journey whether the destination is the correct one.

When we see ourselves and our organizations in the process of becoming, we can act with greater awareness about our process. We can better understand that how we go about change—how we make the journey—determines the outcome, the destination we reach.

When we view our enterprise as multiple relationships in action, we are better able to honor our interdependence, build common cause, and create a future of everyone's choosing. To change the destination, we must change the process by which we make the journey. To do this, we have to be willing to examine and give up some of our entrenched assumptions. Many of these beliefs may be old friends—so old we cannot be sure when they originated. Our entrenched assumptions are like boxes that contain and limit our current thinking. They allow us to act and react only in certain ways. We can do more than react or adapt to the world around us. We can use our hopes and our awareness to enlarge our thinking and in so doing align our desired destination with the means by which we get there.

2

Choosing a Third Path:
The Inventive Organization

The third path described in this chapter is something I call the "inventive organization." It is different from the fixed and adaptive organizations presented later in this chapter. It results from new ways of thinking about and looking at the collective we call the enterprise.

When I speak of choosing the third path, I do not mean "do more." We have designed enough programs, implemented enough improvement initiatives, and added enough new words to our business vocabulary over the last ten years that organizations should be unrecognizable from those of the Industrial Era. Yet oddly enough, the more we change things, the more we wind up feeling that nothing is changing—or that nothing is changing fast enough for us to get ahead, much less maintain the status quo. The third path is not doing more of what we already are doing. It is a new way of thinking about and looking at our collective endeavors in the midst of such challenges as ever-changing customer requirements, a global economy, and the rapid development of new technology.

Often when we think we are doing something new, we find ourselves unconsciously acting in old ways. Empowerment, a popular and powerful concept, is perhaps best explained in Peter Block's book, The Empowered Manager. *Although this concept has tapped a deep yearning in many of us, the ways in which most companies seek to illuminate and implement empowerment are potent examples of "doing new things in old ways."*

Not long ago, I was invited to do a series of one-day sessions on empowerment as part of eight week-long seminars that an international organization was conducting for senior executives located around the world. The first three days of each seminar were devoted to strategic management, influence management, and the state of the business and the industry. I was to facilitate the fourth day of each session, during which participants would experience empowerment and learn what it is and is not, what constitute acts of courage, the difference between autonomy and dependency, and the meaning of interdependence. Further, we would explore the kinds of contributions each of us makes to the current realities in which we work and the kinds of commitments we want to make to create a future that matches our collective vision of greatness for our organizations.

I spoke at length with the conference coordinators to ensure that my session on empowerment would result in what they expected. First, I wanted to learn more about the other segments of the program so that this session could build on the overall conference themes and integrate the concepts of empowerment with the other material presented. Second, I wanted to present options for working with the group and various ways in which the day could unfold. At the end of our second conversation I was asked to name five behaviors against which participants could be measured to assess whether or not they had become empowered as a result of this session. I was told that each presenter was being asked for the same information. The behaviors identified for each of the days were to be used as the basis for an assessment that would be conducted several months after the conclusion of the program. Subordinates and peers of those who had participated would be asked to rate attendees on behaviors designated as indicators of strategic management, influence, and empowerment skills. As I thought over this assignment, I was struck by how easy it is for us to fall into the trap of "doing new things in old ways."

I advised the conference coordinators that such an assessment would be counter to everything they wanted participants to do and feel as a result of a session on empowerment. I explained that empowerment is not something we do or grant to other people, and it is not a specific behavior that can be "required" of everyone. Yet, while empowerment cannot be "given," it can be taken. It is a choice each of us makes when we come to grips with the reality that our fate is in our own hands, not someone else's. We empower ourselves when we decide to live and work for a larger purpose and to act according to the truth we know, regardless of the situation we are in. By designating five empowered behaviors, I would be defining and, by means of the assessment, controlling the behaviors of the participants—rather than having them determine for themselves what they needed to do to become empowered.

I offered an alternative to the conference coordinators—one that aligned the meaning of empowerment with the acts and outcomes of empowerment. I suggested that at the end of each day, participants should develop their own lists of behaviors that would manifest strategic management, influence, and empowerment skills. After the week-long program, they could use these behaviors to start dialogues with their peers and subordinates to inquire (1) whether these were the right behaviors, (2) what other behaviors, if any, their subordinates and peers associated with strategic management, influence, and empowerment, and (3) how well their peers and subordinates felt they were doing with respect to all of these behaviors. Then, some six months after the program, I recommended that a one-day follow-up session be offered, in which participants could talk about (1) what had happened since the program—what they had tried, what worked, and what did not work; (2) whether the behaviors they had evolved were the same as those identified by their peers and subordinates; (3) in

*what areas they were doing well; and (4) in what areas they
needed more support, as well as what would constitute support.
In this way, the materials presented, the expected outcomes,
and ways of assessing the effects of this undertaking all would
be aligned within the very framework of empowerment; namely,
that participants would act on choices they made based on the
understanding that their fate was in their own hands, not in
the hands of the conference coordinators or the presenters for each
session.*

Today, it is common practice to talk about our need to focus
on and meet customer requirements. We can implement programs to reduce cycle time, increase speed to market, lower
costs, and improve quality, but in the long term, none of these
will differentiate one organization from another or grow market share if all we do is meet expectations. When we meet
customer requirements, the customer is leading and we are
pursuing.

To differentiate our organizations and grow market
share we must learn to continuously renew our ability to
convince customers to choose our product. We must do
more than simply design strategies to meet customer requirements, more than improve the quality and lower the
cost of what we already produce. We need to go beyond
merely flattening our organizations and creating teams while
we perpetuate the "command-and-control" mentality associated with steep hierarchies. Real differentiation and growth
necessitate more than inviting commentary from our customers about how we are doing so we can apologize when
we do not meet their expectations. We must rethink what
we create, the processes by which we produce, the principles by which we organize ourselves, and the means by which
we engage our customers.

WE NEED TO GET OUT
OF THE BOX OF
OUR CURRENT THINKING

Out of our background and experience, each of us has carefully constructed a set of frameworks. I think of these frameworks as boxes that contain and constrain how we think. When new information challenges or contradicts what is already in the box, we are often unable to take it in. Rather, we engage our defenses because we are so invested in what is already in the box—in our assumptions, beliefs, values. The more we defend, the more we reinforce the framework and thereby become trapped in the box of our current thinking (see Figure 2.1).

Organizations, like individuals, develop boxes. However, organizations are not "they"; rather, they are "us." Often, what looks like a new idea is put into the box, but when it comes to putting the idea into practice, it is mutilated. This occurs

Figure 2.1. Box of Current Thinking.

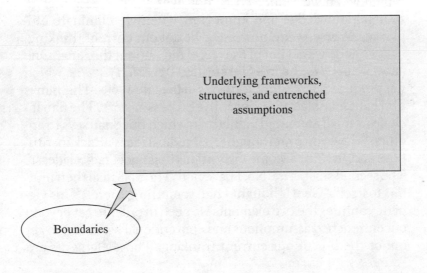

Underlying frameworks,
structures, and entrenched
assumptions

Boundaries

because the framework has not changed. For example, this happens when an organization espouses such new values as *risk* and *experimentation* while the organizational norm is *make no mistakes.* On the one hand, the organization seeks improvement, which may be driven by a belief in "perfection." Therefore, risk and experimentation seem attractive. On the other hand, the notion of "perfection" implies that any efforts at improvement need to be perfect: "there will be no messing up." If "mistakes" are made, blame is affixed, which mutilates the ideas of risk and experimentation.

Another example is an organization whose espoused value is that "people are our most important asset"; yet, when it comes to accounting procedures, people are recorded as "costs," not as assets. On the one hand, we want to believe in the value of human capital. On the other hand, Generally Accepted Accounting Practices reinforce the notion of labor as an expense. It is no wonder, then, that in times of cost reductions, people become expendable. The espoused desire to view employees as assets whose knowledge is wealth in the Information Era is overpowered by a framework from the late Industrial Era in which capital was organizational wealth. We may preserve capital when we reduce costs; however, we decrease organizational knowledge and know-how when we eliminate employees. Worse, we reinforce the box of our current thinking.

How do we get out of the box of our current thinking? One answer can be found in a film entitled *Why Man Creates,* which was produced by Kaiser Industries in the late 1960s. This film is a brilliant montage of the inventive process at work. The film includes a small animated vignette in which one snail says to another, "Have you ever thought that radical ideas attack institutions and, in turn, become institutions that reject radical ideas?" The second snail says, "No, I have not." The first snail then mutters to itself, "Gee, I thought I had something there!" This vignette captures the two elements we need in order to get beyond our entrenched assumptions and conventional wisdom — to get out of the box of our current thinking. Those elements are

1. The ability to look anew at what we already have framed and solidified in our current mode of thinking: to see from another perspective

2. To receive some kind of support or reinforcement for our awareness

Without the ability to look anew and without reinforcement for being outside the box of our current thinking, we relinquish inventiveness and constrict ourselves and our organizations to the status quo.

Achieving change in ourselves and in our organizations involves unlearning and relearning or learning anew. In essence, we need to destroy our old underlying structure or framework—the box that contains how we currently think—as we create new underlying structures and frameworks. One way to envision how we get out of the box of our current thinking is to look at our process as one of de-structuring (de-structing) and reconstructing (re-structuring). For me, this process of change is captured in a model called the Four-Room Apartment, which was developed by Swedish social psychologist Claes Janssen.

Janssen's model is based on his belief that individuals lead their lives as a series of steps through four rooms, which he named "contentment," "denial," "confusion," and "renewal." This model was later adapted by Tony Petrella to illustrate the change cycle within organizations. I have drawn on the work of both men to illustrate the process of individual and organizational change in Figure 2.2.

Status Quo

The first phase of the cycle is Status quo; it represents our state or condition before we undertake change. This can be a state of contentment or confinement. We may feel happy with the status quo or we may feel we have no choice but to accept it.

Figure 2.2. Cycle of Change.

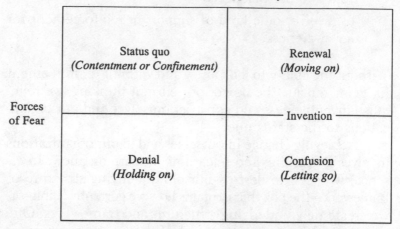

Forces of Opportunity

Status quo *(Contentment or Confinement)*	Renewal *(Moving on)*
Denial *(Holding on)*	Confusion *(Letting go)*

Forces
of Fear

── Invention ──

Source: Adapted from Tony Petrella's Change Cycle and Claes Janssens's Four-Room Apartment.

Denial

The next phase is Denial, a state of holding on. Holding on is a form of resistance, a force for sameness. When we seek sameness in our experience, what we really want is certainty. Our need for certainty often indicates the degree to which we consciously or unconsciously feel uncertain — a feeling that may be overwhelming, depending on the lack of certainty in everyday life. We get up each morning believing the ground beneath our feet is solid — that is, until we experience an earthquake. We drive home each night believing our house is standing — that is, until a firestorm destroys entire neighborhoods in hours. We go to sleep believing we will wake in the morning — that is, until we experience the unanticipated death of someone we love. The need for certainty can take many forms. It may show up as a need for control. It may be shaped by our memories of how things worked before. Most often we identify this need as an unwillingness to change — a deep desire to keep things the way they are.

We go into denial when we fear loss. When the status quo is threatened and we are content with the status quo, we will want to retain it. Even if we feel confined by the status quo, we may "hold on" because we believe that neither the status quo nor our sense of confinement will change, so why should we waste time and energy to go nowhere? Sometimes we resist because to do otherwise would cause us to reexamine and perhaps change the assumptions on which we have built our beliefs, and we fear the loss of our beliefs. Therefore, we not only resist *conscious* loss, such as a change in the status quo, we also resist *unconscious* loss, such as the invalidation of our beliefs and the assumptions that underlie them.

When we move into denial, we store energy. It takes energy to resist, just as it takes energy to act. But the energy used to resist is stored or frozen around that which is being resisted. Examples of stored energy abound in organizational settings. Every time we participate in a hallway powwow after a meeting, to lament what needed to be discussed and wasn't, we store energy that we could have used to take action in the meeting. Each time we hold on to our feelings and opinions rather than express them, we store energy. In essence, we tie up our energy in thinking and talking about what we have not done or expressed where it most needed to be done or expressed. This energy is released and can be used for other purposes when we dare to act in accordance with what we think and feel at the time we experience these thoughts and feelings.

If we recognize denial as holding on, we are more apt to look for ways to work with resistance rather than try to overcome it. In physics, resistance points to where you need to go. There is no sensation of movement without it. In ourselves and in our organizations, resistance indicates where we need to probe. If we are reluctant to see others' resistance as useful, it may be that we are too heavily committed to a change to comprehend its full impact. In the book *Beyond the Magic Circles: The Role of Intimacy in Business*, authors Milani and Smith write, "Changes . . . within the organization . . . run counter to the basic premise of immobility. Furthermore, the changed and enlightened person eventually recognizes that any attempts to change a group threaten the organizational glue that holds the whole system together" (1989, p. 19). In other words, when the need to hold on—the force for sameness—collides with the need to move on—the force for change—movement through the change cycle stops at Denial.

In 1989, the status quo at a household cleaning products plant was a state of contentment. From the standpoint of productivity, profitability, and employee satisfaction, the plant was among the company's best. Nonetheless, the plant manager wanted to position the plant for maximum participation in the company's future growth. To achieve that end, the plant undertook a work redesign initiative that involved thorough analyses of customer requirements, workflows, variances, quality of worklife issues, and organizational values. A design team, made up of nine individuals who represented all functions and levels within the plant, participated in the four-month project, which resulted in a proposal to the steering committee to restructure the plant from functional units of individual contributors to product teams that were each responsible for the entire production process. The proposal was accepted and implementation of the new design began.

To begin the transition from one-on-one boss-subordinate relationships to self-regulating teams, each newly created team participated in a team-building process. I met with one second shift team at 6:00 P.M. after a twelve-hour day at the plant. Members on this particular team were either skeptical about the redesign or openly resistant to its implementation. The most resistant team member was the plant's first nonexempt employee who, most recently, had been lead line operator on second shift. He was greatly admired by a younger and shorter-tenured employee who walked into our meeting wearing a headband that read "MIR." When I asked what MIR stood for, he replied, "Missing in Redesign." He had worn the headband the entire day and my question had been asked repeatedly by others.

I began the same team-building process I had used with the other teams over the previous two days. Admittedly, I was tired. When this occurs and the process I am using is repetitive, my energy comes from the group I am working with. When their energy is low or there is significant resistance, I have to remind myself not to "catch their dis-ease."

The lead line operator's attitude was antagonistic. He challenged my every word. The fellow with the MIR headband emulated his hero. At one point, I felt myself on the verge of ending the meeting. I knew immediately that my fatigue was getting the best of me. Finally, I stopped talking for several minutes. I looked at a woman who had been working hard to get others on the team to give the redesign a chance. She and I had both been attacked for being naive and for believing any part of the redesign would benefit employees. I turned to the resister, looked into his angry eyes, and said, "You know, it does not feel good for me to be conducting this meeting. Everything I have said has been challenged. I am barely able to state a complete sentence without interruption and attack. This simply does not feel good."

The resister sat back. His facial expression was reflective. Somehow I knew that he, too, had experienced trying to be heard but not being given a chance to speak. I continued and said, "This plant was not broken. It did not need to be fixed. The reason the plant manager wanted to undertake this effort was to position this plant for maximum participation in the company's growth. She made a courageous decision. The only other plant to have undertaken a redesign in this region was a plant that was on the verge of being closed. Your plant manager saw a window of opportunity to evaluate this operation from a position of strength and not one of fear."

The resister leaned forward and said, "Thank you for saying that. Everyone has been acting as if this plant were broken. I knew it was not broken. I have been here for ten years and this plant has always done the impossible. I apologize to you for how I have come across." I thanked him for his apology. His admirer began to smile at me. The attacks stopped and the team-building was successfully completed.

The next day I met with the business unit coordinators and gave them my assessment of each team's readiness for the implementation phase. I reminded them of the change cycle model and indicated that when an old structure begins to disintegrate and the new structure is not clear or has not fully emerged, people frequently resist out of a fear of personal loss. Some of this resistance, particularly if it is expressed by an informal leader, can seriously hamper the change process. I told them that over the course of three days, I had found four strong voices of resistance in the plant—three of them in one team and of those, two belonging to informal leaders.

A week later, the plant manager called to give me a progress report. She told me the individual from the second shift team who had voiced the most resistance during the team-building session had not only joined the implementation steering committee but had taken the first rotation as facilitator for his team. This is an example of what can happen when resistance is honored as a need to hold on, the need is explored and not ignored, and the energy associated with holding on—the force for sameness—is unleashed and becomes part of the force for change.

Confusion

The phase after Denial is Confusion—characterized by high energy and often a chaotic quality. It is a phase of letting go, of dismantling those underlying implicit and explicit entrenched assumptions that support our beliefs. The sense of confusion is uncomfortable, but it signals an end to denial. It is acknowledgement of our uncertainty. It is a messy condition that we must move through if we are to create the space to consider new options.

The move forward, out of confusion is a move from what was to what can be. This transition means we are in the process of reconstructing—a process also called invention. We are able to invent and evaluate new options when we let go of what we have been holding on to—when we have worked through the confusion that accompanies the dismantling of the box of our current thinking. We invent when we leave what is familiar and move toward what is unfamiliar. We invent when we shed the boundaries of our old frameworks and underlying structures and adopt or create new frameworks and underlying structures — which may be more expansive or narrower than our previous boundaries.

Renewal

Renewal is the last phase of the change cycle. It occurs as a result of illuminating and testing the assumptions underlying our beliefs. This movement indicates a changed state — a change in behavior, the addition of a new behavior, or a change in boundaries. Renewal may also indicate that learning has occurred — if we define learning as change. When we talk about our need to create "learning organizations," we are talking about creating organizations that have the capacity to illuminate and test their entrenched assumptions and that remain aware that the renewal phase becomes the next status quo.

Fear and Opportunity

Our progress through the cycle of change is affected by our perceptions of two major forces in the environment in which we operate: the forces of fear and opportunity. It is important to note that what one person experiences as a force for fear, another may experience as a force for opportunity. For example, an individual in a very large health maintenance organization (HMO) may see the corporation's size as a force for opportunity because the HMO controls its regional market. Another individual may experience the organization's size as a force for fear because implementing companywide change is a long, arduous process.

Within different phases of the change cycle, perceptions of fear or of opportunity dominate. For example, when we are in Status quo or Denial, fear predominates; we are afraid of change. When we are in Confusion, we experience chaos, which signals that our underlying frameworks are breaking apart. This sense of things breaking apart creates discomfort. Our way of dealing with discomfort can move us in one of two directions. We can become afraid and revert to Denial, which will engage behavior aimed at maintaining the Status quo. Or, we can see other possibilities, which moves us into Invention. We become inventive when we experience opportunity, and inventiveness leads to Renewal.

Sometimes when we get out of the box of our current thinking, we feel as if we are going "back to the future." In 1990, Fortune *magazine published an article, "Personalized Production," that helps to illustrate the point. The article is about the National Bicycle Industrial Company, a subsidiary of Matsushita, which uses robots and computers to provide customized manufacturing. The company offers 11,231,862 variations of bicycles and has been touted as the "factory of the future." Production occurs in lots of one and does not start until a customer places an order. Within two weeks, that customer is riding a one-of-a-kind machine. How is this possible?*

> *John Q. Suzuki visits his local Panasonic bicycle store, where the shopkeeper measures him on a special frame and faxes the specifications to the factory. There, an operator punches the specs into a Digital Equipment minicomputer, which automatically creates a blueprint and produces a bar code attached to a shapeless mass of tubes and gears that will become Mr. Suzuki's bike. At every point in production, a computer reading the code knows that each part belongs to Mr. Suzuki's bike and tells a robot where to weld or a painter which pattern to follow. The process is not highly automated. The factory looks a little like a traditional workshop, with crafts-people hand-wiring gears and silk screening the customer's name on the frame with the same care that would be given to the finest kimono or lacquerware. Yet production is amaz-*

ingly swift. CAD creates blueprints in three minutes that would take a draftsman 60 times as long. A custom bike requires three hours to make vs. 90 minutes for a mass-produced model. So why the two-week wait? Says Koji Nishikawa, head of sales: "We could make the time shorter, but we want people to feel excited about waiting for something special." The finished bikes sell for $545 to $3,200, compared with $250 to $510 for standard bikes. Margins are fat, workers are proud and customers happy with their unique machines [Moffat, 1990, p. 132].

WE NEED TO DIFFERENTIATE WHAT INVENTIVE IS AND IS NOT

An inventive organization is one with enhanced capacities to imagine and create. It is capable of more than adapting to the external operating environment and meeting customer requirements. An inventive organization is one that:

1. Continuously questions the assumptions that gave rise to the enterprise

2. Surprises and delights customers in service and product, warranty, and function

3. Focuses on how something is used and not simply what it was designed to do

4. Leads change through a well thought out strategy that is aligned with organizational structure, policies, and practices

5. Knows when and how to obsolete its existing product or service without alienating its current customers

6. Learns how it learns

7. Encourages experimentation by asking Why not?

8. Chases dreams instead of the competition

To invent is to go beyond expectations and dare to go where we have not been before. We cannot exceed the status quo in what we produce until we exceed the status quo in how we manage ourselves and our organizations. Our ability to invent products and services for others depends on our ability to invent new ways of managing ourselves and our operations; the two are intertwined.

Products and services have long been categorized according to a hierarchy that starts with what is basic and moves to the expected, the desired, and finally to the unanticipated. When we apply these categories to how we manage ourselves and our operations, we have the potential for reinventing our organizations.

We can start with what is basic. In a product or service, *basic* means the essentials are taken care of—for without the essentials, we cannot do business. In terms of how we manage ourselves and our operations, the basics include (1) money, (2) people, (3) our technology or the means by which we produce, no matter how primitive, and (4) our built environment, or the place where we do our work.

The next level is whatever is *expected*. In a product or service, this is what we take for granted. In terms of how we manage ourselves and our operations, we expect, among other things, (1) to be paid; (2) to be provided with some benefits, such as basic health care and time off; (3) to have someone in charge, which for the self-employed is oneself; (4) to have the tools we need; and (5) to have our questions answered.

The next level of expectation is *desired*. In terms of products and services, this means qualities that are not taken for granted and are appreciated. In terms of how we manage ourselves and our operations, this level might include (1) benefits such as eye care or leaves of absence, (2) a comfortable and pleasant work environment, (3) a caring and knowledgeable boss, and (4) opportunity to grow and develop.

At the top level of the hierarchy is the *unanticipated*. In terms of products and services, this means attributes that are beyond the customer's requirements. In terms of how we manage ourselves and our operations, the unanticipated level could include (1) pay for knowledge rather than for time and task, (2) gainsharing, which is a means of allowing everyone to share in the company's monetary gains, (3) authority commensurate with responsibility, (4) inclusion in making decisions that affect us, (5) some form of direct customer and supplier contact, regardless of our role in the organization, and (6) the ability to enhance efficiencies and correct errors without asking permission.

Just to be in business, we have to provide the basics and what is expected—not only in the products and services we provide but also in managing ourselves and our operations. To do more than survive, we need to provide what is desired. When we provide that which is desired in products, services, and how we manage ourselves and our operations, we are capable of adaptation. However, to create dynamic competitive advantage, we must go beyond adaptation. We must provide the unexpected. However, we cannot provide the unexpected to our customers until we learn new ways to manage ourselves and our organizations.

To be inventive, we must use what is known to nurture rather than inhibit what can be imagined. To be inventive we need to preserve and perpetuate those assets—those ways of being and doing—that create organizational strength, while we grow by daring to be what we have not been before. Invention requires that we look within ourselves and our organizations, that we look beyond ourselves and our organizations, that we look back and look forward simultaneously. Invention is a process we can undertake as individuals as well as in our collective endeavors. When we do it well, we act courageously to create what we can and to preserve what we need—and we know the difference between the two. Sometimes, however, organizations engage in activities that seem inventive but are not. The following lists contrast what inventive is and is not.

What Inventive Is	*What Inventive Is Not*
Incorporating what is fresh with no break in continuity of identity	Flooding the market with new products but not maintaining old products—for example, rapid obsolescence of personal computer models, which results in customers becoming confused, a devaluation of a product within a few months of purchase, a lack of support/knowledge about older models, and failure to tap product features fully before a new model is released
Understanding the pros and cons of fast cycle time, which means recognizing that shorter life cycles increase dependence on a smaller number of products and therefore increases overall business risk	Falling into the acceleration trap, where an average shortening of life cycles initially leads to a surge in sales but ultimately results in more rapid sales declines
Doing new things in new ways or doing old things in new ways	Doing new things in old ways—for example, "empowering" employees by management edict rather than understanding that empowerment is self-induced, or creating employee involvement programs where management dictates who will be involved, when, and how

Creating efficiencies in what already exists before implementing new "management-by-best-seller" techniques

Adopting new business jargon without developing shared meaning of the words, or using the jargon as if what it conveys has already been implemented

Making the barnacles in the system visible and questioning their reason for being—for example, burdensome paperwork or record/report keeping, or multiple levels of sign-off, far removed from where work actually is done

Implementing new programs and techniques without regard to how these support the alignment of customer requirements, strategy, structure, support mechanisms, pledges and payoffs, or how these create misalignment in various aspects of the system and add confusion, stress, and activities rather than create results—for example, implementing a team-based structure without defining how it supports business strategy while simultaneously continuing to reward individual performance

When a product becomes a commodity, wrapping a new service around it—for example, bumper-to-bumper automobile warranties; or when a service becomes a commodity, adding the unexpected—for example, a hotel that puts a TV program guide in

Neglecting to consider the use made of a product or service to understand more about how to exceed customer requirements

every room with the page
for that day folded down

Focusing on results and ac-
countabilities rather than
on activities and responsibilities

Creating a "hothouse" of
problem-solving ideas but
accomplishing little

One price of being inventive is understanding that "quick fixes" do not work. It is seeing parts and wholes simultaneously. To be inventive requires us to think systemically about what we do and to ensure that alignment exists between our customer requirements, strategy, structure, support mechanisms, and pledges and payoffs. It also requires that we ensure alignment between different aspects of the system, including structure and roles, people and skills, tasks and technology, decision-making processes and information flows, the built environment, and rewards and organizational values.

Another price of being inventive is scrutiny. This means that when an individual or organization takes the risk of going beyond the conventional wisdom, that individual or organization can withstand the inevitable criticism that the voices for sameness levy against new, untried ideas. To be inventive—whether in product, service, or approaches to managing ourselves and our organizations—requires complex execution involving the whole of a process. It demands that we have the courage to fail as well as succeed and that self-interest be subsumed within those interests that are greater than oneself. Don Frey, previously with Ford Motor Company, sums it up best when he says, "The price for innovation is criticism . . . a price any creative spirit must be willing to pay. Nothing puts a greater drag on innovation than the inertia in your own organization, especially difficult manufacturing reforms or the policies surrounding the security of people's jobs" (Frey, 1991, p. 49).

WE NEED TO UNDERSTAND THE DIFFERENCES BETWEEN FIXED, ADAPTIVE, AND INVENTIVE ORGANIZATIONS

One way to define an inventive organization is to compare and contrast it with fixed and adaptive organizations. The continuum shown in Figure 2.3 is useful. The fixed organization is focused on the technology that created its greatness and on enhancing that which initially captured its market share. It continues to operate on the basis of the assumptions that gave rise to its initial success. Because its focus is inward and it is not attuned to changes in its external operating environment, the fixed organization becomes caught in a syndrome of staring at its own belly button.

The adaptive organization is focused on adjusting to changing conditions in the external operating environment. Most often, this leads to continuous tinkering with the organization's form and results in efforts to imitate the structure and processes used by those who are successful in the marketplace. Thus the adaptive organization is chaotic. In its efforts to respond quickly to changing market conditions, it traps itself in multiple improvement initiatives—the dried peas syndrome—that lead to a loss of focus and misalignment between strategy, structure, espoused values, and operating policies and practices. In essence, the perceived chaos in the external environment is drawn into and exacerbates the potential for chaos in the internal environment.

The inventive organization is focused on creating a future that utilizes the organization's past learnings and incorporates the aspirations and requirements of its constituents—customers, stakeholders, suppliers, and employees. Inventive organizations are capable of producing and pacing continuous improvement and developing core competence—the know-what and know-how that create wealth in this, the early phase of the Information Era (see Figure 2.3).

Figure 2.3. Organization Transition Continuum.

Fixed	Adaptive	Inventive
Focused on the technology that once created greatness Belly button syndrome	Focused on changes in form and structure to respond to the chaos and problems that are part of the organization's current reality Chaotic	Focused on creating a future that utilizes everyone's past learnings and incorporates everyone's aspirations and prospective requirements: customers, stakeholders, suppliers, and employees Capable of producing continuous improvement and core organizational competencies

Xerox in 1970: An Example of a Fixed Organization

When an organization creates a new product, the lack of competitors can induce organizational myopia. In 1970, Xerox experienced this phenomenon when it created the first dry paper copier. The demand for this product outpaced Xerox's capacity to produce. The company's strategy was to continue to dominate this newly created and rapidly expanding market. Because the organization had achieved greatness through its technology, the organizational assumption was that the best tactic would be to continue to focus on that technology.

The company developed faster, bigger, and more expensive machines. It did not focus on the market, which began to shift.

Customers' preferences changed. Instead of one large reproduction center with high-cost equipment, customers wanted the convenience of smaller, user-friendly, less costly machines, which would be practical and affordable for multiple locations within a building. In particular, they wanted copiers that people could use without having to take a course in how to use the machine's features, load paper, or add toner.

Japanese companies, and Canon in particular, focused on the customer's use of copy equipment. These companies quickly began to produce machines that met or exceeded changing customer requirements. Almost overnight, Xerox's market share and profitability began to erode. To regain its market dominance, Xerox began to develop smaller and less costly machines. They also entered into a joint venture with Fuji. To their chagrin, they found that Fuji Xerox could manufacture higher-quality copiers in Japan and sell them at a profit in the United States at a price lower than Xerox's costs for manufacturing the same machine in the United States. Worse, the same copiers manufactured in Xerox's U.S. facilities were of lower quality than Fuji Xerox's. Xerox is an example of a company that was forced to move from the fixed mode to adaptive. Its survival was at stake.

From Fixed to Adaptive

Once Xerox recognized that its loss of market share and profitability were more than temporary, it embarked on a new strategy. First, it began quality circles to improve U.S. manufacturing operations. These efforts were remarkably successful. Next it created five regional partnerships, each of which included administrative, sales, and customer service operations. David Kearns spearheaded a corporate improvement initiative called Leadership Through Quality. This entailed a comprehensive effort to identify and implement quality-assurance and problem-solving processes. Benchmarking (a process of identifying and reviewing processes and practices in other companies as a means of improving one's own processes and practices) was used to create measurement criteria based on identified excellence in other companies' business operations. An obsession with customer satisfaction began to drive technological innovation. Xerox had begun to move from adaptive to inventive.

Becoming an Inventive Organization

In the mid eighties, Xerox's commitment to employee involvement was embedded in its organizational structure. Work groups were created in both manufacturing and customer service. Work groups are self-regulating units whose direct end-user contact inspires greater innovation in work processes and more focus on continuous improvement. Today, the goal is not simply to meet customer requirements; it is to exceed customer requirements. To do this the company has engaged customers in co-designing new document processing equipment. This effort creates stronger partnerships between customers and suppliers and enables Xerox to better conceptualize document processing machinery and methods as well as their potential use in tomorrow's world of work.

The image of a continuum is useful because it indicates that organizations, like people, are in the process of becoming. Transitions, however, may not be strictly linear or only in one direction. For example, an adaptive organization can become fixed when its focus turns inward and it stops concentrating on the whole system—the entire external environment—of which it is a part. Examples of fixedness occurred during the 1980s, when executives and boards of directors focused on the rapid accumulation of wealth through mergers, acquisitions, and leveraged buy outs—amalgamating rather than growing their enterprises—and did not fully consider the implications of creating conglomerates in which different products, services, strategies, operating infrastructures, and marketplaces were suddenly joined at the bottom line. The new behemoths became focused on internal operations—on merging their differing policies, practices, and operating infrastructures.

Another kind of transition occurs when an inventive organization becomes complacent about organizational renewal. When this happens, the ingenuity, vision, and courage that caused the organization to lead (rather than merely adapt to change) are squandered and the organization becomes fixed. As we saw in the example given earlier, this occurred when Xerox Corporation became fixed on the technology that made it great instead of on changes in customer requirements. Conversely, a fixed organization can arise from its slumber. Most often, its leaders and followers are awakened by forces that threaten the organization's very existence. This was what happened when Chrysler was threatened with going out of business and everyone from management to union members had a common interest: survival. When an organization does awaken, it usually becomes adaptive before it learns how to become inventive.

Because organizations are collections of individuals, another way to compare fixed, adaptive, and inventive organizations is to envision a continuum made up of three stages of being: reactive, responsive, and inventive. (See Figure 2.4.)

Figure 2.4. Individual Transition Continuum.

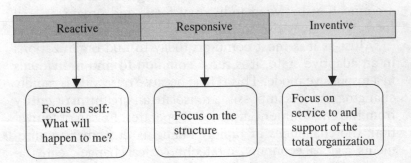

It is important to note that when the structure changes in an organization, individuals tend to become reactive and focus on themselves. They will move forward toward inventiveness if they have been involved with creating the organization's desired future state, and can clearly see the benefits for both the organization and themselves.

A reactive state is driven by fear. At this stage, one's focus is on "what will happen to me." It is an inward focus and corresponds to the fixed state on the organization continuum. A responsive state is driven by the need to adapt to one's external environment. For example, for a person at work, the focus is on responding to changes in the work environment, which is defined by the organization's structure. The person's responses to changes in this environment are based on his or her position within the structure and the desire to fit with the environment. This stage corresponds to the adaptive state on the organization continuum.

An inventive state is driven by the need to create something greater than what already exists. If we translate this to an individual need, an *inventive* state results from the need to act on that which is greater than oneself. At work, this need creates a focus on service and support to the entire organization. Rather than focusing on "what's in it for me," the person focuses on "what's in it for us." The inventive state on the individual continuum corresponds to the inventive state on the organizational continuum; the focus is on the whole of the constituency of which one is a part.

The individual continuum helps us better understand the dynamics of the collective — the organization. There is a connection between individual focus and organizational focus. One gives rise to the other.

Just as it is most common today to find organizations in an adaptive state, it is most common to find individuals in a responsive mode. This is true because our world is rapidly changing and it is impossible to isolate an organism or entity from the environment in which it operates. For an organization, the challenges of rapidly changing customer requirements, a global economy, and technological change create the need to adapt. For the individual — whose power, status, and privileges at work are dictated by organizational structure and the person's place in the hierarchy — the need is to be responsive to changes in organizational structure and strategy that are driven by the need to adapt. Organizations, therefore, wind up focused on improvement initiatives aimed at duplicating competitors' successes, while individuals tend to focus on who is in which box on the organization chart, which boxes have been divided, and which boxes have been moved, deleted, or added.

When organizations feel whipsawed by the need to adapt to the rate of change, they tend to retreat to a focus on what once created their greatness, and thus they become fixed. Similarly, when organizational structure and form are changed—as when hierarchies are flattened or team-based management is introduced—employees tend to become reactive and focus on what will happen to them as individuals. The organization can become inventive if it is able to engage its constituency in developing the ability to lead rather than just respond to change. Individuals become inventive when they are involved with the creation of organizational change and see clearly how such change benefits both the organization and themselves.

If we combine the individual and organization continuums, as is done in Figure 2.5, we find the fixed state is characterized by an inward focus that is born of dominance in an industry. The culture is authoritarian, status driven, hierarchical, and empire building. More often than not, the culture is forged by ego. Fixed organizations are directive. They easily become complacent. The adaptive state develops out of a need to respond to changes in the external operating environment—particularly to changes in the industry and to changes in the nature of rivalry among competitors. The most frequent mode of response is to alter the organizational structure. Companies merge and acquire. They move from functional operations to divisions to strategic business units (SBUs). Some adopt matrixed operations. The adaptive state is characterized by a focus on tasks and results, role clarity, and personal linkages. Company chatter is predominantly about who is being groomed for what job or whose turf is becoming larger or smaller. In an adaptive state, everyone is inordinately concerned with organizational boxes—their occupants, titles, and positions in the hierarchy. The adaptive organization's culture is political and chaotic.

Figure 2.5. Combined Individual
and Organizational Transition Continuum.

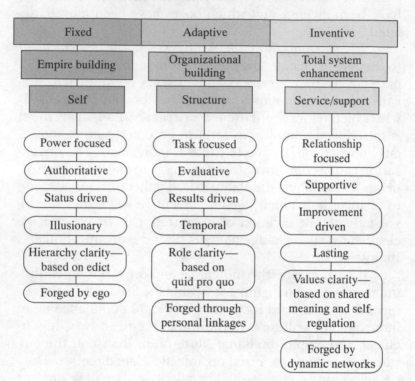

Fixed	Adaptive	Inventive
Empire building	Organizational building	Total system enhancement
Self	Structure	Service/support
Power focused	Task focused	Relationship focused
Authoritative	Evaluative	Supportive
Status driven	Results driven	Improvement driven
Illusionary	Temporal	Lasting
Hierarchy clarity—based on edict	Role clarity—based on quid pro quo	Values clarity—based on shared meaning and self-regulation
Forged by ego	Forged through personal linkages	Forged by dynamic networks

Source: Partially adapted from work by Peter Gibb.

An inventive state results from a focus on total system enhancement through everyone's acting in service to and support of the entire system. It is achieved when there is a value on utilizing everyone's past learnings and incorporating everyone's aspirations and prospective requirements to establish common ground. In an inventive state, the organization is capable of renewal, of continuing to evolve competence while developing mutually supportive and lasting relationships among constituents—including employees, suppliers, customers, and stakeholders. An inventive state has staying power because it is driven by values. It creates conditions that nurture shared meaning and self-regulation. Inventive cultures evolve when organizations

1. Learn how they learn and then act on their learning
2. Engage the talent and commitment of everyone in the constituency
3. Improve and pace the improvement of how they do what they do best
4. Promote partnership and interdependence in every transaction
5. Reward learning—risk taking—and not just success

In an inventive organization, everyone understands customer requirements, the economics of the business, its technology and workflows, the built environment, and the needs and drives of people who constitute the enterprise. The test of an inventive organization is to what extent the following things happen in it:

1. Everyone sees the big picture—knows how they contribute to the final product or service and understands the whole of the enterprise as well as its parts.
2. Everyone enhances efficiencies and corrects errors without asking permission.
3. Everyone acts in ways that provide service and support to the whole system.
4. Organizational boundaries—namely, those that define job roles and functions—exist only to enhance organizational learning, the development of core competencies, and long-term viability.

WE NEED TO KNOW
HOW TO SUPPORT INVENTIVE
RATHER THAN FIXED
AND ADAPTIVE ORGANIZATIONS

As individuals—whether leaders or followers—we seek to know who are we, what we can do, how we can do it, where we can best make a valued contribution, and who will benefit from our efforts. As groups and organizations, which are collections of individuals, we ask the same questions. Strategy and planning are the foundation for meaningful work and meaningful relationships. How we strategize and plan is determined by our assumptions. These assumptions lead to fixed, adaptive, or inventive organizations. Choosing a well-considered strategy is the first step toward building organizational success.

Strategy is a decision about how we will compete in the marketplace. Organizations strategize by determining what their customers want and how they can best compete for market share. For example, will they compete on product innovation, process innovation, or some combination thereof? Strategy dictates appropriate organizational structure as well as the mechanisms required to support the organizational structure and to implement the strategy. Strategy also dictates other factors critical to success: those individual and collective commitments—pledges—that result in individual and organizational success—payoff. Factors that affect the alignment between customer requirements, strategy, structure, support mechanisms, pledges, and payoffs are listed in Exhibit 2.1.

Strategy is expressed in an organization's vision and determines its mission. And strategy encompasses the words and deeds we call our organizational values. Therefore, when we talk about invention, we are talking about a mind-set that is an underlying framework—a strategy—for how we conduct ourselves and our enterprises.

Exhibit 2.1. Success Criteria for Dynamic Competitive Advantage.

A	■ Customer requirements (end user)
L	■ Strategy by which you compete in the marketplace
I	vision, mission, values
G	■ Structure
N	roles and relationships
M	■ Sustaining mechanisms
E	work processes, electronic infrastructure, policies, and procedures that serve strategy and structure
N	
	■ Pledges and payoffs
T	
	investments and commitments (made by stockholders, stakeholders, employees) and critical success factors— goals—that make investments pay off

Source: Based on work by Eldon Arden, 3M Corporation.

The second step to building organizational success is planning. Planning how to implement strategy and measure results is what guides individuals and groups in achieving organizational goals. Organizations plan by means of the following:

1. Creating a vision for the future—meeting/exceeding customer requirements

2. Defining the mission—strategy

3. Designing the organization—structure and support mechanisms

4. Setting goals—pledges and payoffs

The way in which we plan is indicative of the organizational state we are in—fixed, adaptive, or inventive. Over the past thirty years, we have developed tools to help us plan, including goal-setting methods, strategic planning models, mission statements, and vision statements. These tools are not mutually exclusive; however, our emphasis on which tools we use and how we use them solidifies our position on the combined individual and organization continuum. These tools evolved in what I consider a backward order.

In the late 1960s and early 1970s, we focused on individual and organizational goals—statements of what needs to be done by what date. We developed elaborate and time-consuming processes, such as Management By Objectives, to write and approve goals for individuals, departments, and the enterprise as a whole. Goals are useful targets. When the process of writing goals is taken to an extreme, however, it is not uncommon to find people spending more time writing objectives than producing results. More important, goals are derived from strategy. They do not precede strategy.

In the late 1970s and early 1980s, redesigning organizational structures and strategic planning gained in popularity. At the same time that organizational divisions became strategic business units and fixed organizational structures gave way to matrix management, strategic planning efforts began. Both of these efforts gained prominence as organizations became more complex and conglomerates became more commonplace.

Organizational structures and strategic plans should be based on a carefully chosen and articulated strategy. More often than not, however, the strategy is unclear, implicit, or nonexistent. This results in considerable activity focused on changing organizational charts—both the arrangement of boxes and the names in the boxes—and many off-site meetings to develop a strategic plan that is a three-year forecast of what needs to be done based on unquestioned and, often, unarticulated assumptions. The fact that these assumptions are untested is clouded by another organizational icon, the organization's mission statement. Most mission statements, rather than being an explicit enunciation of strategy, contain several paragraphs that attempt to justify the organization's reason for being. To be of value, a mission statement must make explicit the strategy chosen by the organization. The statement should contain critical definitions of what the organization does (objectives), for whom (markets), how (by what means or strategy the enterprise competes), why (for what purpose), and where (geographic boundaries).

In the mid 1980s, "vision" became part of our corporate vocabulary. A vision statement goes beyond goals and mission. "A shared vision is not an idea," Peter Senge writes in *The Fifth Dimension;* "rather, it is a force in people's hearts. . . . It is not what the vision is but what it does" (1990, pp. 206–207). To create a vision is to imagine what might be. To act to achieve a vision is to invent what is yet to come.

If we compare the evolution of goals, mission, and vision to the stages on the Combined Individual and Organizational Transition Continuum (see Figure 2.5), we can identify what kind of state each of these planning tools supports— fixed, adaptive, or inventive.

- Setting goals supports fixedness. This may seem an overly harsh and simplistic view; however, it is not uncommon to find that goals for one year are based on goals from the previous year.

- The development of a mission statement supports adaptation. Adaptation is a focus on responding to the opportunities and challenges inherent in the organization's current operating environment.

- The development of a vision supports invention. A vision is a guiding philosophy on how to create the future. Vision statements have meaning when every organizational action can be measured in terms of its congruence with the vision. The creation of a vision is most effective when it draws on everyone's past learnings and incorporates everyone's aspirations for the world they wish to live in.

Goals, missions, and visions are not mutually exclusive. Rather, they are immediate, near-term, and future statements that guide individual and organizational efforts. Each by itself ties to a particular organizational state—fixed, adaptive, or inventive—and all three are in place and aligned in inventive organizations.

WE NEED TO STAY OUT OF THE BOX OF OUR CURRENT THINKING

If we are to become inventive, we need to do two things well. First, we need to know where we are. A way to develop organizational awareness of current reality is to use the four phases of the Cycle of Change (see Figure 2.2). From a simple exercise, utilizing Figure 2.6, we can determine whether our organization is in a fixed state, which occurs when the organization is in Status quo or Denial; whether it is in an adaptive state, which is associated with Confusion; or whether it is in an inventive state, which is associated with Renewal.

When I employ this exercise in workshops, I ask individuals, sitting at tables in groups of six or eight, to first identify the forces of fear and the forces of opportunity that currently affect their organization. Once they make their lists, I ask them to identify where they would place the following groups in the change cycle, using the symbols indicated:

1. *Leadership,* symbolized by a triangle
2. *Customers,* symbolized by a diamond
3. *Themselves,* symbolized by a star
4. *Employees* within the organization, symbolized by a square
5. *Suppliers or support functions,* symbolized by a circle
6. *Competitors,* symbolized by a pentagon

Each group discusses major themes that arise from their individual plottings. Each group then appoints a spokesperson. The spokespersons come to the front of the room and sit in a semicircle facing the entire audience. First they dis-

Figure 2.6. Transition Continuum with Change Cycle Phases.

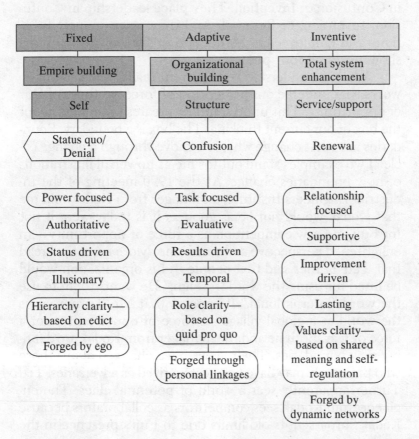

Fixed	Adaptive	Inventive
Empire building	Organizational building	Total system enhancement
Self	Structure	Service/support
Status quo/ Denial	Confusion	Renewal
Power focused	Task focused	Relationship focused
Authoritative	Evaluative	Supportive
Status driven	Results driven	Improvement driven
Illusionary	Temporal	Lasting
Hierarchy clarity— based on edict	Role clarity— based on quid pro quo	Values clarity— based on shared meaning and self-regulation
Forged by ego	Forged through personal linkages	Forged by dynamic networks

cuss the forces of fear and opportunity. These are recorded on a flipchart so the commonalities and differences are apparent for the entire group. Often the same forces are listed as forces of fear and opportunity. In the process, the entrenched assumptions and underlying frameworks that create these perceptions become apparent.

Each spokesperson then states where in the change cycle their group placed the six categories—leadership, customers, themselves, employees, suppliers, and competitors. These are recorded on the change cycle, which is drawn on a flipchart. When I work with middle managers, three patterns frequently emerge. The middle managers place themselves in Confusion or Invention. They place leadership in Confusion, Invention, or Renewal. And they place support functions and employees in Status quo or Denial. Competitors show up in all four phases.

We must understand our current reality and the frameworks that underlie our perception of forces as those of fear or opportunity. This understanding creates awareness about the box of our current thinking. The box is a boundary. Boundaries are what change when we move through a change cycle. Two examples stand out for me as powerful illustrations of how boundaries change. At the 1990 meeting of the Industrial Engineers Institute, a manager from Kodak told me that Kodak would not be as good as it is today were it not for Fuji. He saw competition as a force of opportunity—an enlightened perspective and a rare one. More recently, I read that Ted Turner said that people in his organization would be fined for using the word "foreign." He wants them to use the word "international." It appears that Mr. Turner views the world as a global village—a force of opportunity, not a force of fear. Both he and the manager from Kodak are defining new boundaries. Their views have changed about those who previously may have been categorized as adversaries. Ted Turner apparently sees a world of potential allies. The engineer from Kodak sees competitors as collaborators because Kodak surpassed its old limits due to Fuji's presence in the market.

In addition to understanding our current reality, we must be able to ask ourselves "Why not?" instead of "Why?" The following questions are examples of how to do this. They may sound like radical ideas. If you ask them of yourself, they can help you get out of the box of your current thinking and create inventive ways to manage yourself and your organization.

1.   Why not let those who do the work plan, organize, and control the work? Why not let peers staff, reward, discipline, and terminate failed relationships?

2. Why not spend all your time creating customer-supplier partnerships and creating value for shareholders and employees?

3. Why not provide only those resources that are dictated by customer requirements and communicated by those who serve the customer? Think in terms of internal and external customers.

4. Why not treat employees as owners instead of renters of their work space and let them furnish their space, within some minimum critical specifications, so the space works for them?

5. Why not make known the kinds of financial data available about the company and disseminate this data to any employee who wants it?

6. Why not delete the creation and dissemination of all the data in your in-box or electronic mail box? Why not create and disseminate only information that serves and supports the entire system and is available to the entire system? Why document anything that can be communicated verbally?

7. Why not let those who receive training help plan and design the training they receive? Why not make all training "real time, just-in-time" instead of classroom training?

8. Why not throw out all policies and procedures except those that indicate what cannot happen instead of what must happen? Why not limit the number of words in a policy or the number of paragraphs in a procedure? Why not set a maximum limit on the number of pages in the company's one policy and procedure manual? Why not let those who are supposed to meet specifications help create those specifications? Why not have a rule that all constraints have to be perceived as "enabling" by those who must live with them?

9. Why not throw away all current methods for doing and measuring work? Why not let those who do the work

develop only those methods and measurements that create and verify customer satisfaction while supporting the organization in living out its values?

10. Why not let those who receive rewards help decide what rewards are meaningful to receive and how to distribute them? Why not publish everyone's total income each year and distribute this information to all employees? Why not let employees select their own titles? Why not institutionalize a norm of writing on a post-it the name of a person and what she does that serves and supports the entire system? Why not put these post-its on an appreciation board in a highly trafficked area or on an electronic monitor or ticker for others to see? Why not deliver these post-its to the employee once they have been "broadcast."

11. Why not spend all our time finding ways to improve what we do and invent the future rather than identifying and responding to specific problems?

12. Why not start each meeting with this statement from each participant: "I want _____ and we, as a group, need _____?"

13. Why not train "peer facilitators" to handle third-party consultations involving interpersonal conflicts? Why not ask those who attend meetings to rotate the roles of facilitator, scribe, and timekeeper? Why not use agendas to manage meetings — subjects and time frames — and capture decisions or follow up actions? Why not ask at the end of every meeting, "What did we do well and what could we do better?" and put answers on a flipchart that is used at the next meeting?

14. Why not create "fat awareness" at all levels of the system about the system's current reality so that energy is mobilized to make those changes that meet and exceed customer requirements?

15. Why not create a forum(s) where everyone in the system — including customers, suppliers, regulators, share-

holders, and stakeholders — can talk about their visions of greatness and use these to build a company vision? Why not make it a practice to ask one another if what we do is meaningful and if it is, what makes it meaningful, and if it is not, why are we doing it?

16. Why not invite our customers in and ask if our operation works from their perspective? On a regular basis, why not ask, "What are we learning, how do we know what we know, and how do we know we are sharing what we know?"

17. Why not insist that nothing can be computerized until we have eliminated the inefficiencies in the processes we want to mechanize?

18. Why not insist on "time-outs" for reflection, each time we reach a milestone or achieve a goal, to ask ourselves what we would do differently if we were to do it again?

19. Why not insist on everyone having enough support and control to do the work and keep looking for ways to improve?

20. Why not look at everything we do as a service instead of a product — focus on use rather than form?

21. Why not target a major portion of pretax profits for research and development and investment in plant and equipment?

22. Why not insist that what we do has to create core competencies that can be applied elsewhere?

23. Why not treat every person as my partner? Why not let groups determine their own development needs? Why not create a company "plaza," where people from all parts of the organization can interact informally?

24. Why not insist that every employee invent a way to have contact with external suppliers and customers? Why not invite customers and suppliers to visit on a regular basis?

25. Why not insist that employees have the rights, resources, and commitment to:

a. See the big picture?

b. Enhance efficiencies and correct errors without asking permission?

c. Cooperate across those boundaries that exist to enhance learning, core competence, and long-term viability?

d. Act in service and support to the entire system?

26. Why not make up your own list of why-not questions?

PART TWO

HOPE:
BUILDING FRAMEWORKS
FOR INVENTION

This section of the book covers the six frameworks for inventive organizations. In Chapter Two, frameworks were described as "boxes" that contain how we think and what we believe. This notion of frameworks is echoed in Jay Conger's statement that "frames are essentially snapshots that [we] take of [our] organizations. In a larger sense, frames also provide a map for action. If we believe and describe the world as flat or square, we will 'frame' our understanding of reality through that perspective and act accordingly" (1991, p. 31).

In the late Industrial Era, we believed that the job of planning and thinking was different from the job of doing, that mass production provided competitive advantage, that we needed to organize groups of people into steep hierarchies to ensure control, and that we needed staff functions, such as finance, quality, human resources and information technology to take care of the money, the quality, the people, and the information. These beliefs served us well when capital, rather than competence, created organizational wealth. The frameworks underlying these beliefs looked like this:

1.   Command and control
2.   Separation of work—line and staff, thinking and doing
3.   Detailed descriptions and valuation of work
4.   Profitability
5.   Clear policies and practices
6.   Leader and follower

These frameworks resulted in management from above, as distinct from self-regulation; fragmented jobs and work processes rather than a unified understanding of core work; a focus on job and function rather than on service and support to the entire system; profitability instead of customer requirements; compliance rather than commitment; and dependency instead of partnership.

We have entered a new era: the Information Era. The underlying frameworks from the Industrial Era no longer serve us. In this new era, competence and knowledge are the basis upon which we compete, mass customization is more critical than mass production, the application of knowledge across a broad array of services and products is our core competence, and the nature of our customer and supplier relationships will dictate the long-term viability of our organization. This new era and its attendant new demands require a new set of frameworks. We are now confronted and confounded by rapid changes in everything. To address these changes, we need to do more than adapt, which is the most that our old frameworks can support. We need first to address how we think and what we believe. We need to illuminate our entrenched assumptions and develop new frameworks that will support us in becoming inventive and capable of continuous renewal.

The difference between inventive and adaptive organizations is more than a matter of semantics. An adaptive organization re-

sponds flexibly to changing conditions in its external operating environment. An inventive organization does more than respond to what is required. It creates the unexpected.

My experience with a publisher of educational materials for kindergarten through eighth grade provides an example of the differences between what is required of adaptive organizations and what is required of inventive organizations. One day, after lunch, I took a walk with members of the restructuring design team. As we stepped outside the headquarters building, which is located in the middle of a huge park, I noticed a man on a tractor-mower. He was mowing a lazy 8 between two trees. Recognizing that the lawn was too large to be mowed at one time and that parts of it were in shade and much of it was in sun, I began to wonder how he decided what to do each day. I walked over and asked him what he needed to know to determine what to do each day. He looked at me as if I were crazy and then replied, "Well, first I need to know that my equipment is in good working order and that I have fuel for the equipment. Then I need to look at what happened last week. If I mowed the lawn low and it didn't rain, I have to figure out what will happen next week because if I mow this lawn again and it doesn't rain, the grass will burn. On the other hand, if I mowed the grass just a little last week, I still have to figure out what will happen next week because if I don't cut the lawn low enough and it rains, it will be hard to cut the grass next week." I smiled and said, "Thank you." He asked me what I had learned and I told him that he was an adaptive system. After explaining what I meant, I went back to our conference room and wrote "Mowing the Lawn" on the flipchart.

When the design team returned, I used the analogy of mowing the lawn to explain an adaptive organization. If this organization wanted to be adaptive, it had to figure out how low and how tall to mow the lawn each week. To adapt is to look at what is and what was and make the necessary adjustments to maintain viability. *To be inventive, the publisher would have to go beyond responding flexibly to changes in the external operating environment. It would have to imagine what could be and develop those organizational conditions and competencies that would create what has not been before. If we use the analogy of the lawn, to invent may mean that we consider more than lawn as ground cover. Perhaps we landscape with something that does not need to be mowed. Perhaps we create a series of walkways and ponds that require less maintenance and remain aesthetically pleasing regardless of the season. Invention means going beyond what is and going beyond what is expected. Invention leads to renewal, which is the source of dynamic competitive advantage and enhanced long-term viability.*

There are six frameworks associated with inventive organizations (see Figure II.1). These frameworks underlie how we think about ourselves and our enterprise. They lead to organizational beliefs and practices that align with and support invention and renewal.

The first framework causes us to know our customer's requirements, the customer being the end user of the product or service produced. But it is not enough just to know customer requirements. We must ask ourselves, "How do we know these requirements?"

The second framework causes us to focus on core work. Core work is the essential work that meets or exceeds customer requirements. The best-designed organizations are designed from the outside in — that is, from the viewpoint of the end user — and from the core work out.

The third framework causes us to focus on organizational values. We need to live these values, which address how we want to relate to our customers, our work associates, and the work itself. In her book *How Corporate Truths Become Corporate Traps*, Eileen Shapiro lists two key questions that we need to ask ourselves every day: First, "What does each of us do each day that demonstrates what we really want to reward?" Second, "How do we help stack the deck to make it easier for people to do the right things?" (1991, p. 219).

The fourth framework causes us to focus on systemic

Figure II.1. Six Frameworks for Inventive Organizations.

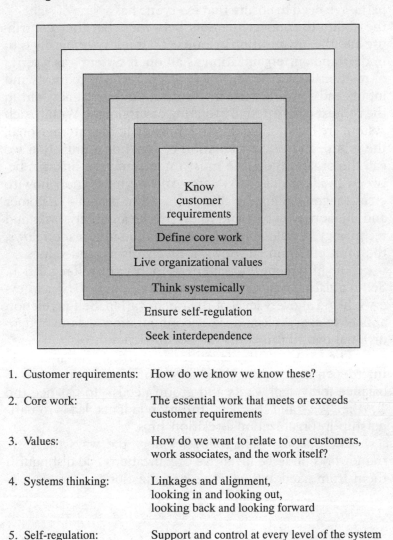

1. Customer requirements: How do we know we know these?

2. Core work: The essential work that meets or exceeds
customer requirements

3. Values: How do we want to relate to our customers,
work associates, and the work itself?

4. Systems thinking: Linkages and alignment,
looking in and looking out,
looking back and looking forward

5. Self-regulation: Support and control at every level of the system

6. Interdependence: Find common cause by balancing "I," "we,"
and "us."

Note: An inventive organization is one where people are able to get out of the
box of their current thinking, test their entrenched assumptions, and act in
service and support of the entire system.

thinking. We must be able to see the whole as well as the parts. We need to ensure that everyone has a "line of sight" — the ability to connect the dots between what they contribute and the organization's results. To think systemically is to understand our organization as an open system — as a series of relationships in action. The system receives requests and inputs and converts these into outputs and outcomes, within the context of its external operating environment. Within each system are levels, including the individual, the interpersonal, the group, and the combination of functional units that we call the organization. We must understand the linkages between the levels of the system. And we must know how to create alignment among all aspects of the system — customer and mission, structure and roles, people and skills, tasks and technology, decision-making processes and information flows, the built environment, reward mechanisms, and values.

The fifth framework causes us to focus on self-regulation. Self-regulation means that support and control exist in every job and at every level of the organization. Self-regulation applies to every role and every configuration — teams and individual contributors — in the constituency.

The focus on interdependence is the sixth framework. Interdependence means the ability to find common cause — to balance individual wants and group needs — to balance the "I," the "We," and the "Us." Interdependence leads to partnership in organizational relationships.

The chapters that follow explore the ways these six frameworks underlie inventive organizations and distinguish them from fixed and adaptive organizations.

3

Customers: Designing the Organization Through Their Eyes

The first framework for inventive organizations causes us to focus on customer requirements. To achieve this, we need to find ways to ensure that everyone knows customer requirements. When I use the term *customer*, I am referring to the end user of the product or service. This definition is important. In many organizations, the focus is on internal customer/supplier relationships. This can lead to a kind of myopia, or what I have referred to as the belly button syndrome. It is not enough to hand work off from one function to another within the organization, to meet those internal customers' requirements. To meet or exceed end user requirements, we must look at our operations through end user's eyes.

DESIGNING OUR ORGANIZATIONS FROM OUR END USER'S POINT OF VIEW

In most organizations, few employees have any contact with end users. This results in a lack of direct knowledge of the customers and their requirements. In effect, people work in a vacuum, producing a part of something that is sold to someone unknown. One truth is universal: we take more care with our work when we have a relationship with those we serve. In an inventive organization, leaders and followers have a "line of sight" to customers. I first heard the term "line of sight" from my colleague Judith Schuster; it means the employee's image or knowledge of how his or her efforts help to produce a service or product that meets or exceeds customer requirements. To understand product specifications is not enough. Everyone in the organization must know end user requirements.

"'Market-In' is a major focus in Japanese quality improvement activities. It means bringing customer needs into every possible part of the organization, thereby heightening uncertainty. These activities include informing production workers or front-line service employees of warranty claims relevant to their work, informing a broad range of employees how customers use products and services, and educating as many employees as possible on customer-desired product and service features. The market-in approach contrasts sharply with the reliance on specialized organization experts to process information about the environment and solve specific problems" (Cole, Bacdavan, and White, 1993, p. 73).

In most organizations customer requirements are identified and described by people who do not make the product or service. The same is true for information about customer satisfaction. The result is that those at the top of the hierarchy— leaders—are as insulated from direct customer contact as those who are isolated on factory floors—followers. Paradoxically, these same organizations espouse strong customer-supplier partnerships. How can we create such partnerships when those who lead and those who produce do not work as partners and both lack direct customer contact? And organizations cannot create partnerships with customers and suppliers if they do not form internal partnerships between work associates and between support functions and line functions.

Customer requirements drive inventive organizations.

In inventive organizations, customer response to organizational outputs is the ultimate measure of organizational success. Whenever there is direct customer contact, people have "line of sight." "Line of sight" forms the basis for creating common cause and for creating partnerships that support everyone in assuming accountability for individual and organizational results.

Lessons from the Plant Floor

A former client of mine is the Fort Washington manufacturing plant of Johnson & Johnson. I worked with four work-redesign teams who wanted information that would help them better understand the plant's manufacturing requirements. The teams invited many members of the corporate staff to their design sessions. Among those invited was a representative from Marketing, who made a formal presentation on customer requirements and the nature of competition within the industry. He used numerous overhead slides that were crowded with columns of figures to indicate buying patterns and customer preferences regarding size and shape of both tablets and bottles. At the end of his presentation, one of the design team members spoke up. He worked in the Processing Department and had been with the company for over twenty-five years. He told the Marketing representative that he had been conducting his own survey of customer preferences. He mentioned that the previous weekend he had attended a wedding with 250 people. He had asked many of the guests what made them decide to buy a particular product when they had a headache. The consistent response was "price." When he asked, "What about quality?" he was told, "Oh hell, Joe, the FDA regulates quality, so anything on the shelf is good." Joe—a follower in Operations—told the Marketing representative—who had the lead role in determining product specifications—that if price was the customer's key requirement, the company had to do everything in its power to be price competitive. Changeovers in the production processes, which were driven by Marketing edicts, drove up production costs, which were passed on to consumers in the price of the product.

Several months into the implementation of the redesign, people from Marketing visited the manufacturing floor. Teams of workers demonstrated the merits of standard tablet sizes and shapes, fewer variations in product containers, and standardized caps and package seals, all of which reduce changeover time, increase productivity, and reduce costs. Many of their recommendations have been implemented.

This is but one example of leader-follower partnerships that are being forged in inventive organizations. The partnership is a vast departure from the hierarchy of yesteryear, when to lead meant to control and to follow meant to do as told. Today, to lead is to unleash the wisdom in the system, and to follow is to take responsibility for having firsthand knowledge of the organization's customers and strategy so that the totality of everyone's efforts meets or exceeds customer requirements.

How to Create Customer Contact

There are ways to put people who do not have direct customer contact in touch with the customer. My good friend, John Hassett, bought a Toyota Celica GTS in 1987. After driving a thousand miles, John took the car to the dealership for its first servicing. A service writer took his order. The car disappeared into the service bay. John went to work and returned to the dealership at the end of the day. As is standard operating procedure, John never saw or talked with the mechanic who worked on his automobile. He dealt with the cashier when he picked up his car.

When John got into his car, he noticed a hang-tag on the rearview mirror. On it was a picture of a man in a mechanic's uniform. The hang-tag read, "Hi, my name is Dave Smith. I worked on your car today. I hope you find everything to your satisfaction. If you have any questions or problems, please call me at 874-9125." John, the customer, was now in contact with Dave,

his supplier. John left the dealership feeling he had a relation-
ship with Dave, even though they had never met, and Dave had
visibility and accountability in his work.

Dave's "line of sight" could be enhanced by a recommen-
dation from my friend, Stanley Wachs, an organizational devel-
opment consultant, who upon hearing this story said, "The dealer-
ship should take a Polaroid photograph of the customer when
the car is brought in for servicing and put the photo on the wind-
shield. That way Dave could see his customer." Direct contact with
the customer and visibility and accountability in one's work pro-
mote self-regulation, job satisfaction, and pride of workmanship—
all of which characterize inventive organizations.

EXCHANGING COMMAND AND CONTROL FOR COMMITMENT TO CUSTOMERS

No shape better represents the nature of American business in the Industrial Era than the triangle: there is room for many at the bottom of the organization and room for few at the top. Because our American culture is based on monotheism— a belief in one god—we have adopted a singular focus in the fabric and structure of our society: one person, one vote, the individual is king, and one person leads. This has translated into a notion of "one above all others," and therein created hierarchy, which American business has perfected as its organizational form.

The old triangle looks like the one in Figure 3.1. In 1987, Jan Carlzon, president of SAS, a European airline, wrote a book called *Moments of Truth,* in which he introduced a new framework for thinking about organizations. That framework is an inverted triangle with the customer, not the CEO, at the top. (See Figure 3.2.)

Figure 3.1. The Old Triangle.

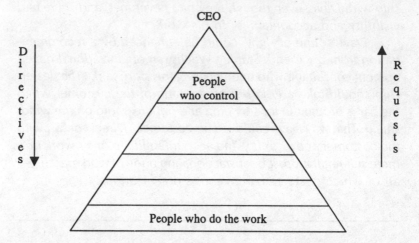

In essence, the communications patterns in the two triangles remain the same; however, the driving forces are dramatically different. In the old triangle, directives and commands flow from the CEO at the top through the layers of people who control (managers) to the people who do the work.

Figure 3.2. The New Triangle.

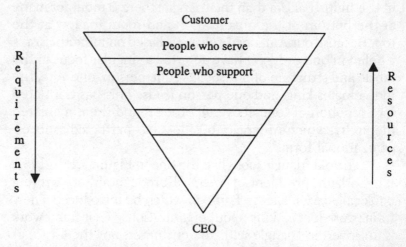

Source: Adapted from Carlzon, 1987.

And those who do the work make requests of those who control it. Requests are born out of the notion of "boss and subordinate"—one up and one down. They come in the form of questions and sound like "Mother, may I?" or "Father, may I?" Requests from those at the bottom of the hierarchy, rather than being pushed up the hierarchy, are most often stalled several layers below top management. "Most of what is important in a company is not written down. . . . Much of it never rises to the top of the company," wrote Badaracco and Ellsworth (1989, p. 128). Is it any wonder then that the notion of "management by walking around" gained such great popularity in the early 1980s? After years of isolation in the mahogany halls of corporate headquarters, CEOs had simply lost touch with their employees and, thereby, their companies. Badaracco and Ellsworth noted that "companies are, in a sense, hierarchies of wastebaskets: as issues and problems rise to the top levels, more and more detailed information is thrown out along the way" (1989, p. 128). More important, both leaders and followers lacked contact with the customer.

The reality for organizations in the Information Era is that the customer counts. The new organizational form, also a triangle, is inverted, and the customer is at the top. This means that customers and their requirements need to be known by those who serve them. These requirements, in turn, are communicated to those who support those who serve. Those who support see their roles as "servant leaders" in that they are responsible for providing the resources, building the vision, and managing the boundaries that ensure value for customers, stakeholders, suppliers, and employees. Those who make products or provide services to customers learn and communicate what is needed to achieve the following:

1. Meet or exceed customer requirements
2. Create paced, continuous improvement
3. Develop competence and learning
4. Create everyone's full understanding of the big picture
5. Promote self-regulation

This also means that those who provide support sustain organizational initiatives, processes, and proficiencies that create more and greater organizational competence.

To turn the old paradigm upside down is a statement of values. Many organizations—battered by global competition, shrinking market share, increased costs, and lower profits—have embraced the value of putting the customer first. But all too often, organizations do not "walk their talk." They do not understand that the structure they seek to turn over is not just a triangle, it is a pyramid. It is three-dimensional; all its surfaces are connected to and support each other—and thus contain all aspects of the organization. (See Figure 3.3 and Exhibit 3.1.)

To embrace the value that the customer comes first is not enough. To live that value, the organization has to examine its assumptions and align its strategy, structure, roles, people, skills, tasks, technologies, information flows, decision-making processes, measurement criteria, reward mechanisms, and the built environment with its espoused values. To do otherwise is to create contradictions. An organization cannot live the value of putting the customer first if it continues to operate with command-and-control assumptions, such as the idea that managers control processes and results as well as resources.

Experience tells us that executives and managers, no matter how skilled, only control resources. Those who make the product or provide the service control processes and results. While it may be appropriate for managers to determine *what* needs to be done, those who make the product or provide the service are in the best position to say *how* it should be done. To be inventive we must reexamine and redesign our organizational structures and practices to achieve alignment. Our strategy—which is to exceed customer expectations in product features, process innovation, or some combination thereof—needs to align with every aspect of our system: our structure, roles, people, skills, tasks, technology, information flows, decision-making processes, built environment, values, and rewards.

Figure 3.3. The Full Pyramid: Organization as a System.

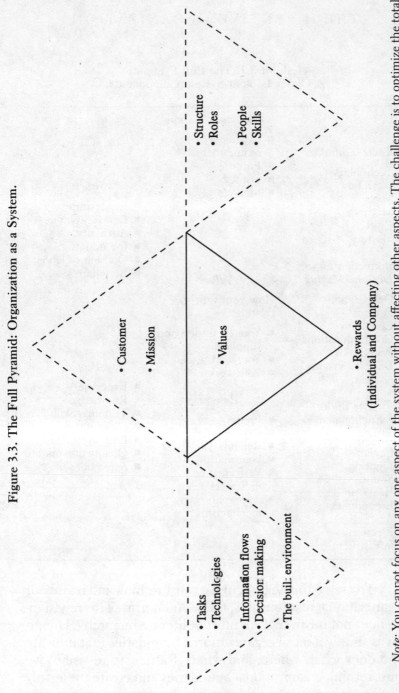

- Structure
- Roles
- People
- Skills

- Customer
- Mission
- Values
- Rewards
  (Individual and Company)

- Tasks
- Technologies
- Information flows
- Decision making
- The built environment

Note: You cannot focus on any one aspect of the system without affecting other aspects. The challenge is to optimize the total system's balance and to be responsive and inventive with respect to customer requirements and outside environmental factors.

Exhibit 3.1. The Full Pyramid:
A Closer Look at System Components.

Customer/Mission

- Customer requirements
- Purpose
- Strategy
- Markets

Task/Technology

- Technology
- Work flow
- Tools
- Methods
- Craft
- Mastery

Structure

- Leadership
- Levels/Roles
- Authority
- Job design
- Division of labor
- Boundaries

Information Flows/ Decision Making

- Deliberations
- Forums
- Coalitions
- Communications
- Feedback
- Decision-making process

Values

How you want to relate to:

- Your customers and suppliers
- Your work associates
- Your work

The Built Environment

- Facilities
- Layout
- Lighting
- Sound
- Heat/Air
- Ergonomics
- Aesthetics
- Electronic infrastructure

Rewards

- Profits
- Pay
- Benefits
- Gainsharing
- Performance indicators
- Appraisal mechanisms

People

- Expertise/ Knowledge
- Training/Skills
- Diversity
- Empowerment
- Quality of work life
- Aspirations

To create this alignment we must rethink and revise our organizational relationships, roles, and norms. This re-visioning does not mean that we must obliterate hierarchy. Hierarchy is simply a set of organizational boundaries that indicate who does what, where, and when. Rather, to re-vision, we must rethink organizational boundaries and create these only to support organizational learning, the development of core competence, and long-term viability. Regardless of shape, boundaries are useful only if they support, promote, and create everyone's accountability for being inventive.

INVESTIGATING CUSTOMER REQUIREMENTS

We need to ask ourselves and everyone in our organization whether we know our end user's requirements and, if so, how we know that we know these. We also need to ask ourselves what our impact is on meeting and exceeding customer requirements. We need to pay attention not only to our answers but also, and more important, to what we discover as we try to answer these questions. If we find that we do not have firsthand information about what the end user wants, we are not alone. The majority of those who work in organizations do not have firsthand information about their customer's requirements. When we do not have this information, we become adaptive: we try to interpret secondary information to figure out what we need to do to meet customer requirements. When we do have direct, firsthand information, we can become inventive. Inventive organizations find ways to put everyone in contact with the end user. The best contact is direct. It can be formal or informal. Focus groups and invitations to customers to visit your operation enable everyone to identify customer requirements and to develop human and technical capabilities to meet and exceed these requirements.

In addition to direct customer contact, we can gain useful information from formal customer surveys, depending on how they are developed. Makers of surveys necessarily begin with assumptions about what customers should be asked. Herein lies a pitfall. Surveys, like other organizational processes, run the risk of becoming institutionalized: year after year, the same questions and data gathering methods are repeated. When the data does not lead to desired organizational results, it is time to question the assumptions implicit in the survey questions and methods.

How often have you been asked to participate in a survey or answered questions on the warranty card of a new product you purchased? And how often have you thought that you were not being asked the right questions? The best surveys are co-designed with the customer. This produces double learning. Organizations need to find out what customers want to be asked about their level of satisfaction. The answers then provide the information needed to meet or exceed customer requirements.

The best *use* of surveys occurs when information from customers links back to the processes being managed. For example, we may ask our customers, "How user friendly is our automated telephone answering system?" Answers to this question may be useful only to those who are responsible for creating a user-friendly phone system and who have authority and responsibility for the process that creates the system rather than the phone system itself.

Today it is common to find organizations where those who state what must be done—executives and managers—and those who make the product or provide the service have little if any customer contact. Without customer contact for everyone, organizational focus is compromised. Customer contact is essential not only for those who decide what needs to be done but also for those who do the work—those who make the product or provide the service. The informal, in-person survey is a potent tool for everyone in the organization who does not have direct customer contact in the course of their daily work. In fact, one of the best ways to help senior executives provide better support to their operations is to have them regularly meet with customers and find out firsthand what customers want. Customer contact is so essential to developing good customer relationships that it cannot be confined to staff support functions such as marketing and sales. Consistent customer contact is essential to building strong customer relationships. These relationships support invention, which is an outgrowth of caring about customers and their needs and attending to those actions that result in meeting or exceeding customer requirements.

When everyone is focused on customer requirements, it becomes easier to distinguish essential work from nonessential work. We can streamline our efforts because we understand more about what we can take out of our operations and what we need to add. We see more clearly which activities create value for our customers, and we can focus our energies and resources accordingly. Customer focus leads us to discovering our core work, which is what the next chapter is all about.

4

Core Work:
Defining and Doing
the Essentials

My colleague Tony Petrella coined the term "core work" to describe the essential work—the doing—required to make the product or provide the service requested or potentially desired by the customer. It is work that results in meeting or exceeding customer expectations. All other work is ancillary; it is done to support the core work. Core work is the internal customer in the organization. All other functions are suppliers whose inputs support the needs of this internal customer.

DEFINING CORE WORK

One of our current struggles is to define essential work. In manufacturing environments, essential work includes those processes, or line operations, that create the product. This is also called "linear work" because one process leads to another in a linear, repeatable pattern.

In service organizations, core work is the service provided directly to the customer. Often it is tangible. Advice or counseling is an intangible service. Sometimes the service includes tangible components. Accountants who prepare tax returns provide advice and a tangible product. Lawyers provide advice and legal documents. Much of the work that is intangible involves analysis, deliberations, and decision making. Such work is sometimes termed "nonlinear." The processes by which such work is done are not easily prescribed. They can involve any number of interactions that occur in inconsistent patterns. This differs from a linear process, in which work occurs in a fixed and repetitive sequence.

The differences between linear and nonlinear work often are confusing because some work falls into both categories. For example, in producing durable and nondurable goods, nonlinear work occurs in marketing, a combination of linear and nonlinear work occurs in package design, and linear work occurs in manufacturing the product. As we make the transition from the late Industrial Era, where the majority of our efforts lead to manufactured goods, to the early Information Age, we will find more of our work to be nonlinear because we will be creating and manipulating data.

The shift from linear to nonlinear work also changes the nature of core work. For example, at one time, core work in the insurance industry centered around the following:

1. Underwriters, who performed the nonlinear work of gathering information and setting rates as well as the linear work of writing policies

2. Agents and brokers, who performed the nonlinear work of selling insurance services to policyholders

3. Claims representatives, who handled the linear work of processing paperwork associated with filing a claim

4. Service representatives, who did the nonlinear work of interacting with policyholders—answering questions, tracking claims in progress, and tracking changes made in policies

If we had redesigned that core work, we would have focused on underwriting, selling, claims processing, and policy tracking. Today, however, the gathering, manipulation, and communication of information is aided by more and more advanced technology. Technology makes it possible for potential policyholders to go "on line" to an insurance carrier's database. Potential customers can use information sent by modem to decide whether to buy insurance, without ever interacting with an agent or broker. A policyholder can increase insurance, file a claim, or cancel insurance, without interacting with an agent, broker, or customer service representative. Therefore, agents, brokers, and customer service representatives, who at one time were necessary intermediaries between the product (the policy) and the policyholder, are no longer strictly necessary. If we were to redesign core work under this scenario, we would focus on the underwriting, the claims processing, and the technologies that support purchasing, filing claims, and self-monitoring of insurance transactions.

Locating Misplaced Core Work

Another of our struggles is that some core work has been taken away from the core and placed in support functions. When organizations grow from very small—twenty people or fewer—to very large—thousands—and it becomes necessary to produce goods and services on a mass scale, the conventional wisdom has been to divide work into segments and to place like segments into functions. At one time, it was possible for one person—a craftsperson—to make an entire product or provide a complete service. When larger and larger quantities were required and methods of production became more and more complex, the conventional wisdom was to divide work into smaller units. It simply was no longer possible to become a "jack of all trades" without becoming a "master of none." The results of dividing up the essential work were that jobs became narrow and repetitive, people became extensions of machines, and procedures were devised to monitor the flow of divided work. In reality, these procedures are superfluous to providing products or services. They become necessary because whole jobs and processes are now fragmented into several jobs and processes.

In some cases, work has been taken away from the core and placed in functions such as engineering, maintenance, materials management, and quality assurance, even though it is part of the process that creates the product. In reality, this work is still part of the core work. In other cases, which result when organizations grow from small proprietorships to institutions with hundreds and thousands of employees, economies of scale have dictated the creation of other types of support functions. Such functions are dedicated to (1) providing linkage—for example, marketing connects the customer and knowledge of the external operating environment to multiple functions within the organization—and (2) centralization of certain processes required throughout the organization, such as finance or human resources. Support functions can be structured as centralized or decentralized, or as a combination. Regardless of how well support functions are structured, they result in a loss of control at the point where production actually occurs.

Aside from redefining what is core and what is support, we need to recognize that core work can also become splintered when task forces are created. Sometimes these temporary structures are created so that some aspect of the organization's functioning can be studied and possibly altered. The benefit of a task force is that it involves a broad spectrum of people—often line and staff—and thus makes possible an enriched and more comprehensive approach to the issue under study. The downside of a task force is revealed when decisions that should be made by those who do the essential work are made instead by those in the temporary structure.

Impediments to Core Work

The net effect of support functions and temporary structures is the creation of more organizational boundaries. For the organization to produce, transactions need to occur across boundaries. The more boundaries, the more difficult it is for everyone to have a "line of sight" from their task to the end user's satisfaction, the easier it is for "things to fall through the cracks," the more likely it is to find organizational fragmentation, and the greater the chances for debilitating internal competition for scarce resources and the "not-invented-here" syndrome. Worst of all, ill-constructed boundaries lead to more and more "signature approvals," more and more policies relegating turf to various functions and dictating how functions are to interact. Procedures may proliferate merely so that those who see themselves as responsible—the leaders—can ensure control over those whom they perceive as not able to be responsible—the followers. These myriad approvals, policies, and procedures give rise to more of the same until they impede the core work of the enterprise. Like barnacles on a ship's hull, they become the invisible and calcified assumptions about "how we get things done around here."

DESIGNING THE ORGANIZATION FROM THE END USER IN AND FROM THE CORE WORK OUT

The first rule in looking at an organization is to see it through your customers' eyes. What does the customer see, feel, hear, touch, and remember in that critical transaction that occurs when the organization delivers and the customer receives a product or service. No customer should have to understand how a company is organized to be able to do business with that company. The organization's internal structure—no matter how convoluted or whether such convolutions are driven by regulatory requirements—should be transparent to the customer, and products and services should be delivered in ways that are seamless. When we look for a jacket or a shirt, we want to see the piece of clothing and not all the seams that go into holding pieces of fabric together.

To design an organization well is to start with the transaction between the end user and the organization (Chapter

Three) and then to focus on core work. Core work—how it is designed and supported—is the most critical element in any organization. With the end user's point of view in mind, then, we design from the core work out. Our Industrial Era strategy of mass production resulted in narrow, repetitive jobs overseen by staff functions and controlled by steep hierarchies. The assumptions underlying that strategy need to be reexamined in this era, which is driven by customer requirements for mass customization, rapid breakthroughs in technology, and markedly differentiated value for markedly different pricing of goods and services. The best way to examine our assumptions is to look at what we believe is the organization's core work—the essential work that meets or exceeds customer requirement.

The critical elements in the design of core work include "line of sight," support and control in every role, whole rather than fragmented jobs, and the evolution of organizational competencies.

Creating "Line of Sight" and Support and Control in Every Role

Work needs to be designed so everyone has "line of sight"; that is, everyone knows the customer's requirements and understands how their work contributes to meeting or exceeding those requirements. Further, they understand the economics of the business, its technical requirements, the people needs, and how the built environment can support the operations.

Johnson & Johnson undertook a work redesign at one of their plants. Prior to the redesign, engineers purchased all production equipment used by the plant. Because they did not work with the equipment every day and were not responsible for equipment repairs, they did not have the big picture. When deciding which equipment to purchase, they relied on their engineering expertise, manufacturers' guarantees, equipment demonstrations, and their knowledge of capital allocations.

It is not unusual for manufacturers to stipulate equipment capabilities based on short-batch runs rather than continuous processing. At this plant, a particular packaging machine had been purchased on the basis that it could run 350 units per minute. Over the course of several days, the equipment broke down. By experimenting, workers found the machine ran consistently well at 275 units per minute. The supervisor approved the employees' requests to lower the per-minute volume to avoid costly downtime; however, the weekly production goals remained the same. These were based on 350 units per minute. The only way to make up for the shortfall was to work overtime, which is a cost to the system.

After the redesign of the plant, a team of engineers, packaging operators, maintenance personnel, and the manager of the focused factory for which the equipment was to be purchased all worked together on equipment purchases. Each had particular equipment needs and no one person could speak for another. The team traveled to Europe to investigate equipment. During a meeting with one manufacturer, post-sale support was discussed. The manufacturer said that at the time the equipment was installed, a team would go to the United States and train all the employees to operate the equipment. One of the operators asked the manufacturer if there would be continued support for people hired after the equipment had been installed. There was silence for a moment and then the manufacturer responded that while they would not provide in-person support, they could make a videotape that the company could use to train new employees. When the operator asked the cost of the video, he was told approximately $25,000. He responded that the company did not have $25,000 in its budget for a videotape. The manufacturer agreed to work with the company to find a way to support ongoing training without exceeding the capital allocation for new equipment.

This story was told to me by the manager who had been part of the purchasing team. As he finished the story, he smiled and said, "Now there is an employee who thinks like a manager." I replied, "There is an employee who thinks like an employee. He understands the economics of the situation, the technical needs, the skills requirements, and how the built environment supports or thwarts meeting and exceeding customer requirements."

One of the major obstacles in today's organizations is that few individuals, if any, can see the big picture. To see the big picture, everyone must understand how tasks, functions, and processes link up to create a product or service. The sheer size and silo-like shape of structures that are characteristic of most organizations make such "sight" almost impossible. The problem can be traced to the late Industrial Period, at the turn of the century, when organizational size and structure changed from small proprietorships to large factories, from family run businesses to professionally run steep hierarchies.

The transition owed much to Henri Fayol, Adam Smith, and Frederick Taylor, who designed methods for mass production at a time when that was the best way to compete. These methods were based on assumptions that were right for the time, even though much of what Taylor developed was misinterpreted and misapplied (see Weisbord, 1987). The ideas of unity of command, spans of control, repetitive jobs, and the division of labor between those who think and those who do are examples of what led to steep organizational hierarchies.

Steep hierarchies result in the division of labor, the evolution of staff functions, and the development of "made up" career ladders, all of which contribute to fragmented organizations. In a fragmented organization, few people, if any, (1) can see the big picture — which means they understand organizational strategy, the work flows and processes, and their contribution to the finished product or service; (2) know how their interactions with their co-workers and other work units support the success of the enterprise; or (3) have "line of sight," which means they understand the end user's requirements, the use of what is produced, and how their work contributes to customer satisfaction. Steep hierarchies are now impediments to strategies required to compete today — such as mass customization, revolutionary new products, services, and process technology — which revolve around organizational core competence.

In a redesign project for a consumer products company, the design team at one of the company's manufacturing facilities charted the organization's entire work flow. The plant that undertook the redesign had responsibility for making two of the company's many products and for warehousing and shipping what they produced as well as products from other facilities. Nonetheless, the design team charted every step in the process, from product conception to customer usage. One entire wall of the redesign meeting room was covered with three-by-five-inch index cards that were connected by black lines to show all the steps involved in "time to market." Pink cards were used to depict all the steps in the process that preceded the plant's receiving an order to produce x number of case goods. Blue cards depicted the work flow within the plant. And yellow cards depicted what happened to the product once it left the plant and was purchased and used.

Several weeks into the redesign, two senior vice presidents from the plant's corporate headquarters asked to attend one of the updates of the steering committee. They had heard about the project and wanted to familiarize themselves with the redesign process. They sat down and looked for a while at the wall depicting the company's entire work flow. Then one asked the other, "Have you ever seen that before?" The other responded, "No, have you?" If two senior vice presidents have not seen the entire work flow — the big picture — who has?

Work also needs to be designed so that support and control exist at the point where work is done and not several layers or functions away. It is critical in efficient operations that where something happens, those who observe and those who control it are all present. It is better still if all this resides in one person or one team of people. For example, on an assembly line, it is common to find that operators can observe a machine malfunction but have no authority to stop the line. They must inform their supervisor, who approves the shutdown, and then maintenance is called to correct the problem. When work is fragmented and three people are responsible for a part of a situation, three things occur. The hand-off of work creates downtime. There is less investment in and ownership of the work process by those who have responsibility without authority. And, more often than not, confusion exists about who does what.

DESIGNING WHOLE VERSUS FRAGMENTED JOBS

Closely aligned with both line of sight and support and control is the concept of work designed around a whole task. The legacy of the Industrial Era is narrow, repetitive jobs where people perform a segment of the whole job and, in effect, become extensions of machines. Work designed to give the worker the whole job creates line of sight, pride of ownership, and accountability for results. This contrasts with fragmented jobs, where individuals often have a "throw-it-over-the-fence" mentality when things go wrong and are unable to see their contribution to customer satisfaction when things go well.

   Fragmentation can occur in individual jobs and in the delineation of functions. For example, it is common to find core work being done in staff rather than line operations. In effect, the tasks are splintered, which results in confusion over who is supporting and who is controlling the core work. Fragmentation also occurs in supposedly decentralized operations wherein a full coterie of staff people are assigned to head-quarters and a full coterie of staff people are employed by each product division or SBU. Whenever people do not have control over their responsibilities or appropriate support for meeting and exceeding customer requirements, it is impossible to hold them accountable for results. (For more information on how to create commensurate authority and responsibility, see the section on Responsibility Charts in Chapter Seven.)

In early 1979, I was hired by a worldwide manufacturer of cloth-ing as director of human resources development. At that time, the headquarters for this company was located in downtown San Francisco, while most of the factories were located along the southern border of the United States. Having come from finan-cial and service-based institutions, I found manufacturing to be a very different world. I knew nothing about sociotechnical sys-tems work and nothing about manufacturing. This much I did know: I visited the plants and saw work so specialized and frag-mented that it hurt. One person would spend an entire day sew-ing the right pocket on a pair of jeans. The workers were well treated, the factories were clean, the wages competitive, and the benefits were more than competitive. Yet I knew there was some-thing inherently wrong with having to sew the right pocket on a pair of jeans all day.

I left the company after six months because I felt guilty. I sat in a glass-enclosed corner corporate office because other peo-ple sat all day in factories and sewed right pockets on pairs of jeans. Had I known about work redesign and re-engineering in 1979, I could have contributed to the much-needed changes in our assumptions about productive and meaningful work.

Fragmented jobs create fragmented functions and fragmented organizations. People are unable to be accountable for results nor can they take pride in their contribution to the whole. If my job is to sew the right pocket on the pair of jeans and I do this cor-

rectly, am I accountable for the finished product? No. Whether or not that product meets standards, all I can account for is the condition of the right pocket. Even then, I may not be able to perform my job correctly because the incoming supply—the sewn pant leg—may contain quality defects that affect my task. Worse yet, neither my supplier nor those whom I supply further down the line have any idea what it takes for me to be successful on my job. Each person knows only that portion—that fragment—of the job that he or she performs.

Ensuring That Responsibility and Authority Are Commensurate

Responsibility without commensurate authority is another outgrowth of steep hierarchies, fragmented organizations, and narrow jobs. Where one person or one function ends and another begins is often most unclear to those who do the work. In Chapter Seven, a Responsibility Chart—an R chart—is introduced. An R chart is a useful tool for clarifying who does what; however, this tool is only as good as the organization's definitions for *responsibility, authority,* and *accountability.*

It is useful to think of responsibility as the obligation to do the task or make the decision. Authority is the right to approve how the task is done or how the decision is made. Accountability means to "be held to account for the results." Managers can delegate all kinds of authority and responsibility. What they cannot delegate is their accountability. And they cannot hold employees accountable for the results if the employee's authority is not commensurate with responsibility. In simple terms, those who do the work must control what they do. If they do not, two outcomes result. First, because they need authority to execute their responsibilities, and this authority can only be obtained from a designated person, employees are forced to ask their managers to do their work—to make and/or approve decisions that are a part of the employees' role. Second, when those who do the work do not have control over what they do, they will rightfully balk at being held to account for the results.

Providing Support Versus Control for Core Work

Staff work supports core work whether core work is linear or nonlinear. (Human resources, finance, and legal functions were mentioned earlier as examples of staff work.) While the intent of staff work is to provide support to core operations, staff functions frequently take on a life of their own. Rather than perform as internal suppliers of information or services needed by the core work functions, staff units become internal customers. This occurs when core functions perform work simply to meet the demands of a staff function. The staff function is then viewed as a drain on core work rather than a support for core work. In effect, the internal supplier has become the internal customer. I know this has occurred whenever I hear people in core work functions say "I have to get this performance appraisal done for Human Resources," rather than "I need to get this appraisal done so Joe will know how well he is contributing to meeting our customer requirements." In inventive organizations, work is done only to meet external customer needs, regulatory requirements, or the organization's responsibilities as a member of society.

A simple example illustrates the difference between core work and staff work. In a work design simulation called the Flying Starship Factory, the core work is cutting, folding, assembling, painting, and selling starships. The staff work—or ancillary work—is materials handling, quality assurance, and supervision. This work is ancillary because it can be handled by those who do the core work. In other words, it is not necessary to create separate functions and jobs for taking materials from supply and moving materials through the factory, nor is it necessary to have a separate inspection process, nor is it necessary to have someone supervise the making of starships unless the work has been so fragmented and organizational policy is so restrictive as to prevent those who do the core tasks from working together on the entire product. In almost every redesign of the simulated starship factory, design teams wind up re-creating the factory so that quality is at the source — everyone is their own quality assurance person — and materials are obtained by those who do the work whenever they need to replenish supplies. And in most redesigns, the traditional supervisory role is eliminated. Among the many lessons the starship factory offers, perhaps the most critical is that work once split off from the core can be returned to it.

In Chapter Three, customer requirements are presented as the driving force in the organization. Core work is the essential work that meets or exceeds customer requirements. All other work should be in support of core work. In a redesign or re-engineering process, the focus is on core work. Once that work is redesigned, there is greater clarity about the type of support required and how it is best provided. It is a mistake to redesign support functions before examining and redesigning core work. When re-engineering starts in support functions, the enterprise, rather than becoming integrated and inventive, becomes fragmented and fixed.

The best work redesign efforts start where the product is produced, rather than with support functions. In the former, you build the support function to meet the needs of the internal customer. In the latter, you retrofit the customer to fit the supplier. The redesign effort at a Johnson & Johnson subsidiary in North Carolina is an example of what can occur when redesign does not start with the core work and move out. The plant in question makes nonwoven gauze products, many of which are used in hospitals. I was asked to facilitate a redesign at the plant in 1988. The group designated for the redesign was Materials Management — a support function. At this plant, the tail was wagging the dog.

The plant manager chose Materials Management as a place to start because he wanted to test the pluses and minuses inherent in whole-systems work, but he didn't want to risk disruption in the core work. The design team included individuals from Materials Management, Finance, and Engineering. The steering committee included the plant manager and the managers of Finance, Engineering, and Human Resources.

Among many recommendations, the redesign proposal indicated that Purchasing and Accounts Payable should report to Materials Management. This recommendation created havoc with the manager of Finance. He reported on a straight line to Corporate Finance in New Brunswick, New Jersey, and on a dotted line to the plant manager. His first argument was that Generally Accepted Accounting Procedures (GAAP) would not allow Purchasing and Accounts Payable to be in the same function because the necessary controls would not exist to ensure against fraudulent purchases. The design team called the corporate controller to find out what kinds of controls had to be in place to put Accounts Payable and Purchasing together. The controller was not against the proposal and, in fact, stipulated the kinds of controls that would make the recommendation feasible. The manager of Finance then argued that no changes in Accounts Payable should be made until Finance had undergone a work redesign.

The real issue was one of turf, not how best to serve customer needs. If Accounts Payable went to Materials Management, the manager of Finance had lost some turf. His boundary had been assaulted in ways he perceived as negative for him. And to place Purchasing in Finance made no sense in terms of properly aligning Purchasing and other aspects of Materials Management. His solution was to delay implementation of the redesign proposed by Materials Management until the same effort was undertaken in Finance.

When I was asked to facilitate a redesign in Finance, I told the plant manager it was a poor use of company money to disaggregate work design efforts when such efforts were aimed at integration. I said the plant should start redesign in Operations and then work into Finance, Human Resources, and Materials Management. To do otherwise was to continue to fragment an already fragmented system and to anoint boundaries that were no longer appropriate to sustaining competitive advantage. The plant manager agreed; however, he could not obtain approval from Corporate to proceed.

Brenda Allen, secretary to the plant's chief engineer and a member of the Materials Management design team had become the informal leader of that team. Brenda is a quick study, dedicated, hard working, and a natural leader. She asked me if I would be available to her by telephone if she took on the role of facilitating further work design efforts at the plant. I was delighted. (One of my values is to link up with internal company resources so clients can carry on continuous improvement without becoming dependent on external consultants.)

I heard from Brenda two or three times during the next several months. Then she sent me the design proposal for Finance. That proposal is among the best I have ever seen. I wrote Brenda a note and told her that when the plant said it needed a consultant, she should say, "I are one!" Today the plant has been completely redesigned and the boundary issues have been resolved, even though redesign started in support functions. The good news is that the head of Finance became a convert and wound up leading the redesign of the core work. The process would, however, have been less difficult and more efficient if boundary issues— between the plant and Corporate and those within the plant— had not precipitated the start of the redesign in the support functions.

REMOVING ORGANIZATIONAL BARNACLES

Organizational barnacles are policies, practices, structures, and roles that build up over time and are not examined from the standpoint of how these support the core work. These barnacles are often invisible to those within the enterprise. They develop when implicit assumptions are not questioned. They protect the status quo. For all of these reasons, they are difficult to remove.

Just as ships need to be dry-docked and scraped, organizations need to review their operations periodically. Such reviews need to be conducted by those who actually do the core work as well as those who support the core work. Areas of review include

1. Customer requirements
2. Core work flows — what goes on and what goes wrong
3. The quality of employees' work lives
4. The values the organization wants to live out in its relationships with customers, work associates, and the work itself

Systematic analyses of these four conditions are part of the process called work redesign.

During one redesign project with a consumer products company, the design teams found that 550 sheets of paperwork were completed for every batch of product produced. The essential work that created the product involved six steps, most of which were automated. Prior to the redesign project, no one had ever tracked the amount of paperwork for the entire six steps, which were performed in three departments that were subdivided into sections. I will never forget the astonished response from a steering committee member when he heard the design team present this finding. He said, "My god, every time we produce a batch of product, a forest falls in Washington!"

The implicit assumption was that the Food and Drug Administration (FDA), which was the primary regulatory agency for this company, was the culprit. In reality, the FDA required only about 20 sheets of paper. At least 400 of the 550 sheets were barnacles. They had evolved over time. Most were legacies left by MBAs who had been hired fresh out of school to serve two-year stints as production supervisors. The job was part of the rotation required to move up the leadership ladder in the organization. The plant workers called these two-year stints "getting your ticket punched." These same workers were saddled with the paperwork left by those they felt they had trained for promotion.

Paperwork

Paperwork is one of the more onerous organizational barnacles. Once a form or report is created, it often endures long after its usefulness has passed. Worse, a great deal of paperwork turns out to overlap with other paperwork, which creates redundancies that often double the time and cost to process information. Tracking the amount of paperwork it takes to produce product or provide service is a good way to learn more about the most efficient use of resources, both human and technical; about assumptions that give rise to paperwork, such as a belief that most paperwork meets some form of regulatory requirement; and more about essential and nonessential work.

More often than not, the amount of paperwork in an organization is proportional to the degree to which staff support functions have become internal customers rather than internal suppliers. When those who make the product or provide the service are required to complete paperwork they did not create, there is a danger that the support functions that created the paperwork are the customer. As a result, those who make the product or provide the service have two customers: the end user and the internal support function whose paperwork requirements often add no value.

Automated Processes

Another barnacle begins to grow when manual processes are automated without evaluation. A sound evaluation includes a review of how the process contributes to meeting or exceeding customer requirements. Sometimes the process is no longer needed. More often it needs to be streamlined prior to automation. Otherwise the organization spends time and money to automate its inefficiencies.

When I joined the Federal National Mortgage Association in 1982 as director of Human Resources, I had a gut-level feeling that there was entirely too much paperwork in the function. I hired a summer intern. I told him he was to become an application form and follow the process until he was hired and put "on record." I wanted to know how many pieces of paper he had become. A week later, he informed me he was now forty pieces of paper. The cost of storage alone, never mind processing, made me wince. I asked the staff if they thought this was excessive. Everyone agreed it was ridiculous. And everyone had contributed to the pile.

Human Resources had an unreliable and antiquated Human Resources Information System. Actually, to call it an HRIS is an insult to systems. This particular system did not interface with Payroll; they had their own antiquated system. My predecessor's relationship with the director of Payroll was so poor that no one in HR spoke to anyone in Payroll. The duplication of information in HR and Payroll was bad enough. The duplication within HR was even worse.

The receptionist, in addition to logging applications into a log book, kept a three-by-five-inch index card on every application—just in case the log book was misplaced. The two women who entered data into the HRIS were "well burned" skeptics. The system was so unreliable that even correctly entered data was lost or recorded inaccurately. They each kept their own manual logs of what was supposed to be in the system. Finally, when all the forms were lined up side by side, the overlap of required information was mind-boggling.

Within a few months, the staff consolidated most of the forms into documentation that was far more useful and efficient. I mended relations with the director of Payroll and we appointed a joint task force, made up of Payroll and HR employees, to investigate and recommend the purchase of a combined Payroll/HRIS system.

Levels of Approval

When multiple levels of approval are required to begin, change, or stop an action, another barnacle is growing. In one *Fortune* 100 organization, to avoid layoffs, the CEO must sign off on every addition to the full-time staff. And to get that signature requires that everyone else in the chain of command, which can include up to sixteen levels, must sign off as well.

Another worldwide organization set a goal of reducing speed to market from one year to six months. It was found that pricing approval on new products took six weeks because eight people had to sign off. When questioned, members in the organization admitted that the first person signed off because they had gathered the requisite information. The second person signed off to indicate this decision had been reviewed by someone other than the person who gathered the data and made the recommendation. The remaining sign-offs were pro forma. In other words, the third individual would not have signed off had the second person not signed off, and so it went up to the eighth individual. Six of these signatures were meaningless, and they cost the organization five weeks of time when the espoused goal was speed to market. This is an example of an organizational barnacle — a calcified object that adds useless bulk and impedes progress.

Form Without Substance

Form without substance is another barnacle. An example is the need for employees in department stores to have their supervisors sign off on credits to charge cards. Often the supervisor is not available. More often, the supervisor signs without reviewing the credit or the returned merchandise. If employees are trusted to sell thousands of dollars worth of merchandise without a supervisor's signature, why is it impossible to permit the employee to credit a hundred dollars for merchandise that has been returned?

Other examples of form over substance can be found

in policies and procedures — rules and "how to's" for doing — that often stifle invention. Rather than write policy for what *can* be done, inventive organizations write policy only about things that cannot happen in the work environment.

Most job descriptions, too, are examples of form over substance. More often than not, they are written to calculate a pay scale for a job. They describe tasks and boundaries — what can and cannot be done — rather than expected results, actions, and behaviors. As such, they focus the job holder on the wrong outcomes — activities as opposed to contributions to organizational success.

Nonaligned Authority and Responsibility

Yet another barnacle is nonalignment between authority and responsibility. In one regional stock exchange, the senior vice president (SVP) of technology had sign-off authority for $2,500. Yet he was responsible for a $6 million annual budget. To make matters worse, information systems technology is the core work in a stock exchange. To avoid involving the president in signing off on every purchase that was part of the SVP's approved capital budget, vendors were asked to issue "parts" invoices for anything that cost over $2,500. Approximately 90 percent of the purchases exceeded the SVP's approval limit.

The ripple effect of this limited authority was enormous. Vice presidents, division managers, and functional managers had practically no approval authority. The SVP could not delegate what he did not have. Signature after signature was required on forms that circulated up and down the hierarchy. The processing of the approval form delayed the implementation of efficiencies the purchased equipment was supposed to effect.

Organizational barnacles are insidious and constricting because

1. They are the result of unexamined and often intractable assumptions and therefore impede flexibility.

2.   They grow slowly over time, so it is difficult to see exactly how onerous they have become.

3.   They form a hard cover over the real work that needs to be done and are difficult to remove.

4.   They absorb rather than free resources by creating unnecessary, nonadded value work.

5.   They often cover up underlying issues of trust.

HOW TO DEVELOP CORE COMPETENCE

Core competence is "know what and know how" to meet and exceed customer requirements—in processes, products, services, delivery, and customer service. Core competence is knowing how to

- Harmonize streams of technology

- Organize work to create value for customers, suppliers, stakeholders, and employees

- Blend individual expertise with that of others in new and interesting ways

- Assemble and spread resources across multiple businesses

- Find original ways to provide customer value instead of following others into the marketplace and competing only on quality or price

- Generate multiple approaches to meeting and exceeding customer needs

- Create ways to collaborate, internally and externally, through strategic alliances

- Create flexible structures that support organizational strategy

- Develop outsourcing resources
- Form partnerships with customers, suppliers, and financiers
- Involve key stakeholders—customers, employees, suppliers, stockholders, and community members—in the right combination and at the right time so that products, services and organizational vitality exceed everyone's expectations (Prahalad and Hamel, 1990, pp. 80–88).

Core competence is the basis for achieving dynamic competitive advantage. As Prahalad and Hamel put it, it is the ability "to create an organization capable of infusing products with irresistible functionality or, better yet, creating products that customers need but have not yet imagined." It is the ability to look ahead ten to fifteen years and "see emerging customer needs, changing technologies and the core competencies that would be necessary to bridge the gap between the two. The strategic architecture for doing this is not a forecast of specific products or specific technologies but a broad map of the evolving linkages between customers' functional requirements, potential technologies and core competence" (Prahalad and Hamel, 1990, pp. 80–88). The most valuable core competence is not product or service specific; rather, it is competence that can create a broad array of products and services.

5

Values:
Walking Our Talk

Our collective values are the soul of our organizational entities. They underlie how we will learn about and act on our customers' requirements and how we will design our organizations around the core work that meets or exceeds these requirements. Our organizational values constitute a force that links individuals into a collective. They create common cause. They inspire us to achieve our potential.

Many organizations spend considerable time, effort, and money flirting with values by sponsoring values clarification activities. The ways in which these activities occur speak volumes about what will be achieved. Most often, executives go off-site, often with an external consultant, and create a list of organizational values. These values turn up on wallet-sized cards and organization posters to remind everyone to adopt them as operating principles. Unfortunately, not only does this sort of activity reinforce the old "some think and others do" organizational mentality, the very slogans that people are asked to adopt often have multiple meanings, depending on who is using the words.

It is easy to subscribe to the idea of organizational values.

It is easy to adopt terms such as *respect, openness, quality, efficiency, honesty,* and *excellence*—to name a few. We make it difficult, if not impossible, to walk our talk when we do not ask ourselves what these words mean and how we can tell they are in practice in our organizations.

How can we tell if we are living our values in our relationships with our customers and suppliers, our work associates, and our work itself? Our values need to become more than words. They need to become deeds. They need to become behavioral statements: our organizational practice of our organizational ethics. Here are some examples of how ideas can be expressed as actions:

Word	*Deed*
Diversity	We seek the maximum mix of people in our collaborative efforts.
Quality	We do it right the first time.
Service	We do unto others as we would have them do unto us.
Learning	We create time out to reflect on and enhance our efforts. When we do not know, we ask.
Risk	We ask why not and not simply why.
Timeliness	We do it now.
Excellence	We want to create good habits.
Dedication	We honor "how much you care" before "how much you know."

Team	We look on each person with the same eye of favor. We work together, train together.
Goal oriented	We focus on results, not activities.
Continuous improvement	We structure projects so there are visible payoffs along the way.
Experiment	We try out rough prototypes of new systems to get early feedback from the people who will use them.
Efficiency	We postpone automation until processes are redesigned.

When we talk about deeds (rather than espouse words), we have ways of knowing whether we are practicing what we espouse. In "Notes on Running an Organization," Peter Vaill says, "If we do not face the fact that leadership and management is about values and standards and morals and is a modern pursuit of the ancient dream of the good, we truly are just rearranging the deck chairs on the *Titanic*." I would expand that statement to say that how we lead and follow in our organizations is indeed about values and standards and morals and is a modern pursuit of the ancient dream of the good, for I believe walking our talk is not management's domain; rather, it is everyone's. Further, if we do not state what our values look like when they are in practice, we lose the key to knowing whether we are walking our talk.

I once worked with a worldwide manufacturer whose motto was "The company is its people." One day I had an experience that not only illustrates how different people can interpret a motto, which is a statement of corporate values, but also what can occur when we have only words and no actions to show if we are measuring up to what we espouse.

I had a luncheon meeting with a senior vice president, a man who started his career in the stock room and worked his way up the corporate ladder. There was no doubt he was an experienced businessman if experience means understanding profit and loss, the cost of goods, what will sell, and how to stay ahead of the competition. What was missing was his seeing the organization — the system — as a series of relationships in action.

We took the elevator to the company's cafeteria. As the doors opened, we saw a young man writhing on the floor. It appeared to me that he was convulsed. The senior vice president stepped over him and continued to the cafeteria. Several others went to help the young man, who, it turned out, was having an epileptic seizure. He needed immediate medical attention. All I kept hearing in my head was that motto: The company is its people. This value seemed to be lived out by those who stopped to help the young man. But for one senior vice president, lunch seemed to be more important than ensuring the well-being of the company's most important asset.

FINDING OUR LOST KEY: WALKING OUR TALK

In *Wisdom of the Sands*, Antoine de Saint-Exupéry writes, "Place no hope in man if he works for his own lifetime and not for his eternity" (1950, p. 28). Our values represent our eternity. Our values are our higher selves. They are the basis for finding our common cause. They make clear the consequences of our actions. When we live our espoused values, we act on behalf of others and not just ourselves. In effect, extracting from Saint-Exupéry's words, we are bartering our souls for something greater than ourselves.

Values are not complicated. They are the essence of who we are and what we stand for. They are a kind of genetic imprint. They are the Golden Rule, the Ten Commandments, the Seven Deadly Sins, and the simple basics Robert Fulgram wrote about in his book *Everything I Need to Know I Learned in Kindergarten*. We complicate values by turning them into things we need to go off on retreat to clarify. We detach our actions from our values when we believe that a card in our wallet makes our commitment to our values real. We estrange ourselves from our values when we point to them as something to aspire to rather than live.

My friend and colleague Jack Sherwood coined the "pinch theory." He defines a pinch as a "signal of the possibility of an impending disruption." Our values create the pinch. A pinch occurs when we are quick to tell a cashier that we have been given too little change but fail to speak up when we have received too much change. A pinch occurs when we have eaten a banana while driving in our car and flung the peel out the window, telling ourselves that it is biodegradable. A pinch occurs when we eat meals on the company's expense account that we would not eat at our own expense. A pinch occurs when we see an imperfection in our work but it is "close enough" that no one else will know. A pinch occurs when we have "off the record conversations" about issues that are part of our record. A pinch occurs when we use language to mask reality—euphemisms such as *right-sizing* and *downsizing* when we mean *permanent lay-off.*

A pinch occurs whether or not we are found out. A pinch is the signal of a disruption in walking our talk. A pinch is our own self-knowledge that we have violated the deepest wisdom we have—our internal gauge of fairness, right action, justice. This gauge is our integrity. It is our ability to live out the truth we know regardless of the circumstances in which we find ourselves. Unfortunately, each time we ignore a pinch, we condition ourselves to stop feeling the pinch. We become desensitized to violating our values. And in the end, we violate no one else as deeply as we violate ourselves when we do not live according to the truth we know.

Why have our values become things we need to clarify, package, distribute, and record in our corporate diaries? Why have our values become "how we wish to be"? It is as if our obsession with marketing, packaging, and distribution, which is aimed at products and services, has eclipsed our common sense. We can package and distribute things, but we cannot package and distribute our higher selves. We cannot package that pinch that signals the possibility of an impending disruption. We can, however, feel that pinch and live our daily lives by acting in accordance with our internal gauge of fairness, justice, and right action.

A NEW BLUEPRINT
FOR DEVELOPING
ORGANIZATIONAL VALUES

Because our values create common cause—a term coined by Tom Watson of IBM—we must align what we walk and talk with our customers' requirements. This means that we must also align our corporate strategy, structure, and sustaining mechanisms with these requirements. Then our individual and collective pledges and commitments are aligned and we have the possibility of satisfying our individual and collective aspirations. Sometimes our values are the same as our mission; for example, McDonald's values of service, quality, cleanliness, and value. Sometimes value is the same as a vision; Herman Miller's vision statement is "To be a gift to the human spirit."

Our values create community. They can represent both the individual and the collective whole. They can fuel actions that serve and support the entire system of relationships in action. When we review the transition continuums in Chapter Two in concert with values, we can determine the underlying causes of fixed, adaptive, and inventive organizations (see Figure 5.1).

Figure 5.1. Transition Continuum with Values Orientations.

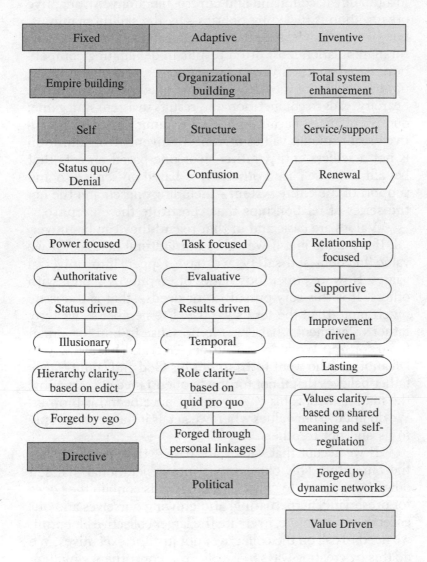

Source: Partially adapted from work by Peter Gibb.

A fixed organization is fueled by directives—by a belief in a top-down, command-and-control hierarchy. An adaptive organization is fueled by politics—by the skillful manipulation of oneself in relation to the organizational structure. Skillful manipulation most often results in debilitating competitions based on scarcity—scarcity of power, of positions in the upper echelons of the hierarchy, and of corporate resources. Scarcity leads to competition and results in a zero-sum game; one is enhanced because another is diminished. An inventive organization is values driven. An inventive organization is not a selfless entity; rather, it is one based on acts that benefit both "self" and others. It is based on service to and support of the entire system—including oneself and the entire series of relationships that constitute the enterprise.

Values are basic and in that regard they can be universal. If we value life, if we value our cultural heritage; if we value freedom and safety, we have tapped into universal values. How we pursue our values often puts us at odds with others. It is this very pursuit—our deeds—that is the issue much more than the terms we use. I remember so well my father's statements that it made no sense to him for a man to go forth in World War II under God and his country to kill another who went forth under his God and country. My father believes that if not for the happenstance of geography, the man named as his enemy might have been his brother. We do not live our values when we act as if they pertain only to us and not to others.

If we accept that values are basics, then everyone has the blueprint. This blueprint is intergenerational, handed down from parent to child. Our blueprints contain the codes for preserving, perpetuating, and growing ourselves and our collectives. Therefore, to create the larger collective blueprint, we need to call on the collective, not just the executives. We do this by creating ways to involve our constituency in identifying what is needed to make our deeds reflect our words. By involving the collective, we build not only common cause but common commitment.

Our values should not be confused with our preferences. Each generation has had its chosen styles of music, architecture, art, literature, and fashion. Each generation has experimented with new ways of living and creating relationships. And each generation has rebelled against the previous generation's preferences. And yet, with time and age, we find ourselves honoring what our parents honored — the basics.

Not long ago, I was contacted by the head of Human Resources for the Information Systems Division of a large insurance company. He was interested in clarifying the division's values and asked me to facilitate a values clarification retreat for the division's top management. After talking with him about the difference between commitment and compliance, I proposed that I first interview a diagonal slice of the organization. ("Diagonal slice" refers to a representative sample of people from each function and each level within an organizational entity.) In this way, I could learn what values were important and how best to collectively determine and then illuminate these values. He agreed.

When I arrived at the corporate offices for a day of interviews — some of which were individual and most of which were group interviews — I noticed framed poster after framed poster hanging on hallway and conference room walls. One was an Information Systems mission statement, another a vision statement, another a list of improvement initiatives, another a list of targeted objectives, another a focus statement on strategy, another a statement of quality principles. I knew a great deal of effort had gone into what these posters represented. I also knew they were too many and too detailed to be remembered and implemented. They were symptoms of the dried peas syndrome (see Chapter One). To add a statement of values to these walls would be to further confuse activities with results.

After completing the interviews, I spoke with the head of Human Resources. I told him I would be happy to facilitate the retreat; however, rather than using the retreat to develop a state-

ment of values, I thought it would be best to use it to determine what values were important to the senior management in attendance and then how best to engage the system—in this case the Information Systems Division—in developing statements of deeds by which they wished to live. I also suggested that the other initiatives that had resulted in the many framed posters on the division's walls be integrated into a usable whole. This meant synthesizing and aligning mission, vision, and values so that they were usable tools and not merely decorations.

We went off-site. The senior managers felt my feedback on what I had learned from the interviews was "right on target" when it came to what was being experienced in the division. They clarified their own values and developed a preliminary list of these. They understood the need to involve others, including a need to align the division's values with those of the larger corporation. However, they were reluctant to take the time required to involve and gain the commitment of everyone in the division. I cautioned them that they could invoke a list of divisional values, but they could not invoke the behaviors required of everyone in the division if these words were to translate into daily deeds. Those behaviors develop out of commitment, which comes from involvement of the whole system in illuminating our collective blueprint.

ALIGNING POLICIES, PRACTICES, PHILOSOPHIES, AND VALUES

Because we are moving from the late Industrial Era into the early Information Era, our underlying assumptions about how to operate are up for grabs. While it is important to preserve that which warrants preservation, it also is important to understand how changes in our thinking affect our organizations. For example, we have demonstrated a core value by rewarding individual performance during the Industrial Era. In the Informa-

tion Era, organizational wealth is in organizational competence, not just in the amount of capital in our corporate coffers.

To enhance corporate competence, we are creating structures today based on human networking and supported by
distributive technology, such as the personal computer. This
human networking has led to team structures. Yet many
organizations, if not most, are still rewarding individual performance.

Incompatibilities — such as team-based performance but
individual rewards — signal problems with alignment. Our
values — our basics — have not changed; however, we need to
align the internal components of our organizations so that
every aspect — our structures, roles, people, skills, tasks, technology, information flows, decision making, the built environment, and our rewards — exemplifies our values.

When we do not align our daily practices and organizational policies with our espoused organizational values, we
cannot align our overall operation with our customers' requirements. Without alignment, there is no common cause. And
without common cause, our organizational communities become divided.

Kenneth Patchen writes, "The best hope is that one of
these days the ground will get disgusted enough just to walk
away, leaving people with nothing more to stand on than what
they have so bloody well stood for up to now." Mr. Patchen
is writing about walking our talk. He is writing about values
as the essence of who we are and what we stand for.

USING VALUES TO
EVALUATE OPPORTUNITIES
AND ALTERNATIVE ACTION

Our statement of organizational values should be brief enough
so our values can be embedded in our daily deeds. And our
values should be comprehensive enough to measure how well
we do what we espouse. As our organizations evolve, new op-

portunities and threats arise. If we evaluate how we can address these opportunities or threats in accordance with our values, our values become the final arbitrator for what we do and how we do it.

Implicit in every corporate decision is an assumption that is based on a value. When I was in graduate school, one of my professors, a noted organizational consultant, told of attending a new products meeting of one of his high-tech clients. Senior managers made up the committee that decided which new ideas the company would fund. Two engineers presented their idea. At the end of their presentation, they were confronted with rapid fire questions from all of the managers present. An animated discussion ensued about the merits of their idea. Ultimately the discussion became heated and a lot of shouting occurred.

When the meeting ended, my professor told the two engineers that he was surprised by the tone of the meeting. He felt new ideas were fragile and needed to be handled with care. He was uncomfortable and somewhat aghast with the treatment received by the engineers, even more so because their organizational ranks were far below those of the people on the committee. The engineers told him that one of the organization's underlying assumptions was that truth could stand scrutiny. They were unaffected by the exchange in the committee because the behaviors exhibited were in accordance with an organizational value of producing the best.

In this case, a value on the "best" translated into an underlying assumption that truth could withstand scrutiny. If it were true that the idea presented was the best idea, it could withstand the scrutiny of those who decided whether or not to fund it. The engineers were in no way ruffled or dissuaded from pursuing their idea. They perceived their idea had been scrutinized, not that they had been treated poorly. They were able to make this differentiation because scrutiny exemplified how the company walked its talk of pursuing the best.

6

Systems Thinking:
Seeing Organizations as
Relationships in Action

Regardless of organizational type or size, we need to think systemically. For many years, the conventional wisdom has been that bigger is better. My father subscribed to this theory every time he picked up groceries for my mother. She asked for the regular-size box of detergent and he came home with the jumbo economy size. Never mind that the box was too big to fit in the cupboard or that my mother found it easier to handle the regular-size box. My father favored getting the best value for the money while my mother favored convenience.

During the last half of this century, this same conventional wisdom was applied to organizations, and organizational size exploded. Two factors contributed greatly to this explosion. First, the quest for shareholder wealth fueled merger and acquisition mania in the late 1970s and 1980s. Parent companies now oversee huge conglomerates that produce everything from oil to books to movies. Second, the desire for economies of scale spurred the evolution of national franchises. No longer are the corner drug store and local hardware store independent small businesses. Now they are part of Thrifty Drugs or Ace Hardware. In terms of organizations, bigger means "competitive advantage" and "economies of scale."

While the jumbo-size organization is not without merit, unless it is carefully designed, it may lack agility and flexibility at a time when changes in the global economy require increasingly quick responses. In the context of rapid change, one way to better understand the jumbo-size organization as well as the smaller organization is to think about our organizations from a systemic point of view.

WHAT IS SYSTEMS THEORY?

Systems theory is not a technique or a program, nor is it new. As early as the 1930s, the physiologist W. B. Cannon and the biologist Ludwig von Bertalanffy outlined the complex interaction of physical systems that maintain "dynamic equilibrium" in living organisms. Soon thereafter, this concept, known as "open systems thinking," was applied to psychology and the social sciences by Fred Emery. It was then a short step to application in business and industry. (See Weisbord, 1987, for more on the history of open systems thinking.)

Systems thinking provides a roadmap for how to interact simultaneously with the whole of the enterprise as well as the parts of the enterprise. When I am called to work with one level within an organization, I am aware that the outcomes will affect other levels of the organization, whether or not I start with an individual or a group, an executive, or nonexempt employees. To act in ways that create better alignment, less fragmentation, and more awareness of interdependence within the organization, the client and I first need to understand fully:

1.   The current linkages within the organization

2.   What constitutes the "system" (an individual, a group, several functional units or the entire organization) in terms of the work requested by the client

3.   Where the "system" is and what it wants to achieve

These three things are essential to determining how to help the "system" improve.

Often I hear that whole-systems thinking is a "luxury that public-sector organizations cannot afford." What is meant is that it is more time-consuming and, therefore, more costly, to look at an organization systemically than to look at a particular problem that needs to be fixed. The main difference between public- and private-sector organizations is that the former are budget driven and the latter are market driven. There is no doubt that constraints on budget-driven organizations are different from those on market-driven organizations; however, I would argue that because public-sector funding is harder to come by than private debt, we can ill afford the costly mistakes that arise from a quick-fix or shortcut mentality. The wisest approach we can take is to look systemically at public-sector organizations.

To look systemically means that we do more than examine a particular issue out of context. For example, it is easy enough to determine that training may be needed to enhance skill levels within an organization. But such training is often undertaken without an understanding of how it may affect the current division of responsibilities — structure and roles — or the assumptions that underlie current decision-making processes and information flows. Thus the training frequently results in unintended consequences or even no change in the status quo. When we "skill up" the workforce, we create expectations. These can be fulfilled or thwarted only when there is alignment between newly developed capabilities and the interactions — designed roles and processes — that support the use of these new capacities. To look systemically means we consider the whole of the system as well as the various components that go to make it up. Such looking takes more "up-front" time; however, when actions are taken, there is a much higher probability that intended results will be achieved.

Not too long ago, a large division of a government agency requested my advice as to the options for reorganizing their headquarters staff to better support the needs of their field operations. Two years prior, two field divisions had been merged, yet the headquarters staff had not been realigned to support this merger. Further, the whole of the agency was under pressure to reorganize owing to proposed and anticipated cutbacks in funding that were associated with the inauguration of the Clinton administration.

I met with Jim, the head of the division—a very bright, capable, and energetic man who gives the appearance of being in a hurry. He told me that whenever he had reorganized functions in the past, he and two or three of his direct reports had hashed out what needed to occur and then announced their decision. He was intrigued with the idea of getting others involved with and thereby committed to the reorganization of the headquarters staff. But he became dismayed when I talked about getting a microcosm of the division engaged in designing the organization to meet the needs of its customers—in this case the field staff—and to expedite the essential work that supported the field. "We do not have the time," he said, "nor can I ask people to take the time from their current jobs in which they are already stretched too thin."

A few months later, Jim asked to meet with me again. He told me he had asked ten officer level employees who represented both headquarters and field functions to restructure the headquarter's staff along five product lines. He had taken these people off their jobs for one week to enable them to give him a plan for such a reorganization. He wanted my reaction to what he had done, and I told him he had taken a major step forward in engaging a part of the system—ten officers—in looking at the whole of the system. I also told him I believed he would get a better proposal, more buy-in and easier implementation if a microcosm of the system were engaged in looking at the whole system. My comment was based on my belief that it takes the people who do the work to redesign and restructure how work is done. With-

out representatives from clerical, administrative, analytical, and managerial functions, the officers were missing critical information and perspectives as to the essential work of the division and what was required to deliver the division's five products.

Jim asked me to meet with the task force and talk to them about what they were doing and ways to enhance their output. I suggested that they might be resistant to an outsider coming to "help" them when they had not asked for any assistance. But Jim felt I might help them to uncover some of their entrenched assumptions about how to go about their assignment.

When I entered the task force's meeting room, I found ten people busily engaged and highly energized. It was obvious they were relishing their assignment and were well along in their deliberations. My presence was an interruption. The train had already left the station.

Instead of talking to them about systems thinking and how it applied to their task, I told them what struck me as I entered their meeting room; namely, that it seemed obvious they were actively involved with and enjoying their assignment. They readily agreed. When I asked what made the assignment so rewarding, they informed me that it was the first time they had been asked for input on a restructuring, that many of them had never even met let alone had an opportunity to work together, and that they were a "good fit" in terms of working together on this important assignment.

I then asked them if they thought others in the division would enjoy the same opportunity. They were sure they would. They also indicated that it was not necessary to involve others because between the ten of them they had all the necessary information to make the right decisions as to how the headquarters function should be restructured, even though their group included only officers.

My next question was whether they would be willing to be accountable for the results of their proposal should it be enacted as presented. I told them accountability for me would mean they would be willing to stake their jobs on the outcome of their endeavors. I was immediately informed that this was not their project, it was Jim's. All they were doing was making recommendations.

In effect it was Jim's job that was on the line, not theirs. I asked them if Jim would agree with their assessment regarding their accountability and they were not sure.

I offered them some ideas as to how they could look at the restructure systemically and how they might involve others in the system to look at the whole of the operations. They were resistant, and rightly so. After all, they had been at work for two days. They already had major agreement on many aspects of what needed to be moved where. And most of all, they were enjoying the assignment and not wanting to give up any of their newfound influence.

I reported back to Jim and again commended him for setting up this task force rather than deciding alone how to reorganize the division. I told him the officers were well along in their assignment and did not feel the need for additional input—mine or otherwise. Because they felt they were working well on their own, it would be fruitless to insist that they work with me or anyone. Jim was concerned by my statements and he agreed that he would be countermanding himself if he required the task force to work with me when that had not been part of their original assignment. Nor did he feel it would be a good idea to try to sell them on the advantages of working with an outside consultant when they felt they had what they needed to get the job done. He did, however, indicate that he would hold them accountable for the success of their endeavors and that he would correct the impression that this was "his project alone."

About two weeks later, I received a call from a woman on the task force who had been designated as the group's leader. She asked me if I would be willing to work with others in the division to validate, enhance, or make changes to what she termed the task force's "blueprint" for the division. She told me that after my visit, the task force realized that all they were doing was creating wiring diagrams. They did not have sufficient information to know exactly how work would be accomplished if their proposal were to be accepted, which had caused them to realize that placing boxes on an organizational chart was a far cry from implementing new ways to do work.

The task force's blueprint became the "straw dog" of a restructuring that ultimately involved five design teams of eight volunteers each—including representatives from clerical, administrative, technical, and managerial jobs—and a steering committee comprised of Jim, his direct reports, and two members of the task force. Each design team was assigned a particular product line. Over the course of two months, they met for seventeen days and fleshed out the restructuring of the division. As of this writing, implementation is under way and 87 percent of the headquarter's employees have been placed in their first or second choice positions in the newly restructured operations. The chances that this restructuring will achieve its intended results are very strong—much stronger than those for other divisions within the same agency that are also responding to budget cutbacks and downsizing under the Clinton administration. Other divisions opted to take two days for thirty-five officers to go off-site and create six groups, each looking at a particular aspect of the operation—technology, people, tasks, space requirements, and so forth—or ordered a restructuring based on two or three senior officers' deliberations. In contrast, the division I worked with decided they could not afford to be anything but thorough in determining priorities in a downsized operation and allocating limited resources appropriately to accomplish their task. They had thought and acted systemically with regard to their reorganization. It is my bias that the commitment to and success of their undertaking exceed that which occurs when people are dragged into the future.

Our organizations are open systems. An open system is not static; it is continuously changing, affecting and being affected by the external environment. An open system takes things from the environment, converts them, and puts what is created out into the external environment. In organizational terms, this means we input, throughput, and output. Each organizational system contains subsystems. Subsystems carry out organizational conversion processes—throughputs—

Figure 6.1. The Organization as an Open System.

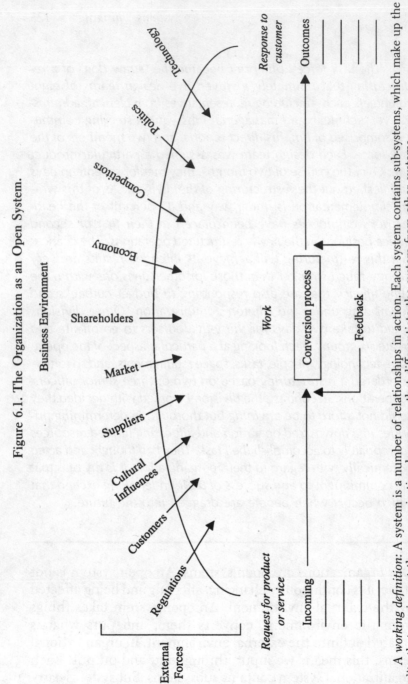

A working definition: A system is a number of relationships in action. Each system contains sub-systems, which make up the totality that carries out those organizational processes that differentiate the system from other systems.

which differentiate one organizational system from another. (See Figure 6.1.)

WHAT CAN SYSTEMS THEORY DO?

Systems theory is useful in four major ways. First, it helps us understand relationships between things, between people, and between people and things. Let us start with things. Systems theory helps us understand the relationships between inputs, throughputs, and outputs; between raw materials, conversion processes, and finished goods. Systems theory also helps us understand relationships between people—those in the external environment—such as customers, suppliers, regulators, and stockholders—and those within the organization. If we view a system as a series of relationships in action— raw material to finished goods, one work associate to another, a supplier to a customer, an individual to the means by which he produces—then we can understand the implications of relationships in action. These relationships are not static; they are always changing, always in the process of becoming.

Second, systems thinking clarifies how change that affects one aspect of a system impacts all other aspects of the system. Simplistically, if I stub my toe and the rest of me is perfectly all right, I am, for a moment, only the pain in my toe. In other words, all of my attention is consumed with my pain, even though 99 percent of me is functioning perfectly well. In organizational terms, when something in the external environment changes—such as a new government regulation taking effect—the whole of the organization becomes focused on implementing what is required, even though those requirements may involve only 3 percent of organizational activity. Or, when internal results, such as quarterly earnings, are lower than anticipated, the organization becomes consumed with the price of its stock, even though production, research and development, shipping and receiving, and sales and inventory account for 99 percent of organizational activity. A system does not exist in a vacuum, nor does any one aspect of a system exist in a vacuum. What happens to the whole affects the parts, and vice versa.

Third, systems theory helps us to simultaneously see the whole system and the parts that it comprises. In Chapter Three, an organization is depicted as an upside down pyramid—a three-dimensional object where each surface supports and is integral to every other surface (see Figure 3.3 and Exhibit 3.1). The organization's components include customer and mission, structure and roles, people and skills, tasks and technology, decision-making processes and information flows, the built environment, rewards and values. All of these components—these parts—make up the "whole" of the organization. And all of these components exist in relationship to one another. For example, if an organization is restructured and teams replace individual contributors, people must develop their interpersonal skills to work together effectively. Systems theory illuminates the interdependence of these components and helps us understand how best to align these components, which can easily become misaligned.

Fourth, systems theory helps us understand integration and fragmentation. One way to understand fragmentation is to look at the differences between core work and support work (see Chapter Four). In designing how work will be done, core work is often divided, and much of what belongs to the core is given to a support function. This leads to fragmented roles and less than optimal efficiency in work processes because the work occurs in one place but is controlled in a different place. A prime example is quality control. Rather than being incorporated into every job in the production process, it is often splintered into a support function that audits quality after a product is produced.

Another way to consider fragmentation is to see how our mass production methodologies divide work into small and highly repetitive jobs in ways that preclude individuals from seeing their contribution to the whole. The story in Chapter Four of one person whose job was to sew the right pocket on a pair of jeans illustrates this. Our effort to create teams of people who are responsible for an entire product is really an effort to create wholeness and avoid fragmentation. It is an effort to better integrate the collective endeavors that create the product or service. And it is an attempt to create line of sight—a relationship—between those who produce and who use what is produced.

Systems theory is a useful lens through which to view an organization because it allows us to focus on:

1. The organization as a series of relationships in action

2. The impact of one aspect of the organization on all other aspects of the organization

3. The whole of the enterprise as well as those parts that constitute the whole

4. What creates wholeness—the integration of efforts— and what creates fragmentation

---

More often than not, I am contacted by a potential client because he or she needs help with integration and alignment, though that is almost never the request. Usually the request is to help create self-managed teams, develop a training program for "leaders," or facilitate relationships between individuals and groups. If I view the organization from a systems perspective rather than simply respond to the request, I can often help uncover misalignments and fragmentation in the system that are thwarting the achievement of desired outcomes. One thing is certain: the desired outcome is never teams or training. The desired outcome is greater organizational effectiveness and the ultimate goal of long-term viability.

A utility company is an example of a client who called for help with a safety program when the underlying cause of its difficulties was fragmentation. I was called shortly before a natural disaster to assist a senior level manager who had been named Region Safety Chair for 1990. He was interested in finding new ways to make safety a number one priority for everyone in the company. We met three weeks after the disaster at a time when employees at all levels of the company had been working heroically, long days and nights, to restore power to the devastated parts of the disaster area, which included several counties and several million people.

In starting our meeting, my client talked at length about the disaster. I complimented him on the company's incredible ability to respond to the crisis, and he told me about their preparedness plan, which had been set up long before the disaster occurred. I heard insider stories about how employees from key executives to maintenance workers had left their homes with no change of clothes and no toothbrush to answer phones, lay gas pipeline, and reestablish electric power hour upon endless hour. Often they slept in their trucks or at their desks because to go home took too many hours away from their much needed efforts. Within three days of the disaster, the company had restored service to the entire area, even though it would take years to rework the gas pipeline infrastructure. In one district, which was the most heavily damaged, city dwellers had hung banners from their balconies with words of thanks to the company. Residents baked muffins and passed them out to workers, who continued to use every available minute to check pipes, lay new lines, and inspect and reinspect gas caps and plugs.

Eventually our conversation turned to safety. My client told me that previous Safety Chairs had used training programs to get high-level managers enthused about safety. The company then gave each manager a budget to support their efforts to get their employees enthused about safety. Luncheons were held, rewards were handed out, the safety record improved temporarily, and then more accidents occurred. These fell into three categories: personal injury; damage to vehicles owned by the company or by citizens whose vehicles had been hit by company employees; and lost time, which occurred when employee injuries resulted in an inability to work for more than one day. My client believed that boredom, job dissatisfaction, and frustration could lead to momentary inattention to the task at hand and result in a lost-time injury.

I was intrigued with the contrast between our earlier discussion about the heroic efforts that were still going on three weeks after the disaster and our talk about accidents. I asked my client how many hours, on average, employees had worked each week since the disaster. He told me that most employees were working seventy- to eighty-hour weeks, where before they had been working forty. When I asked him what had happened to the company's accident record since the disaster, he told me there had been zero accidents.

I found it interesting that employees had no accidents when they worked twice their normal hours and that their work was performed more safely during times of long hours, high stress, and crisis. My hunch was that work was more satisfying during a crisis because everyone could see the big picture as well as the little picture; employees could act without asking permission to do what they knew only too well how to do, and everyone was cooperating with everyone else because there was a common cause that was greater than any one individual's interest. Further, because employees knew the area's revival depended on their efforts, they took care to work safely so they could continue to work. The result was no accidents and an extraordinary level of output.

To understand more about the connection between safety and job design, I recommended that the client and I interview a diagonal slice of the workforce that would include representatives from all levels and jobs within the organization. I wanted to learn from those who did the work what made routine work less safe than work performed during a crisis. From a systems perspective, safety is not a separate task within a job; it is inherent in every task. As such, safety is embedded in how tasks and jobs are designed. Our conventional wisdom may tell us that routine tasks and narrowly defined jobs are the safest, yet such jobs often create boredom that leads to accidents. In the case of this company, learning more about job conditions during a crisis was the key to creating job conditions where safety was number one at all times.

BALANCING
THE WHOLE AND
THE PARTS

Size creates change in the way we manage ourselves and our organizations. It is fairly easy to get your arms around a 250-person company—to know what is happening in the company and to be known for your contribution, regardless of your level in the company. It is more difficult to manage thousands so that everyone knows and is known. And it is more difficult still to manage thousands when they are geographically dispersed. To manage thousands or to manage hundreds is to simultaneously manage well the big picture and the little picture—the whole of the organization and the entities that constitute the organization.

Most large organizations are not good at managing the whole of the enterprise and the functional units that make up the enterprise. Large organizations tend to overmanage or undermanage. They overmanage and create dependency when they constrain functional units so that the whole of the enterprise moves in lockstep. They undermanage and create fragmentation when functional units become so autonomous as to lose sight of the common cause. To manage well is to balance the whole of the enterprise with the parts, to be simultaneously focused on the individuals in the enterprise and the collective efforts that create the enterprise, and to foster interdependence.

Systems theory helps us balance the needs of each part of the organization with the desired outcomes for the entire organization. It helps us to pinpoint misalignments, which occur (1) between strategy and structure and between structure and sustaining mechanisms that are required to support the structure (see Exhibit 2.1), (2) between functions doing core work and functions performing support work, and (3) between espoused and rewarded values.

As individuals engaged in collective endeavors, we need to know what is happening in our organizations and we need to be known—to be recognized for our contributions—regardless of organizational size. In 1970, as part of my duties in the training and development unit at The Automobile Club of Southern California, I was responsible for creating an orientation program for all employees. The Club, which is the largest AAA affiliate, had 120 offices throughout Southern California and employed more than 5,200 people. The orientation program, which I presented every three weeks to between 50 and 120 new employees, included the history of the club, how the club was organized to serve its members, and what benefits were provided to employees. At the end of an audio slide show, I would take the participants on a tour of the headquarters, which was a historic Spanish building in downtown Los Angeles. Because the orientation was presented every three weeks, headquarters employees grew accustomed to seeing me lead a parade of new employees through the building, stopping at various areas to explain the nature of the work being done.

After several months, I realized that our maintenance crew, which included seventy-five employees, had never been through the orientation. They worked at night and most of them spoke only Spanish. I had studied Spanish but I was by no means fluent. I had a friend who was a Spanish teacher, however, and she offered to translate the orientation program into Spanish so it could be presented to the maintenance crew.

I obtained permission from the director of personnel to bring in the maintenance crew at three o'clock one afternoon, on overtime, so they could tour the building when the people who worked days were performing their jobs. I could not help but feel that the maintenance employees experienced the club as a series of desks that needed dusting, waste baskets that needed emptying, floors that needed polishing, and windows that needed washing.

On a sunny Wednesday afternoon, all seventy-five members

of the maintenance crew filed quietly into the auditorium and took their seats. I welcomed them in Spanish. The expressions on their faces indicated they were perplexed. I began to wonder if my Spanish was understandable. I asked, "Comprende?" Suddenly the room was filled with smiling faces as they responded, "Sí, señora!" They had not expected to hear me speak Spanish and they were delighted. I spoke from the script my friend had translated while I manually operated the slide projector. At the end of the program, I took them on a tour of the building. Their bilingual supervisor accompanied us so he could translate their questions and my answers when my need to respond spontaneously in Spanish was hampered by my lack of fluency.

As we walked through the building, many employees stopped us. Some asked me to tell the crew how much their efforts were appreciated. Some complimented the crew on the outstanding job they were doing in making it possible for others to come to work and serve the club's members. Many spoke of their appreciation for the crew's outstanding job in preserving the historic building and its grounds. And several talked about how much pride they took in working in such a well-maintained and beautiful environment. Each comment was immediately translated. The crew responded with smiles, gentle waves of their hands, and many utterances of "de nada," which means "you are welcome."

Of my five years with the Auto Club, that day stands out as the most satisfying and fulfilling of many satisfying and fulfilling days. That experience exemplifies, at a very personal level, the interdependence of individuals and the functional units that constitute the system. It is an example of everyone having an opportunity to know and be known, to understand the big picture of what their organization does as well as the little picture of how each functional unit contributes to the whole, to experience the value of their work in supporting others, and to feel appreciated for their efforts and contributions.

THINKING IN TERMS OF LEVELS OF SYSTEM

To think systemically, we must see not only the big picture and the little picture, we must also understand levels of system. When we think of organizational levels, we often conceive of levels within the hierarchy. Today most large corporations are trying to flatten their organizational structures from as many as sixteen levels to no more than seven. Levels of hierarchy are important indicators of how organizations align parts into wholes. Levels, however, are just one way of looking at levels of system.

Another perspective on levels of system emerges when we differentiate configurations of people. For our purposes, five levels of system, or five designations, are useful:

1. Individual, which means any employee

2. Interpersonal, which includes relationships between two people, whether or not the relationship is one of peers, customer and supplier, or manager and employee

3. Group, which includes permanent (section, department, or division) and temporary (task force or committee) configurations of three or more people

4. Organization, which is that entity we call the enterprise, including external customers and suppliers

5. Industry, which is that sector of the economy to which the organization contributes

Organizationally speaking, each level of system reflects all levels of system. Nothing exists in isolation in systems thinking. This means that every employee represents that for which the organization stands. It also means that each group is a microcosm of the whole. The organizational norms that exist in one group or functional unit exist to a very great extent in all other functional units. Another way to say this is that what goes on in one configuration of the enterprise is indicative of what goes on in every other configuration of the enterprise.

Covia Corporation is a rich example of how what happened to one individual impacted the entire hierarchy of a large organization as well as the individual, interpersonal, group, and organizational levels of the system. Covia, which is now owned by United Airlines and British Airways, was spawned from the Apollo airline reservation system developed by United Airlines, Inc. (UAL). It was spun off as a separate subsidiary of UAL in 1987. The intent was to use the Apollo technology to develop back-office software applications for dentists, doctors, attorneys, accountants, and other professionals. My assignment was to facilitate a work redesign in the core work for the subsidiary.

During the redesign, turbulence occurred at the board level of UAL. Richard Ferris, then CEO, had wanted to create a "total travel" entity, so that a traveler could make one reservation to secure airline tickets, hotel accommodations, and a rental car. His strategy included the acquisition of Hertz, Westin Hotels, and as many air travel routes as possible.

The combination of Ferris's acquisition strategy, airline deregulation, and resulting increased competition led to a lot of red ink on UAL's bottom line. The board asked Ferris to step down. The head of Hertz was named interim CEO. He changed the membership of the senior management team by moving some of Ferris's appointees to other jobs in the corporation. Two of these executives were "given" to Covia just after the redesign proposal had been approved. To make room for these individuals, the division manager and manager of the Reservation Division were outplaced and the division was split in half. All of the design team's technical recommendations were implemented and none of the recommendations regarding quality of worklife, or what is called the social system, were enacted.

*The Covia story is a powerful example of what can happen
when there is a lack of awareness of how one individual's role
affects an entire company and how changes at the senior level
of a parent company can powerfully influence one section of a
very small subsidiary. As consultant to this project, I take responsibility for not recognizing the potential for what occurred. And
the lesson learned is valuable; namely, every part of the system
affects and is affected by the total system and what happens to
one individual at one level of the organization can impact other
levels of system and other levels of the organization, no matter
how far removed these levels appear to be.*

When we see each level of system as reflective of and impact-
ing every other level of system, it is easier to understand who
and what needs to be involved if the system is to achieve its
desired results. Let us consider for a moment how this works
from the customer's point of view. A customer does not have
a relationship with an entire organization. A customer relates
to an organization through the salesperson who conducts
transactions with that customer. If the salesperson treats the
customer well and the transaction goes smoothly, the customer is likely to have a favorable impression of the company.
If the product or service is as expected or is better than expected, again the customer has a favorable impression of the
whole company. And the opposite also holds. If the sales transaction is problematic and the product is unsatisfactory, the
customer's view of the company is poor.

Systems thinking means we look to more than the salesperson or one sample of product to understand what must
occur for the company to achieve its desired ends. It means
we look at the interdependence between job design, job qualifications, hiring practices, training and development, and reward mechanisms to understand what makes for a good salesperson. It also means we look at the sales process—where and
how it is designed and controlled. Finally, it means we look

at the inputs and all aspects of the conversion process to understand the end product or service.

SEEING THE MEANS BY WHICH A COMPANY BRINGS PRODUCT TO MARKET AS REFLECTIVE OF HOW THE COMPANY MANAGES ITSELF

Frequently I am asked about the differences I experience between one company and another. This question is nearly always preceded by the statement that "our company is different." The differences I experience are attributed primarily to a single phenomenon: namely, that the means by which an organization brings its products or services to market is reflected in how it manages itself. This "mirroring" is another indication that what goes on in one part of the system is reflected in other parts of the system.

Three examples are useful in illustrating this mirroring phenomenon. They come from pharmaceutical, insurance, and high-tech organizations. My observations are not intended as judgments on management practices, but rather, on how management practices reflect the means by which an organization brings product and service to market.

When I first began to work with pharmaceutical manufacturers, I expected to find high-risk cultures. After all, these companies take substances out of the ground and process them so we can ingest them. That seems high risk to me. However, when you look at the process by which these companies bring their products to market, you find risk aversion. Years and years of clinical trials are required, to say nothing of the laborious Food and Drug Administration (FDA) approval process. The people in this industry tend to be risk aversive. They manage and control and are managed and controlled as carefully as the processes by which they produce.

Another example of this phenomenon is found in the insurance industry. In one organization, claims processors for health benefits were leaving in droves after three months on the job, even though their pay was more than competitive with clerical jobs in other organizations. Their job descriptions detailed every action they were to take, from which drawer to open first in the morning to how to lock their desks at night. An insurance company must ensure that every *i* is dotted and every *t* is crossed on an insurance policy to correctly correlate premiums collected with potential liability. In managing employees, the same high degree of specificity was employed. Claims processors felt stifled by operating procedures.

A third example of this phenomenon is found in high-tech companies where success is based on speed to market, the obsoleting of existing advantages, the creation of technological discontinuity, and the ability to continuously bring to fruition that which most of us have yet to imagine. Let us first consider the most critical dimension in the high-tech industry—time. Product life cycles are short, speed to market must be fast, and the willingness to obsolete existing advantages must be strong if an organization is to compete effectively. The adage "time is of the essence" applies above all to high-tech endeavors. This strategic dimension of time is reflected in how high-tech firms manage. An employee's organizational life cycle is often as short as its products' life cycles. The ups and downs of company fortunes are reflected in the frequent gearing up and sizing down of the workforce, a phenomenon that creates a plethora of short-tenured and stress-packed jobs for high-tech employees.

A second dimension of time is speed to market, which is reflected in the speed with which work must be done. The products themselves—from super minicomputers to notebooks and from disk drives to chips—result from efforts to condense more and more into less and less, all the time going faster and faster. These same efforts result in people trying to cram more and more into a finite amount of time by working faster and faster. Long hours are spent at work. Often the line between work and play becomes blurred, which is reflected in norms such as casual dress and in such on-site organizational amenities as volleyball and basketball courts and workout rooms. Often one effect of more and more, faster and faster is high stress. One stress reliever is a sabbatical, which appears to be the means by which people get away from the job of doing more faster.

Short time frames, critical to product life cycles and speed to market, are also used for measuring results. Companies are only as good as their quarterly profit and loss statements. Staying power in the high-tech industry is dependent on two closely aligned capabilities: the ability to obsolete existing advantages and the ability to create technological discontinuity — which is to leapfrog the market with revolutionary and hard-to-imitate breakthroughs in product features or technical processes associated with production. When high-tech organizations are not in control of obsoleting their existing advantages and they do not create technological discontinuity, they wind up at the mercy of rapidly changing market conditions that quickly obsolete the entire enterprise. If you look at a list of companies operating in Silicon Valley ten years ago compared with today, you would find less than five percent of the names on both lists. It is a paradox that the same competence needed to start up a company and compete in a rapidly changing industry — the competence to obsolete existing advantages and create technological discontinuity — is lost in the quarterly profit and loss mentality that can fuel the rapid and often too-early demise of business units and whole companies.

Finally, because time is of the essence, it is common to find almost everything elevated to crisis proportion and priority status. Impatience is rampant, which further fuels the urge to do things quickly. Such a norm may support a business in the short term; however, it can prove deadly to the diligence required on complex business issues that enable an organization to build capacity over the long term.

Another characteristic associated with successful high-tech companies is the ability to create and innovate. The best companies have people who see things as if they already exist, which fuels the ability to bring what is dreamed into existence. This ability to imagine and pretend often carries over into organizational relationships in the sense that employees feel a familiarity and identification with the CEO regardless of whether or not they have any direct contact with him or her. This virtual reality of closeness with the CEO is supported in two primary ways. First, CEOs of high-tech firms are regarded as more technologically competent and visionary than CEOs in most other organizations. Most are engineers, if not by degree, by tinkering. Their professional origins are in the technology rather than in finance or marketing. Their technical expertise, drive, personalities, and ability to compete in a high-stakes industry make them susceptible to being seen as heroes as well as people to fear. Second, they are referred to by their first names by everyone in the firm. This first-name norm creates a sense of closeness and in some companies is a euphemism for "dad."

When a CEO is experienced as familiar or as father to the organization, his every move and every request have heightened impact on others. Employees say "Ken wants" or "Bill thinks," as if to indicate they are part of an in-person conversation when, in fact, the information is secondhand and sometimes interpreted. These virtual relationships of familiarity and fatherhood frequently result in the very relationships that can prove anathema to the long-term viability of the organization—relationships of dependency rather than interdependence, a focus on how best to follow rather than how to help lead, and a reluctance to tell the "emperor" the truth when he is "wearing no clothes."

If we are to become good students of our organizations, we need to understand that what we see in one part or aspect of the organization is indicative of the whole of the organization and, further, that what we learn in one part of organization has application to the whole of the organization. Whether we think about levels of system or the means by which products and services are produced, when we think systemically, we understand that no level or component of the system is inconsequential nor does it exist in isolation. All are interrelated and, thereby, interdependent. Whatever is going on at one level of the organization — individual, interpersonal, or group — is or will be going on to a greater or lesser extent at every level of the organization. And, whatever process is going on in the creation and marketing of products and services will be characteristic to a greater or lesser extent of how the organization manages itself.

THINK IN TERMS OF BOUNDARIES

Boundaries are the most critical aspect of any system. A boundary is a demarcation. It delineates where one person or entity ends. A boundary can be technical, such as the inability of one computer system to link to another. Or it can be physical, such as a wall or physical distance that separates one operating unit from another. Boundaries are not necessarily dividers; they are, however, demarcations.

Within organizations boundaries exist:

1. Between the enterprise and its suppliers, customers, regulators, shareholders, and stakeholders

2. Between internal operating units, such as manufacturing, engineering, materials management, and finance

3. Between support functions and line functions

4. Between sections, departments, and divisions

5. Between members of different teams, task forces, or committees

6. Between individuals

In organizations, action that occurs across boundaries is more critical than action that occurs within the boundaries of given roles and functions. In essence, the nature of the interactions between individuals and functions makes or breaks organizational strength. For this reason, it is important to identify and manage all boundaries — personal, organizational, technical, and geographic.

Boundaries can be formal, informal, fixed, fluid, permeable, impermeable, elastic, clear, invisible, visible, forced, or chosen. Boundaries include written and unwritten rules (norms), and the formal and informal organizational structure. Boundaries delineate the nature of internal as well as external customer and supplier relationships.

Decision-making ability is a primary component of a boundary. Whether a boundary is fixed, fluid, or flexible, within it, decisions can be made. Fluid or flexible boundaries are temporary or changeable, but within them, people are capable of making decisions. This means they have the knowledge to make required decisions and the authority to do so.

When authority is unclear, boundaries grow until they include those who have the right to decide. For example, when employees at all levels feel that only the CEO can decide on or sanction corporate initiatives, the boundaries around corporate functions that are *responsible* for corporate initiatives are either unclear or not real. Boundaries are unclear if those who are supposed to decide do not feel they have the authority or are afraid to exercise it. Boundaries are not real if others outside the boundary have to be included in the decision-making process.

When the power to decide is highly centralized, it is quite possible that many organizational boundaries are not only meaningless but also barriers to fast and efficient operations. For example, in the discussion of organizational barnacles, in Chapter Four, it was noted that time to market was a critical success factor for one company. The right to decide on the price of a new product involved seven levels of the hierarchy and approval took six weeks. In this example, responsibility, authority, and accountability for pricing did not exist within the boundary where pricing analysis was done; rather, responsibility to determine price was within one boundary and authority to approve price spanned six different areas. Such "boundaries" are not demarcations; they are obstacles. Rather than making clear who is responsible for what, these phantom boundaries create dependence, thwart efficiency, stifle accountability, and perpetuate duplication of effort.

Conversely, in highly decentralized organizations, boundaries may serve a single functional unit and preclude service to the entire system. For example, in one company that manufactures microprocessors, functional units were so autonomous that they could not communicate with one another electronically. Four types of E-mail existed, multiple systems architectures and platforms existed, and standards were nonexistent. The result was that information could not move across organizational boundaries and get to the point of use at the time of need. Each functional unit had concentrated on what it needed to succeed without consideration for what created success for the entire enterprise.

In Chapter Two, an *inventive* organization was defined as one in which each individual acts in service and support of the entire system. The management of boundaries is critical to serving the whole of the enterprise as well as the parts of the enterprise. Even though the action that occurs at the boundary of a particular function or team may be relatively more significant, action also occurs within the boundary— between individual members of a function and between members and the function as an entity. Individuals are better able to manage their boundaries in ways that serve and support the entire organization when their goals, roles, relationships, and processes are aligned with those of other individuals within their function, and when their function's goals, roles, relationships, and processes are aligned with those of the corporation. The inventive organization in the Information Era is required to identify which boundaries create organizational learning and core competence and then manage transactions across (interactions between) these boundaries in ways that ensure long-term corporate viability. Boundaries, whether too narrow, ill defined, or seemingly absent, have pluses and minuses. How they are drawn, what they include, and what causes them to change are essential elements in systems thinking.

Most organizations suffer from too many rather than too few boundaries. One consulting assignment illustrated what can happen when there is an absence of boundaries.

A large sanitation district was considering work redesign. To familiarize employees with the process and ensure organizational readiness to undertake this long-term improvement initiative, I was asked by a colleague, who was the consultant on this project, to conduct the Flying Starship Simulation. The simulation involves two phases. In the first, the setting is a traditional factory, where jobs are narrowly designed and highly repetitive, and supervision is restrictive. The goal is to sell as many "in spec" starships as possible to a designated customer. To do this, participants are provided with a supply of paper, which they cut, fold, assemble, paint, and sell. After the first production run, they learn the principles of work redesign. The participants are assigned to design teams, and they redesign the factory. The factory is re-run, using the participants' design, and results from the first and second production runs are compared. Ninety percent of the time, results from the second run far surpass the first run.

Sixty sanitation workers assembled with their supervisor. From the moment they arrived until the end of the day, the room was bedlam. People moved about whenever they wanted; they talked to each other when they were supposed to listen to instructions. They joked and jibed, jostled and poked fun at one another, swore and belched, and appeared to have little interest in anything but having a good time.

At lunch, I told my colleague that I was uncertain whether these individuals would be able to do a redesign without a great deal of training in interpersonal and group process skills. Work redesign involves analyses of customer requirements, work processes, and working conditions, and the ability to redesign work to meet management's criteria for critical success. A consultant's role is to offer a methodology for these analyses as well as to facilitate interpersonal and group processes that lead to a redesign proposal. The simulation exercise indicated that boundaries were nonexistent when it came to the sanitation workers' personal habits and behaviors, nor did they take their Supervisor seriously. It appeared to me that these employees needed more experience in how to work together before they tackled a work redesign.

My colleague told me that many of these workers were in twelve-step rehabilitation programs for alcohol- and drug-related problems. Many had been abused as children. In doing their jobs, most often they worked alone and in the most unpleasant conditions—in sewers, with waste and refuse. Although pay and benefits were good, everyone had a plan to somehow get out of the sanitation district.

Now the connection between personal behavior and job boundaries was obvious. There were no boundaries in terms of what they had to do to get their jobs done. There was no such thing as conditions too foul for them to work in. And many of these employees came into these jobs from personal backgrounds in which boundaries were absent—boundaries around the abuse of substances or other forms of abuse.

In the afternoon, again with much mayhem, the employees ran their redesigned factory. They produced the most creative, intricate, and beautifully painted starships I have ever seen, and I have run this simulation over a hundred times. The same absence of boundaries that gave rise to the bedlam in the room had now given rise to people empowering themselves to make starships that far surpassed the prototype.

This story illustrates that where we draw the boundary determines what actions will occur. Tight boundaries are restrictive. Loose boundaries create more possibilities for greater innovation. We need to know where and how to draw boundaries so that we minimize the kind of bedlam that occurs when boundaries are absent and optimize the possibilities for innovation that are inherent in the suspension of unnecessary rules and regulations.

THREATS TO
SYSTEMIC INITIATIVES

Today more and more companies are becoming involved with work redesign and re-engineering. These are two methods for improving systems. Companies also are heavily invested in Total Quality Management (TQM). The commonality shared by these initiatives is that they are systemic.

There are three primary threats to whole-system initiatives. The first occurs when changes in leadership happen too early in the implementation of a systemic initiative. The second occurs when complacency sets in after an organization has developed the characteristics associated with inventiveness. The third occurs when initiatives that precede whole-systems projects are not properly integrated with a systemic initiative. Let us consider these one at a time.

When organizations undertake successful systemic initiatives that result in achieving an inventive state, danger lurks. Those who were shepherds in achieving an inventive state often are rewarded by being promoted elsewhere. New managers are brought in who have not been through the systemic initiative and who are not aware of how to operate within the vastly different set of relationships and processes associated with an inventive state. These new managers feel most comfortable doing what they know best, which is acting on the underlying assumptions associated with either fixed or adaptive organizations. Premature changes in leadership threaten the inventive state precisely because such a state is a radical departure from the predominant culture. Without continuity of the leadership that created the inventive state, it is likely that the predominant organizational culture — the one entrenched in either a fixed or adaptive state — will cause the dismantling of relationships and processes associated with the inventive state.

The second threat is complacency. The reinvented organization quickly becomes the new status quo, regardless of the effort associated with such an achievement. When invention is seen as an end state rather than a process, the reinvented organization becomes the goal rather than the process that led to invention. When this happens, people stop inventing. Organizations are not static. They are either in a state of renewal or a state of decay. Decay occurs when we get fixed on the status quo or when we adapt to conditions that threaten the status quo. Invention occurs when we get out of the box of our current thinking.

The third threat occurs when we view a systemic initiative as unconnected to efforts that preceded the systemic initiative. When we think of our organizations as systems that are in the process of becoming, we recognize that everything that has occurred previously is part of the system and needs to be honored and linked to the systemic initiative that is about to be undertaken. When such linkage is ignored, there is little if any awareness that all that occurred in the past is what creates the readiness or lack of readiness to proceed into the future. With such awareness, we are better able to undertake initiatives in ways that consciously complete unfinished business associated with past initiatives and in ways that create foundations for future initiatives. The following story best illustrates this point.

Not long ago, I was asked to spend half a day with a group of individuals who represented two utilities that were in the process of merging. This group had been assembled to examine what boundaries, programs, and procedures needed to be changed for the two organizations to successfully become one. Because the CEO and president of the new entity had expressed an interest in core process re-engineering—a systemic initiative—the group wanted more information about what re-engineering is and how to go about it. As we talked, I quickly became aware that re-engineering was viewed as a separate initiative from examining boundaries, programs, and procedures and other changes associated with the merger. Without a systemic approach to the whole of the merger, a re-engineering effort, at best, could create duplication of effort and, at worst, could be at cross-purposes with boundaries, procedures, and programs designed and implemented without consideration for what is involved with re-engineering.

At the time we met, the two utilities had developed a structure for undertaking a set of initiatives aimed at ensuring a successful merger. A senior team of executives from both companies oversaw a group of twenty high-potential young managers—ten from each organization—who in turn oversaw some twenty-four integration teams. These teams were engaged with looking at and making recommendations about everything from employee benefits, to bonus programs, to policies and procedures regarding vacation, sick pay, promotion, performance management, and so on. In addition to the integration teams, there were three issues groups focused on communications, human resources policies and procedures, and regulatory issues.

As the half day progressed, I cautioned those present that if they were to undertake a core process re-engineering, they ought to delay the determination of anything but the minimum policies and procedures required to merge the two companies. To do other than that would be to design all of the ancillary mechanisms that support work getting done without redesigning the work itself. The result would be double work. Once the redesign took place, much of the work of the integration teams might have to be rethought and even redone because the design of core processes determines how work gets done—not only in terms of the technical system but also the human system, the allocation of resources, and the development of the built environment. Further, if re-engineering were done properly, it would build on the best of both companies prior to the merger as well as on the minimum specifications required to facilitate the merger. In effect, every step taken needed to be seen as a foundation for each succeeding step.

Over and over again, I have seen companies achieve a hoped-for state only to dismantle what they have achieved. This occurs because the principles we are talking about become the means to an end rather than an end in and of themselves. When we speak about customer requirements, core work, values, self-regulation, thinking systemically, and interdependence, we are speaking about the conditions that perpetuate invention. When we stop nurturing these conditions, we rob our organizations of their capacity to enhance the hoped-for state that has been achieved. Without those conditions, that state will vanish, for it only exists in the context of the organization's external operating environment, which is constantly changing.

HOW TO CONDUCT
A SYSTEMS ASSESSMENT

From the first moment of contact with a prospective client, rich data is available about the system. Does the system use voice mail? How hard is it to reach someone by phone? How many meetings are scheduled and changed before we actually meet? If the client is located far away and the first meeting is aimed at assessing what a consultant can offer, is the client willing to meet somewhere that is halfway? When the consultant goes to the client's location, are the instructions clear for how to get there? What are the facilities like? Is it easy to get around the facility or is the facility a labyrinth of corridors and undesignated offices? How often are scheduled meetings held on time? How well treated is the employee whose job appears to be lowest in the hierarchy? Is the client timely in meeting the agreements outlined in the contract — from returning phone calls promptly to paying invoices on time? Does a potential client call back after the first meeting to say whether to proceed, or do they simply avoid calling or responding to follow-up calls?

A full-blown assessment is a tool that helps us become more aware of where a system is and what must be involved to get it where it needs to go. The assessment method can be used by a consultant who presents findings to the client and/or "client system," or the consultant can teach people in the system how to assess it. (A client is the person who authorizes the work. A client system includes all individuals, groups, and functions affected by the work to be done.)

The assessment should be based on a system's framework. This approach ensures a view of the whole system as well as the ability to focus on particular aspects or components of it. To conduct an assessment:

1. Determine who and what constitute the system.

2. Design the assessment.

3. Select a diagonal slice of people who represent the system. (A diagonal slice includes representatives from each level of the hierarchy and each job category within the system.)

4. Interview people individually or in groups.

5. Analyze the data by a systems framework.

6. Report findings and recommendations.

Too often work is undertaken in an organization before the system is fully aware of where it is and who and what is involved in achieving its desired goals. The six steps involved in an assessment are easy to perform and the results constitute a clear roadmap for proceeding with initiatives that will align the elements of the system. Wasted, misguided, and fragmented efforts are avoided.

Step 1 involves understanding who the client is and what constitutes the client system. I start by asking for organization charts. I learn about formal and informal boundaries, and I seek to find out who and what functions affect or will be affected by the issue or initiative under consideration. This first step is essential whether this initiative is a strategic plan, work redesign, development of a new compensation program, or other project. *The pitfall* is to leave out any person or function who can impede or impact desired results or who will be affected by the desired results.

Step 2 involves designing the assessment. The design needs to specify ways information will be gathered, who will have access to the data, and how findings and recommendations will be presented. The design also includes writing a questionnaire. Because the goal of an assessment is to create awareness, the system being assessed should have access to the data. At a minimum, everyone interviewed should receive a full copy of the findings and recommendations. When this does not occur, awareness is not created.

With respect to a questionnaire, a good format includes seven or eight questions that can be asked in a forty-five-minute interview. I use three standard questions; the other four questions are designed with the client and are directed at creating more awareness about where the system is and what needs to occur for it to undertake a particular initiative. These are the two questions I use to begin the interview:

> What is going well, what are you proud of? [This question uncovers organizational strengths.]
> What could be going better, what are you sorry about? [This question uncovers potential areas of improvement.]

The third standard question is used to conclude the interview:

> What were you hoping I would ask you today? [If the interviewee says he or she did not hope to be asked anything, the last question is, If you could change anything at all, what would you change and why?]

The pitfall is to omit questions about organizational strengths and focus only on organizational problems or opportunities.

Step 3 involves selecting a representative sample of people in that system. Ten percent of those who constitute the system will provide data that is statistically significant; however, when a system includes more than three thousand people, ten percent may be too high. Maximum mix should be sought, which means that the sample needs to include long- and short-tenured employees, older and younger employees, men and women, minorities and nonminorities, and people who would support whatever is under consideration as well as people who would resist.

The pitfall is to include only those who favor or support what is being considered. Resistance is a healthy part of an organization's reality. It is a force for sameness. Resistance is a need to hold on, and often it indicates a need to hold on to something that should not be eliminated. It is easier to understand and address resistance when resisters are included at the time an initiative is being developed. When an initiative is implemented, it is often too late to understand or properly address the resistance that existed (but was excluded from consideration) when the initiative was developed.

Step 4 is to interview people. An assessment usually involves a mix of individual and group interviews. Group interviews should include no more than eight individuals. Group interviews work well when interviewees perform the same work and are at the same level of the hierarchy. At the beginning of the interview, interviewees should be informed as to

> The purpose of the assessment
> How they were selected
> How data will be gathered and organized
> Whether they will receive a copy of the assessment
> How the assessment will be presented—by whom and
>   to whom

An assessment produces more data if interviewees are assured that their names will not appear beside any statements they make. It also is important to tell interviewees not to share information they deem confidential and do not want to see in print, with or without their name attached. Such information is useless to the interviewer because it cannot be used.

Questions should be "open," which means they cannot be answered by a simple yes or no. Questions that begin with "what" yield more concrete information than questions that begin with "why" or "how." When responses are unclear or provide clues to additional information, those responses should be probed.

Good interviews include both of Edwin C. Nevis's Sherlock and Colombo techniques. Sherlock, named for Sherlock Holmes, means following a predetermined pattern (such as a questionnaire) in gathering data. Colombo, named for the TV character portrayed by Peter Falk, means the interviewer follows his or her own curiosity and pursues whatever seems intriguing. The Colombo technique allows the interviewer to take in more data than can be obtained in a set questionnaire.

A combination of the Sherlock and Colombo techniques provides the richest data. (Often it is difficult for one person to perform both roles—whether that individual is the consultant conducting the assessment or a member of the system who has been trained to conduct assessments. When two people work together to conduct the interview, the potential is greater for rich data.) *The pitfall* is to become so intrigued with a response to a particular question that there is insufficient time for all questions that need to be asked.

Step 5 involves analyzing the data. Data analyzed by using a systems model pinpoint:

- Which aspects of the system are aligned with other aspects
- Which aspects need to be aligned with respect to the initiative under consideration
- Which aspects are misaligned

(See Figure 3.3, Exhibit 3.1, and Figure 6.1.)

A system's various components need to be aligned:

- Customer and mission (including strategies and goals)
- Structure
- Roles
- People
- Skills
- Tasks
- Technologies
- Information flows
- Decision-making processes
- Layout and facilities
- Rewards
- Values

An initiative that creates change in any of these areas can affect any or all other aspects of the system. It is essential to analyze data in terms of the system's framework; this allows us to pinpoint which aspects of the system need attention and how each one affects others. Without this awareness, actions can be taken that unintentionally result in more misalignment between various aspects of the system and, thereby, greater imbalance in the total system.

Additionally, data analyzed by organizational hierarchy (senior management, middle management, supervision, exempt and nonexempt employees) or functional unit (section, department, division) illuminate differences and similarities of opinions within the hierarchy and between functional units. Such data provide important clues as to how to align different roles or functions so that the initiative under consideration can achieve its desired ends.

The pitfall is to collect data without first knowing what format will be used to analyze and report the data. Data analysis is time-consuming. Time is used efficiently when data have been collected according to the format in which they will be analyzed and reported.

Step 6 involves reporting findings and recommendations. It is preferable to present the assessment, in person, to those who participated in it. This creates an opportunity to explain systems thinking as the basis of the assessment. Also, questions can be asked and answered about findings and recommendations. A written report should accompany the presentation. At a minimum, the report should include:

1. The purpose of the assessment and its intended outcome
2. A brief history of what led to the assessment
3. The methodology used, including a list of questions asked and a list of people interviewed
4. An executive summary of recommendations
5. A detailed report of findings that includes:
    a. An explanation of each component of the system (customer/mission, structure/roles, and so on)
    b. Data from the interviews—actual quotes from interviewees that are organized by level in the hierarchy or functional unit and not ascribed to individuals—that have been categorized under a particular component of the system

An organizational assessment achieves two ends. It helps the organization to become aware of who and what is involved and what needs to occur to achieve a desired end. It also teaches those within the organization how to think systemically. There are many methods that can be used to assess an organization. In-person interviews are one way. Others include:

■ Surveys, such as climate surveys
■ Focus groups
■ Simulations
■ Tracking paperwork—amount, cost, and use, by whom and when

- Analyzing levels of responsibility, authority, and accountability — who is responsible for doing work, who has the authority to approve how work is done, and who is accountable

- Detailing decision-making processes — how decisions are made, who is included, and who is excluded

- Analyzing information flows in both the formal and informal organization, including verbal, written, and technology-supported information

- Mapping the system's relationships — who interacts with whom and whether these interactions are electronic or in person

- Delving into technology to determine whether system architecture are integrated, information services are distributive or centralized, standards exist for choices of hardware and software, who chooses hardware and software, who has access to the system, who can change the database, redundancies occur in the system, and so forth

Regardless of the method used to assess the organization, the system needs to be involved, and the assessment should be based on a framework that helps everyone in the organization to think systemically.

7

Self-Regulation:
Control and Support
for Everyone

When we shift our thinking from "command and control" to everyone acting in service and support of the whole system, we are moving from self-serving, authoritarian, dependent behaviors toward partnership and interdependence. This shift signals that rather than being controlled by what is external to us, we are regulating ourselves in response to our working environment. An inventive organization is one based on a philosophy of self-regulation. This means that each individual and every organizational function understand their existences in relation to the system, and each self-regulates so that the entire system is enhanced.

In terms of systems theory, self-regulation means that what is being regulated is the boundary around the organism—whether a person or an organization. Boundaries, as indicated in earlier chapters, are demarcations. They can be permeable, impermeable, fixed, flexible, open, or closed. At an individual level of system, to be self-regulating is to test and know our own boundaries—for example, to establish where we give ourselves permission to act and where we stop ourselves from acting. At an interpersonal level, self-regulation means we act and react in ways that respect our own boundaries and those of others—that is, we do not try to force or coerce others to do what they do not wish to do. At a group level, self-regulation means that our collective boundary honors the boundaries of each individual in the collective and those of others outside the collective—that is, we do not form exclusive cliques within the group nor do we act in ways that trample the rights of other groups. At an organizational level, self-regulation means we manage the boundary with our external environment in ways that enhance the enterprise and that greater system of which the enterprise is only a part—for example, we do not pollute our environment. When we manage our own boundaries—rather than look to others to dictate what we should do—we become self-regulating, which is the foundation for interdependence and the creation of common cause.

My colleague Peter Block defines empowerment as a belief that our survival is in our own hands, not someone else's, that we have a purpose that is compelling and we are committed to that purpose in the moment (Block, 1987, p. 65). Self-regulation is another term that describes empowerment. We become self-regulating and empower ourselves and our organizations when we create the means for all individuals to have control over those processes by which they produce. We become self-regulating when we simultaneously create conditions that support all individuals in contributing at the level of their highest potential. Organizations are self-regulating when everyone:

- Learns and discovers
- Invents and creates
- Experiments and risks safe emergencies
- Sees forces of opportunity in forces of fear
- Pushes at self-imposed boundaries
- Seizes the challenge to go beyond what is expected
- Acts in service and support of the entire system

In 1976, I was hired by Dr. Maurice Mann to head up Human Resources for The Federal Home Loan Bank of San Francisco. On my first day at work, Maury, who became my mentor (see Epilogue), told me my job was to ensure that there were no more lawsuits filed against the bank by employees. At that time, four were outstanding.

When I had accepted the job, I had seen it as guiding the development of a new human resources function, not necessarily as being accountable for ensuring no new lawsuits against the bank. Without articulating it and feeling very scared, I knew that such responsibility could not rest with one person, so I began to think a lot about what in the organization caused people to feel their only recourse was to file a lawsuit and what conditions would make such lawsuits unnecessary.

Over the course of the next year, my staff and I recommended and implemented myriad programs and operating policies that were focused on ensuring that people's voices were heard inside the organization so they would not have to resort to outside intermediaries to feel heard. Each of our recommendations had to be accepted by the Senior Management Committee, of which I was a member. And each of our recommendations was fully and robustly debated amid the kind of skepticism and resistance that accompanies any initiative that impacts the lives of everyone in the organization.

At the end of 1976, after we had implemented job posting, a new salary administration program, new benefit options, various training programs, a first-ever employee handbook, and a complete overhaul of existing policies and procedures, I recommended to my colleagues, whose patience and goodwill I had tried for twelve months, that we implement flex-time. They called the idea "Jill's folly"! Who ever heard of employees being able to regulate their working hours so they could balance their personal and professional lives in ways that fulfilled their responsibilities in both arenas? On this proposal, I did not have Maury's unconditional support. He told me if others wanted to do it, he would go along; however, he would not promote the idea.

After being roundly refused by all my colleagues, I asked if we could find one area in the bank where we might run a pilot program and see how it went. The vice president of finance offered to let us pilot the program in the Credit Department, which had about twenty-two employees. After checking with Building Security, we created some parameters. People could not come to work earlier nor leave the building later than when security guards were on the premises. This meant working hours had to be between 6:30 A.M. and 6:30 P.M. Because the bank was part of a twelve-bank system that was under the aegis of the Federal Home Loan Bank Board in Washington, D.C., we had to ensure adequate coverage for core business hours, which were determined to be between 9 A.M. and 3 P.M. Additionally, California state law requires breaks, and federal statute requires meal periods and overtime pay for nonexempt individuals. Taking all of this into consideration, we announced to the Credit Department that individuals could work between 6:30 A.M. and 6:30 P.M., that they had to take a minimum of thirty minutes for lunch and two ten-minute breaks each day, that they could take up to two hours for lunch, and that the department had to have coverage during core hours. The pilot would run for three months, at the end of which time we would evaluate their reactions and program results.

The experiment began. Although I appeared calm, I was anxious about the potential for mayhem, and in my anxiety, I had been wandering down two floors to the Credit Department at least once a day, just to chat with people about how it was going for them. I heard amazing tales of delight. Some people flexed early so they could take classes in the late afternoon. Some flexed late so they could assist at their children's schools. Some took an occasional two-hour lunch to be with visiting family members or take care of dental and doctor appointments or car maintenance needs. When I asked how the phones were being covered with all the "flexing" going on, I was told that people had begun to cross-train one another so they could ensure that workflows were not interrupted, even when those most expert at particular tasks were not around. After a few weeks, most of the people had settled into a new routine, and the times people flexed were fairly consistent. At the end of the three months, the pilot was deemed a huge success and the Credit Department permanently adopted flex-time.

Exactly two days later, the senior vice president of Supervision and Industry Development, which then was the regulatory function for the Savings and Loan Industry and the largest department in the Bank, asked if we would implement flex-time in his area. We made his employees the same offer with the same parameters that existed in Credit. They accepted and the program was started. Because of the experience in Credit, I was confident all would go well. Within two weeks, the senior vice president was in my office demanding an end to flex-time. When I asked him what was going on, he reported that the supervisor of Word Processing was flexing early and her staff was flexing late. She had work to give to people who were not there to receive it, and at the end of the day people were waiting to receive work and no one was there to give it to them. Everyone was taking long lunches and the phones were going unanswered during core hours. Unlike the Credit Department, no cross-training had occurred. I asked him to let us talk with the employees before deciding to cancel the program. He said if things did not improve within two weeks, flex-time would be abolished. My staff and I fanned out to talk with the people in the department. We told them this was their program, not ours, and only they could make it a success.

After meeting with the employees, my image was one of a teacher leaving the classroom and the students throwing erasers at one another. In essence that was what had happened. I thought about this image and I thought about what might have caused the differences in implementing flex-time in Credit and in Supervision. The answer was simple and it was clear—even though in those days I did not have the language of self-regulation and the word empowerment was not yet part of the business vocabulary. What was clear was that the people in Credit had always been treated as adults. They had the respect and support of each other and of those to whom they reported. Such was not the case in Supervision. The senior vice president was an exemplary regulator, and he regulated not only the Savings and Loan Associations but everything in his department as well. It was a hierarchical, *edict-driven, highly controlled unit, and people had been treated as children. No wonder when given the opportunity to govern when they would work, they took license with their new freedom.*

The experiment in flex-time is an experiment in self-regulation. The degree of readiness for self-regulation directly correlates to how people have been treated all along — as individuals capable of regulating their behaviors in pursuit of common cause or as people whose tasks and efforts must be defined and controlled by others.

Self-regulation is based on support and control. We need both if we are to sustain and enhance the series of relationships we call our organizations. *Support* is tied to our need for relatedness, for alliance — whether with others or with our environment. One way to understand this need is to consider how we support ourselves. Do we feel we have only ourselves to rely on, do we see ourselves as having to rely on others, or do our sources of support include both self and others?

Figure 7.1 depicts behaviors that arise from how we define our sources of support. If we feel unable to rely on ourselves or others, our behavior is *counter-dependent*. This means we depend on no one. Individuals who do not know what to do for themselves and cannot rely on support or assistance from others, often become isolated. They also may feel stuck in a status quo that they experience as confining. (See the discussion of the change cycle, Chapter Two.)

People who believe they can rely on themselves but not on others behave *independently*. This results in a focus on doing what is best for oneself with very little, if any, regard for how one's behaviors affect others. Those who feel unable to rely on themselves and, instead, look to others for support and direction, act in ways that enhance *dependence*.

Self-regulation is derived from and is the foundation for *interdependence*. It is the ability to rely on oneself, to act in ways that show recognition of others' needs and desires, and

Figure 7.1. Perceived Sources of Support
and Related Dependence.

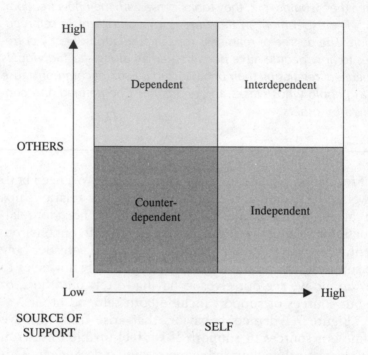

to allow others to contribute—in short, to act in partnership as a means of potentially enriching and enhancing whatever is considered or undertaken. Because self-regulation is the basis for and is supported by understanding our interdependence, it is the basis for partnership.

Control is the other component of self-regulation. Control is something we seek and resist. Our need for control is really our need for certainty. We seek control when we want to be certain. We resist control when we fear loss. We fear loss when we are uncertain. For example, when an organization is uncertain of its long-term ability to compete, it fears loss of its market share and ultimate profitability. When an individual is uncertain about obtaining a much-desired promotion, he or she fears loss of tangible rewards. Our sources for control are ourselves and others. Our behaviors around control result from whether we see ourselves or others as sources of certainty or sources of loss (see Figure 7.2).

When we are uncertain and cannot rely on ourselves or others to help us know what to do, we tend to act in uncertain—*unregulated*—ways. Rather than being self-regulating—which is to act within parameters set by ourselves or others—we are so uncertain as to what we should do that we, in effect, do not have any parameters. We behave as if there were no boundaries on our behavior. Thus deep uncertainty interferes with our ability to create certainty; we are not only uncertain as to what we should do, we are unable to recognize others as a viable source for helping to create the certainty we seek.

When we seek certainty and our source of control is

Figure 7.2. Perceived Sources of Control and Related Behaviors.

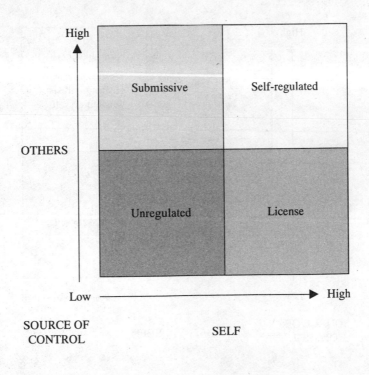

ourselves, we give ourselves *license* to do what we need to do to create certainty. License results when we feel we can trust ourselves but not others.

When we seek certainty and our source of control is others, we become *submissive*. We believe others have the means to create uncertainty; therefore, we relinquish our own control and submit to their control as a means of creating certainty.

When we seek certainty and we believe that we and others can create this, we become *self-regulated*. We neither give up our own control nor do we rely solely on others for control. We act in interdependent ways to create the certainty we need.

When we fear loss, we resist control. (See Figure 7.3.) If we see loss as beyond our own or others' control, we *disengage*

Figure 7.3. Fear of Loss and Resistance to Control.

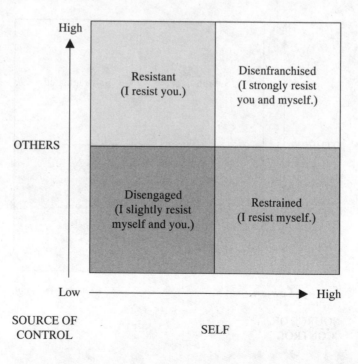

as a means of avoiding that loss. When we fear loss that we might create for ourselves, we become *restrained* in the hope that restraint will prevent loss. When we fear loss that could be brought about by others, we *resist* their control over what is happening. And when we fear loss that we believe will result from our own and others' need for control, we disenfranchise ourselves and others.

Our internal dialogue is a tug-of-war between a need to have it our own way and a need to rely on others. The way out of these seeming polarities is to recognize that our needs for relatedness, alliance, and certainty require us to be inter-dependent. Without interdependence, we suffer loss—the loss of relatedness, alliance, and the potential for certainty.

TESTING OUR ASSUMPTIONS ABOUT THE PERMISSION WE GIVE OURSELVES

It is common for people in organizations to give themselves less permission than they actually have and to accord others more authority than they actually have. Our socialization process is one of dependence—dependence on our parents, on our teachers, and, finally, on our bosses. When we barter our self-control for a hope that someone else will take care of us, we give away our power. When we give our power to another, we become dependent. This act of giving up power is an act of giving away our boundaries. It is to ask another for permission that we need to give ourselves.

When we fail to give ourselves permission to act, we prevent ourselves from achieving our highest potential. To make this point, I recently asked a group of senior managers to think of a time when they had acted courageously at work. A woman in the audience raised her hand and beckoned me to come speak with her. In a hushed voice, she told me she had never acted courageously. When I asked why not, she said that she would be fired if she did. I asked her what evidence she had that this would happen. She said she did not have any evidence; rather, it was just something she knew. A few minutes later, she acted courageously by telling the rest of the group that she had never acted courageously for fear of being fired. When I inquired if firings were commonplace in the organization, members of the group said people rarely were fired; rather, they were "shelved." The fear of being fired or "shelved"—the *fear* of loss versus actual loss—prevented this woman from achieving her highest potential and from making her full contribution to the organization.

At another company, which prided itself on family values and hired people who were family oriented, people shook their heads when I asked, "For what would you stand firm, regardless?" They felt that taking a stand would not get them fired; however, it could get them "shelved," which meant their career paths would evaporate and their ability to influence the system, no matter how limited in the past, would become nonexistent. They said they might be willing to take a stand if it meant that only they would suffer the potential consequences; however, they did not feel they had the right to jeopardize their families by putting their careers at risk. When we think of taking a stand as putting ourselves and our families in jeopardy, we reinforce our own confinement—we reinforce the very status quo we say needs changing. The required change now becomes the responsibility of the amorphous "they"—the ones to whom we have given our power and, thereby, our ability to be self-regulating.

Our own assumptions create our confinement. If we believe ourselves to be literally boxed in by the organizational chart, we will be boxed in. We will act accordingly and, thereby, rob ourselves and our organizations of our full potential. An example of how this can occur comes from a workshop I conducted for a group of professional trainers who were learning how to conduct a new program for middle managers.

As part of the workshop, participants had to present to one another a portion of the program they were learning to conduct. One man detracted from the lecturette he was giving by expending an inordinate amount of energy pacing, whirling, and bouncing up and down. His nonverbal behavior was very distracting, and I mentioned this to him as he sat down. He told me that when he was in front of a group, he felt like a caged lion, and that was why he paced and moved about so much.

I thought a great deal about his analogy. As a child, I often went to the zoo with my father, who was a large-animal veterinarian. I thought it was cruel to cage wild animals because it denied them their freedom. My father told me that in exchange for freedom the animals received good care, never went hungry, were free from pestilence, and were taken care of when they were ill. Sometimes we make our workplaces zoos.

A day later, before this same individual presented for the second time, I put a note on the overhead projector that he was using. It said, "The lion is free." He read the note, put it aside, and delivered his presentation without all the distracting behavior that had accompanied his first effort. When he sat down, he smiled at me. We both knew that he had to believe he was not confined if he wanted to end his confinement.

We can make our organizational hierarchies into cages. In exchange for staying within certain boundaries, we believe we have the assurance of a steady paycheck, benefits coverage, and a job for life. In truth, this is an illusion. We create our own confinement when we settle for structures that limit support and control. We accept these limitations because of our assumptions about control, which are driven by our need for certainty. We may pace and whirl about, but until we believe we have the power to create safe emergencies, we will confine ourselves and our contributions to something far less than we have the power to achieve.

DIFFERENTIATING BETWEEN EDICTS AND EMPOWERMENT

In Chapter Five, organizational values were defined as including words and deeds. A dichotomy exists between the two when we have not aligned what we say with what we do. To create organizations capable of self-regulation at all levels, we must see the necessary linkage between our words and deeds; we need to seek alignment between (1) wanting everyone to be accountable and so ensuring that responsibility and authority are commensurate and (2) wanting everyone to act empowered and so ensuring support and control in every role.

In recent years, the notion of employee involvement has garnered a lot of attention. Employee involvement is an outgrowth of self-regulation. The intent behind fostering such involvement is to enable people to have a say about decisions that affect their working lives. In Chapter Six, each level is depicted as a microcosm of the system as a whole: each person represents the group and each group is a microcosm of the organization. In a self-regulating environment, a representative sample of the entire system participates in making decisions that affect the system.

In most companies where employee involvement is espoused, one or two conditions are likely to occur. Both result from a lack of trust, and both are evidence of an inability to think systemically about how a misalignment of words and deeds affects any initiative we try to get under way. The first condition occurs when employee involvement is treated as a new idea but implemented under the old philosophy of "command and control" or "control, order, and predict." Employees are involved by edict rather than by invitation. They are told when they will be involved, in what issues, to what extent, and in what manner. The underlying assumption is that work is divided between those who can be trusted to make decisions and those who should do as they are told. It is no wonder, then, that employee involvement efforts, including quality circles, die rather quickly. These initiatives contain an inherent dichotomy between espoused and practiced value—that is, "we want your participation but we will tell you how much and when." Employees, then, rather than becoming self-regulating and empowered, become dependent on others for approval of what to do and how to do it. Further, when employee involvement does not become a way of operating that is embedded in the organization's structure—for example, quality circles—employee involvement becomes an ancillary system, a parallel organization. When two systems or organizations run parallel to one another, the system that has the right to decide or approve is the one that prevails and survives.

The second condition that often results from employee involvement is group gridlock. When an organization attempts to include everyone who needs or wants inclusion, the group becomes so large that timely analysis and decision making are impossible. The group's size results from a lack of trust that a microcosm can represent the whole of the system.

THE IMPORTANCE OF AUTHORITY RESIDING WHERE THE WORK IS DONE

In the Industrial Era, we believed that those who designed and approved tasks were different from those who performed the tasks. This reasoning aligned with our notion that some think and others do the work. This framework resulted in the creation of jobs in which responsibility and authority were not commensurate. As organizational size increased, so did the need to feel in control. To be certain that the collective energies of thousands of employees would yield the intended results, we devised steep hierarchical structures in which approval for how work is done rests many levels away from the work itself. The paradox is that rather than ensuring control, steep hierarchies fragment control. Is it any wonder, then, that the more layers we create, the more out of control we feel?

In one multinational company of over 85,000 employees, the CEO must sign off on any new additions to the staff. This policy was devised in 1967 after the company had to lay off workers. To ensure that no one would ever again be laid off, it was decided that no additional personnel would be hired without CEO approval. Twenty-five years later the process for adding staff is so time-consuming that hardly anyone bothers to request additional help.

In this same company, the need for certainty extends to capital expenditures. Even though capital budgets are approved, monies are not allocated until the time of purchase. At that time, approval is required to spend monies already allocated. It takes eight additional weeks to obtain the required signatures. Everyone acknowledges the process wastes valuable time. Worse, the process is in conflict with the company's stated desire for a self-regulating work environment.

In these two examples, the need to avoid loss results in submission to authority that resides farther up the hierarchy. This submission creates dependence on others rather than interdependence and self-regulation.

Self-regulation does not mean that "everyone does his own thing." To be self-regulating is to base one's actions on the boundaries that define the system, whether the system consists of one person, a group, a function, or an entire organization. Self-regulating environments are created when (1) there is common cause—a purpose that is greater than and encompasses one's self-interest; and (2) parameters of success and limitations are clear.

Lately, there has been an intense focus on diversity in organizations. Shelby Steele (1990), in his book *The Content of Our Character*, writes that diversity without common ground is not diversity but fragmentation (p. 148). We collude with failure when we undertake collective efforts without first defining our common cause. Common cause enables each of us to align our self-interests with the interests of the whole col-

lective. Without common cause, individual efforts, no matter how well intentioned, lead to fragmented results or no
results at all.

Common cause is not enough. Our parameters for success need to be defined, just as our limitations do. Even when
a group agrees on its goals, success is often difficult to measure. The question we need to answer is How will we know
we are where we want to be?

When senior management sanctions a work redesign (a
process used by those who do the work to redesign the way
the work is done), the parameters for success need to be clear.
Sometimes they are called critical success factors. My colleague Marvin Weisbord calls these "minimum critical specifications." Whether these parameters include hard measures,
such as reduction in time to market or cycle time, or soft goals,
such as greater work satisfaction, it is important to know what
constitutes success. Without that information, self-regulation
is not possible. To be self-regulating is to be self-monitoring
in allocating energies and time to reach or surpass predetermined goals.

To achieve self-regulation also requires knowledge of
limitations. Before beginning the analyses associated with a
work redesign, design teams need to know if there are limits
to what they can recommend. For example, in one redesign,
the layout of the facility could not be changed. In another,
three large pieces of equipment could not be moved nor could
additional aromatic machines be purchased. One way to think
of limits is in terms of budget limitations. Most limits involve
avoidance of costs — such as those incurred in the acquisition
of more resources or in changes to the existing facilities. Without clear statements of limitations, individuals and groups cannot be self-regulating.

---

*My work with a pharmaceutical company provides a rich source
of information about self-regulation. In 1988, an East Coast plant
redesigned the way work was done. The plant moved to a team-*

based structure in which each team was responsible for making an entire product.

One design team member became a member of the first-shift Liquids Team in the Liquids plant. The manager of Liquids set a monthly production goal for all three shifts in Liquids. The goal was driven by market demand and monitored on a weekly basis through a measurement called "performance to plan."

One morning, the team member approached the manager and told him that the first-shift team could not see their impact on the "performance to plan" because their efforts comprised only one-third of what was being measured. Further, the team was hampered by performance problems related to specific individuals, whose behavior had been tolerated for years by management. Although the team was happy to be self-regulating, it was also frustrated because it was now responsible for solving problems that managers had never solved. As examples, the team member mentioned one individual on the cartoning section of the line who painted her nails instead of paying attention to her job. Another individual snuck out for cigarettes when the line was running. Another took long lunches, which kept the line from starting up on time.

The manager asked the team member what he wanted to do to address these problems. The team member thought that having a team goal might help—something everyone could endorse and work toward. He said he wanted to bring a flipchart out to the line at the beginning of the shift and get people on his team to focus on a daily production goal. At that time, that particular team was packaging about 30,000 units a day. The manager encouraged the team member to go ahead. At the beginning of the shift the following morning, the team member asked the team to set a goal for its output. The team decided to shoot for 40,000 units. They also agreed to stop every two hours to make sure they had 10,000 units. At the end of their shift, the team had produced 40,000 units. Everyone was elated. Not surprisingly, another benefit accrued. With everyone focused on the same goal, the problems of nail painting, unauthorized cigarette breaks, and extended lunches disappeared.

*The next day, buoyed by their success, the team again used
the flipchart to create its goal. They decided to stick with 40,000
units because they had only done it one time. They wanted to
be sure it was not a fluke. At the end of the shift, the team had
made 40,000 units for the second day in a row. Everyone went
home a few feet off the ground.*

*On Monday, the team member assembled the team. All but
one member wanted to up the ante to 42,000 units. That member said she could not live with a goal of 42,000 units. The team
operated by consensus. When a member said, "I cannot live with
that," the team continued to work the issue. The woman argued
that the team had a two-day track record of making 40,000 units;
therefore, they did not have enough of a track record to increase
the goal.*

*The team listened and kept the goal at 40,000. At the end
of that day, they had produced 35,000 units. Deflated but not
defeated, they sat down to determine what had caused this drop
in production. They determined that because equipment "sat cold"
over the weekend, it did not start smoothly on Monday. This
slowed production. They agreed that in the future, two people
would come in early to start up the equipment so that when the
team began the shift, the equipment would not be cold. Today
that team produces 60,000 units a day.*

*A second story about self-regulation involved another of that
same manager's teams. Shortly after the work redesign was implemented, an automatic case packer was moved from Line 2 to
Line 4. The team on Line 2 believed they would have to slow
the Line from 105 to 90 units per minute to compensate for the
loss of this equipment. A line operator informed the team that
if they reduced the speed of the line, they could not meet the
weekly planning value (PV) so they would have to give up working the four ten-hour days they had selected over the five-day workweek. Because the team wanted to keep the four-day workweek,
they decided to experiment. They quickly learned they were able
to produce 105 units per minute without the case packer. Their
incentive was their desire to work a four-day week and their commitment to meet their weekly PV goal. Goal achievement is en-*

hanced when goals satisfy both individual and organizational needs. Without such mutuality, workforces are coerced into complying with standards that benefit the company only. Commitment occurs when thresholds for success are clear and when individuals can be self-regulating in how they achieve success. In essence, this means that leaders specify what *and workers specify* how. *These specifications are the basis of partnership— something completely absent in the old command and control hierarchy, where managers had the illusion of controlling processes and results when, in actuality, they controlled only resources.*

Self-regulation also requires us to determine whether boundaries are real or imagined and to create boundaries that enable us to serve and support the entire system, not just ourselves or our function. More often than not, we act as if the options we can exercise are fewer than actually exist. In organizational terms, this means that we act as if our job boundaries are actually narrower than they are. The creation of new boundaries is an act of courage. Such acts are not commonplace.

We and our organizations want to ensure certainty, and simultaneously avoid loss. We can do both when we create a safe emergency (see Figure 7.4). The term *safe emergency* is an oxymoron, made of two words that do not go together, yet it defines an *experiment*. To experiment is to do something safe enough to avoid annihilation and yet emergent enough to push ourselves through boundaries that are holding us back. Our ability to create safe emergencies is tied to our sources of survival. If we believe our survival is in our own hands, we will err on the side of the emergent, rather than on the side of that which is safe. Conversely, if we believe our survival is in our bosses' hands, we will err on the side of playing it safe. Those who are self-regulating know that survival is a matter of relatedness, alliance, and control.

Figure 7.4. Learning and Risk: Elements of a Safe Emergency.

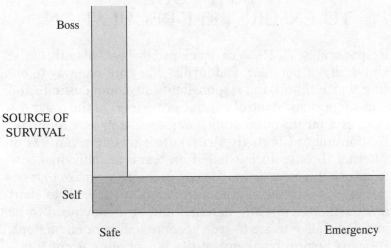

Note: Figure based on definition of *experiment* attributable to Gestalt Institute of Cleveland.

They also know that to thrive is a matter of interdependence. A safe emergency, therefore, is a model for invention, self-regulation, and interdependence.

One way to assess a possible safe emergency would be to use the support and control graphs shown in Figures 7.1 and 7.2. In any enterprise, underlying assumptions about support and control are inherent in organizational structure and roles. To create awareness of these assumptions: (1) plot on the support and control graphs where you see yourself, your function, other employees, other functions, and those who formally lead your organization; and (2) determine what themes are present in what you have plotted. Next, discuss support and control with others in your organization and ask: (1) What is missing in terms of alignment between responsibility, authority, and accountability? and (2) What needs to occur for support and control to exist at every level of the system?

THE RESPONSIBILITY CHART
AS A TOOL
TO ENSURE SELF-REGULATION

Responsibility Charts were developed by Jay Galbraith, at the University of Southern California. They are one way to ensure that authority and responsibility are commensurate and that support and control exist at every level in the organization, as a means of creating a self-regulating environment. Responsibility Charts (R charts) are effective regardless of whether the structure is based on teams or individual contributors. When we assess the key decisions we make to meet and exceed our customer requirements, we are able to chart how tasks are currently handled and how they need to be handled if all of us are to seek accountability for our actions. R charts help us break out of the box of our current thinking and push the boundaries our entrenched assumptions create.

In creating R charts, the first step is to identify the ten to twelve key decisions inherent in a job. The next step is to determine what tasks are associated with each decision. The results of these steps are measured against three factors:

1. Decisions and tasks must meet or exceed customer requirements.

2. Decisions and tasks must relate to essential work — core work or work that supports core work.

3. Decisions and tasks must be based on an alignment of responsibility, authority, and accountability.

Once the key decisions are identified, the current reality can be charted. This shows who is *responsible* for making decisions (R), who *approves* them (A), who needs to be *consulted* about them (C), and who must be *informed*, after the fact, that a decision has been made (I).

In Figure 7.5, under "Decisions That Create Customer Satisfaction," the decision to hire an individual is charted. In

Figure 7.5. Responsibility Chart for Decision.

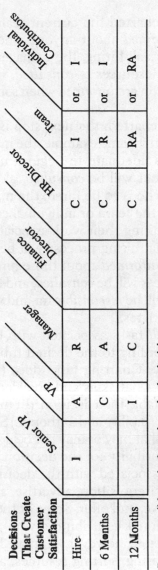

Decisions That Create Customer Satisfaction	Senior VP	VP	Manager	Finance Director	HR Director	Team	Individual Contributors
Hire	I	A	R		C	I or	I
6 Months		C	A		C	R or	I
12 Months		I	C		C	RA or	RA

R = responsible to do the task, make the decision
A = gives approval
C = must be consulted before decision is made
I = must be informed, after the fact, of the decision

Questions relevant to assigning R, A, C, I:

1. Should this be done by a team member or individual contributors?
2. Should this be done by a team leader if team-based structure is in place?
3. Should this be done by a facilitator or manager to whom team or individuals report?
4. Should this be done by policy or procedure? (Caution: Inventive organizations have lean policies and procedures.)
5. Should this be done?

If there is disagreement about whom to assign which responsibilities, ask:
(a) Why not? and (b) What needs to occur to make this assignment possible?

Note: Responsibility Charts are based on work by Jay Galbraith.

this example, the manager has charted the current reality: the senior vice president is *informed* about anyone who is hired, the vice president *approves* all hiring, the manager is *responsible* for hiring, Human Resources is *consulted*, and those on the team or in the function are *informed* when someone has been hired.

After the current reality is charted, the next step is to chart the desired future state. In this same example, the manager believes that six months is adequate to begin a new process wherein the vice president will be *consulted*, along with Human Resources, about who is to be hired; the manager will *approve* the hiring; and the team or individual contributors will be *responsible* for hiring their work associates. In twelve months, when the final hiring process will be in place, the vice president will be *informed* about those hired, the manager and Human Resources will be *consulted*, and the team or individual contributors will be *responsible* for and will *approve* the hiring of work associates.

The next step is to chart *all* tasks associated with the decision. These are charted according to the desired future scenario, not the current reality. Charting tasks does two things. First it clearly delineates what skills and knowledge are needed by whoever is accountable for a decision. (In turn, accountability helps to align responsibility and authority.) Second, each decision involves tasks that may or may not be done by those who have overall responsibility for the decision. In Figure 7.6, the following tasks associated with the decision to hire additional staff are listed: requisition, advertise, sort resumes, interview, select, approve, and offer. Some of these are done by the team or individual contributors who are responsible for the overall decision; however, Human Resources is responsible for advertising, sorting resumes, and offering benefits.

Analyzing R Chart Data

In reviewing our charts of current reality, we need to look for *multiple* R's and A's in the current reality and avoid assigning

Figure 7.6. Responsibility Chart for Task.

Decision: Hire Additional Staff

Role \ Tasks	Requisition	Advertise	Sort resumes	Interview	Select	Approve	Offer job	Offer benefits
Senior VP	C							
Manager	C		C	C				
Finance Director				C	C			
HR Director	R	R	R					R
Team	RA	A	A	R	R	RA	R	
Individual or Contributors	RA	A	A	R	R	RA	R	

R = responsible to do the task
A = approve who does task or how task is performed
C = must be consulted before task is done
I = must be informed, after the fact, of task completion

Note: Responsibility Charts are based on work by Jay Galbraith.

Exhibit 7.1. Instructions for Responsibility Charting.

---

1. On the vertical axis, list the ten to twelve key business decisions you make that drive out (meet) your customer's requirements.
2. List the roles with whom you interact.
3. Chart the "R," "A," "I," and "C" for each role.
4. You can have multiple "I's" and multiple "C's." These tell you what co-alitions and what forums are necessary to keep people included in and/or informed of the process.
5. If you have multiple "R's" and multiple "A's," you have unclear boundaries.

Once you have completed your current reality and desired future states, you need to contract with your leader, your followers, your customers and suppliers, and your support functions. This contracting may lead to adjustments in both the current and desired states. This contracting makes explicit what is required to be an effective leader, colleague, and follower.

Note: Responsibility Charts are based on work by Jay Galbraith.

---

multiple R's and A's in the desired future state. Multiple R's and A's indicate unclear responsibilities and authorities, which result in unclear boundaries. The clearer the boundaries, the better the linkages—between people, between people and technology, between customers and suppliers. Poor linkages create communication nightmares.

We can have multiple C's and multiple I's. If these occur, it is important to think in terms of coalitions and forums. A *coalition* means all those who need to be informed or consulted. A *forum* means the best way to do the informing and consulting—through a meeting, electronic mail, or other means. Multiple C's and I's need to be scrutinized to ensure that the minimum critical specification for C or I is *those who are impacted directly or those who should have direct impact.* (See Exhibit 7.1 for a summary of R charting.)

Another key to R charting is to determine who really needs to be involved. In the R charts in Figures 7.5 and 7.6, the organization is team based. Many organizations are combinations of teams and individual contributors, in which case, the roles of the individual contributors need to be noted on the horizontal axis of the chart. Regardless, these questions need to be asked:

1. Should this decision be made by a team member? An individual contributor?
2. Should this decision be made by a team leader? A supervisor?
3. Should this decision be made by a facilitator or manager?
4. Should this decision be made by policy or procedure?
5. Does this decision need to be made?

A caution applies to item 4. Policy and procedure manuals thwart creativity in organizations. The leaner the policies and procedures, the better. Some policies and procedures are required by law; however, I have worked in nuclear environments where some of the requirements generally thought to be those of the Nuclear Regulatory Commission were really company-initiated policies and procedures. Similarly, I have worked in pharmaceutical environments where much that was attributed to Food and Drug Administration requirements was not mandated by the FDA. When policies and procedures are not legal requirements, organizations can choose to write policies and procedures that cover exceptions only. In these cases, *exceptions* refers to what cannot be done, not what ought to be done.

The fifth question needs to be asked because many decisions have evolved as haphazardly as did the processes for making them. Just as it is wasteful to automate a process before determining the most efficient design, it is ineffective to assume that all decisions being made support invention and self-regulation. The former automates inefficiencies and the latter institutionalizes "fear" and "form" rather than "invention."

Ferreting Out Constraints

The most successful R charting involves our undertaking some deep soul searching, primarily by asking two questions: (1) What supports and what thwarts our having the impact we wish to have? and (2) How do we hold ourselves back?

It is not always easy to understand our own contribution to creating the collective whole we call our organization, particularly when we feel unheard or the organization is not one of our choosing. The powerfulness of the whole often translates into the powerlessness of the individual. But this translation is, by and large, of our own making. So it is important to ask ourselves *how* we hold ourselves back, rather than "why" we do so or "what" makes us do so. This insight into *how* frequently presents the alternative we have been seeking in creating a safe emergency for ourselves—an experiment in which we push against our own self-imposed boundaries and seek to create an organization of our choosing.

Holding ourselves back is sometimes related to denial (see Chapter Two). Denial is holding on. It is a form of resistance, which results in stored energy. We hold on for a reason. Sometimes the reason is historical—it used to work when we did "it" this way. But perhaps we were punished sufficiently never to do "it" again. Sometimes the reason is found in the *constraints* of the context in which we work.

Constraints are of two kinds—those that enable (such as minimum critical specifications) and those that restrict. Enabling constraints support "know what, know where, know when, know how" because they are the "know why." They are limits that have been established and challenged and found to be a necessary condition for the time. Constraints are of our own making and usually arise out of a need for control. It is important to rethink constraints—those we believe are imposed and those we create for ourselves. "As long as we think we already know, we don't bother to rethink the situation. Identify the system's constraints. Decide how to exploit the system's constraints. Subordinate everything else to the above decision. Elevate the system's constraints" (Goldratt,

1990, p. 36). Identify your own constraints and decide how to exploit them. Subordinate everything else to this decision. Elevate your own constraints by challenging everything you put on your R chart with the question *Why not?*

Contract Making and Follow-Through

Once you have completed your R chart, you will need to contract with your followers, your boss, your support functions, suppliers, and customers to create awareness and agreement about:

1. What makes this shifting of responsibilities and authorities supportive of self-regulation and invention?

2. What is needed to support this transition — information, training, increased authority at your own level, more or less staff support, customer awareness, and patience with a process that may disrupt current levels of customer service to improve the system's ability to meet and exceed customer requirements? This list goes on, and can only be created by those who are impacted by and those who have impact on the desired future state outlined in your R chart.

   A well-done R chart will enable you to answer these questions, which illuminate the action steps you need to take to move from your current reality to the desired future state:

1. What new decisions (and their attendant tasks) need to be handled by me or by others?

2. What knowledge or skills do I or others need to develop to make these decisions/do these tasks?

3. What training or experience will I or others need to develop the requisite knowledge and skill to make these decisions/do these tasks?

4. What do I need to do, how, and by when?

5. What do others need to do, how, and by when?

R charts result in a five-way contract between an individual, his or her boss, employees, and internal customers and suppliers (see Figure 7.7). It is important to note that accountability never changes. The manager will always be held to account for the results achieved in his area, just as the vice president and senior vice president will be held to account for the manager's results. What can shift are authority and responsibility—authority being the right to choose, and responsibility being the completion of task—to where the work is actually done so accountability exists at every level of the enterprise.

Figure 7.7. Five-Way Contracting.

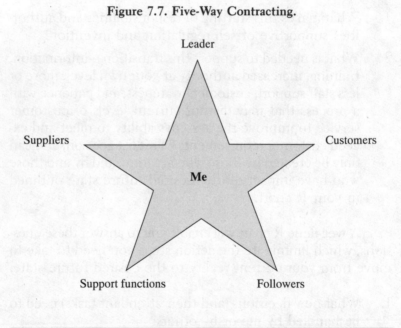

A worldwide supplier of pulp, paper products, packaging, and construction materials provides an example of how to use R charts to create a management development program. The company wanted to create a week-long program for senior managers. The manager of management development asked me to conduct a half-day session on empowerment. To illustrate empowerment in action, rather than talk about it in a half-day segment, I asked if the participants could co-design the program. As I explained how this could be done, the manager's eyes lit up. He was becoming aware that the program he had had in mind might not be what was needed.

We talked in broad terms about a two-day awareness building session in which senior managers would do the following:

1. Look at the past and decide what they were proud of and what they were sorry about

2. Look at the present and focus on forces of fear and opportunity affecting their operations

3. Meet with the new CEO to discuss his broad vision for the company

4. Develop a vision for each of their respective functions

To complete step 4, the senior managers would meet with external customers to find out firsthand what created customer satisfaction. Then they would focus on what support they needed to move forward—technology, skills, knowledge, and training.

The tool for determining support was a responsibility chart. The current reality was charted along with the desired states six and twelve months into the future. Responsibility and authority were placed with the individuals or functions that performed the work that met or exceeded customer requirements. Shifts in responsibility and authority determined developmental needs, both for senior managers and those they led.

The proposed design accomplished four things:

1. It created awareness of current reality at many levels of the organization.

2. It empowered those who were targeted for development to determine what development was needed.

3. It created double learning—senior managers learned what they needed to learn while they learned how to determine their learning needs.

4.   *The process used to develop the program modeled what the program intended to teach: self-regulation.*

USING SELF-REGULATION
TO CREATE SELF-REGULATION

When a work redesign is done well, it models the very process that is the intended outcome. The basis of any work redesign is to align authority, responsibility, and accountability at the point where the work is done rather than to fragment these efforts by assigning authority to employees other than those responsible for doing the work. Moreover, authority and responsibility must be aligned in ways that create the proper boundaries and interfaces between staff and line functions and between centralized and decentralized operations. One of the intended outcomes of work redesign and re-engineering is always self-regulation.

In the Information Era, our organizational wealth lies in organizational knowledge and competence. This requires us to create structures:

1.   In which human and electronic networks can easily transfer information across necessary organizational boundaries

2.   That support increased core competence and, thereby, capacity at all levels of system — individual, interpersonal, group, and organizational

3.   That provide each employee a "line of sight" to end users, which enables employees to see their contribution to the product or service being produced

4.   That eliminate unnecessary boundaries

Our efforts to create these structures have led to a redesign of the traditional one-on-one, boss-subordinate relationship and the evolution of team-based structures. Sometimes these teams are called "self-managed" or "self-directed." Often these terms have led to an inadvertent belief that "hierarchy is dead and managers are unnecessary." Neither is true. The success of collective efforts depends on acts of leading and following—those acts that link individual effort and desire with group goals and needs. Moreover, the success of collective efforts depends on the linkages between groups that result in some form of hierarchy. Our resistance to hierarchy derives from past experiences in which hierarchy has meant "one over another and with command and control." If we look at the need for linkages between groups and functions rather than the need for one over another, we can create organizational structures that support self-regulation and organizational success. Those who are the linkages no longer need to command and control; rather, they become conveyors of information and providers of resources. If we change our traditional structures but not the roles within those structures, we have changed nothing. And if we are to change the roles, the process by which we do this must model those new roles and their attendant behaviors.

Each restructuring or redesign effort provides ample opportunity for those involved to become self-regulating, provided the process for the restructuring or redesign is not imposed but is co-created among those on the project. In working with design teams, I invite team members to rotate the responsibility of updating the steering committee, which is made up of a group of senior managers who have sanctioned the redesign. An update occurs after each phase of analysis so that the steering committee is informed about what is being learned as it is being learned. This same information also is given to everyone in the system that is under study. Design team members who are shy or unaccustomed to making presentations are often reluctant to take on this responsibility. Interim presentations, however, are great training for the final presentation, in which it is ideal for every team member to speak because the product is the result of a joint effort.

In one redesign that took place in a plant located in the South, a team member named Gerald told me, "Ma'am, if I have to speak to the steering committee, I am going to drop dead." I asked if he would be comfortable introducing those who would present the update and, with a bit of hesitation, he agreed. The next day, Gerald did not come to work. After the update, we were told that Gerald's wife had called to say he was very ill. He had developed a high fever during the night and his psoriasis, which had been under control, had flared up. I thought to myself that Gerald was right. He would drop dead if he had to speak to the steering committee.

From then on, Gerald did not speak during the updates to the steering committee. He took responsibility for running equipment, controlling the lights, and other behind-the-scenes tasks necessary for the presentations. When it came time for the team to present its redesign proposal, Gerald again volunteered to work behind the scenes.

On the morning of the presentation, I asked the team if they would be willing to tell the steering committee what it had been like for them to work on this project. I did not need to know what they were going to say. I only wanted someone to volunteer to go first so there would not be a long silence before someone spoke. Brenda, the team's informal leader, volunteered to go first. When the steering committee sat down, I told them that before the team made its presentation, members wanted to say a few words about what it was like to work together on this project. Brenda spoke first. She talked about what she had learned about the plant, its various functions, and her own ability to be part of a team. Another member talked about the difficulties of managing differences and agreements and how some of the decision making had been agonizing. Another person spoke. And then, from a corner of the room, softly and at first haltingly, another voice was heard. "I want to thank the steering committee for giving me this opportunity to work on this team. I have learned a great deal and I appreciate the confidence people had in me to be part of this effort." The voice belonged to Gerald. His courage in that moment exemplifies what empowerment is all about. During the time the group *worked together, he, and only he, had regulated his participation in presentations to the steering committee. In so doing, he had experienced enough support from his team members that he was able to do what he had not been able to do before—to speak in a forum that four months earlier had been so intimidating as to make him ill. For me, that moment was the redesign. It captures what is possible when conditions support self-regulation— the ability for everyone to have the support and control to achieve his highest potential.*

8

Interdependence:
All for One and One for All

If we see our organizations as a series of relationships in action — a system — then we understand more clearly that the nature of our relationships is determined by (1) where we draw the boundaries — who's in and who's out; (2) the nature of the boundary — fixed, flexible, open, closed, permeable, impermeable, and so forth; and (3) how we transact across those boundaries we have drawn. Inventive organizations are based on relationships of mutuality and partnership — relationships that are interdependent. Mutuality is possible when every organizational member has the requisite support and control to act in ways that serve self and others in pursuit of a common cause. Partnership is an outgrowth of our ability to be self-regulating in the entire series of relationships that make up our organizations.

An example of the consequences in our choice of "who is in and who is out" comes from a plant producing household cleaning products for a large consumer products company. In 1990, the manager of the plant began a work redesign. She believed that she could better position the plant for maximum participation in the company's growth by having the whole system study itself.

A work redesign involves a design team, made up of people who do the work, and a steering committee, made up of managers who are responsible for ensuring the continued viability of the organization. Prior to my working with the plant manager, every other person who had held that position had created a steering committee made up of managers within that plant. This composition ensures the plant manager's control of the steering committee, even though it isolates the plant from other functions whose support and cooperation are needed to support implementation of the redesign.

The plant manager wanted the design team to include two managers and a diagonal slice of workers from every function and shift in her plant. Nine people joined the team. She invited one other manager to join her on the steering committee along with five other individuals — her regional manager, the corporate heads of Technology, Industrial Relations, and Training, as well as a manager from another plant (which had been through a work redesign). In so doing, she gave up her control of her steering committee; however, she gained much more. In essence, she extended the boundary of the plant. She involved people in the redesign process whose support and input were invaluable during both the design and implementation phases.

This manager understands interdependence. She saw the plant's boundary as elastic and permeable. Most managers see boundaries as fixed, invisible, blurred, necessary to maintain, impermeable, protected, or unprotected. This manager did not view the existing plant boundaries as delineating "insiders" and "outsiders"; rather, she saw the existing boundaries as flexible, visible, and changeable. In the process of setting up the redesign, she modeled a definition of boundaries that the design team emulated. They created a redesigned plant with flexible, permeable, clear, elastic boundaries. When it came time to implement the redesign, the plant manager's team included all the necessary support functions. Her foresight and understanding of the plant's inter-

*dependence enable her to align the company's support mecha-
nisms with the redesign during the design phase rather than during implementation. This resulted in the fastest implementation
of a redesign that I have ever experienced.*

Boundaries indicate points of contact. Without them, we are
unable to distinguish one entity from another—whether the
entities are persons, dyads, groups, or organizations. So where
we draw the boundary indicates the possible point(s) of contact, and the nature of the boundary determines the kind of
contact that can occur. When we encounter boundaries that
are permeable or elastic, we tend to experience others—individuals and groups—as open or accessible.

When we transact across boundaries that are permeable, elastic, or open, we tend to experience our transactions
as easy and satisfying. Conversely, when we encounter boundaries that are fixed or closed, we tend to experience others
as inaccessible or impossible to influence. When we transact
across these boundaries, we are apt to experience our transactions as difficult and frustrating.

Boundaries also indicate (1) level of system—individual,
interpersonal, group, organization, and so on; (2) how one level
is distinguished from another level; and (3) how similar levels
of system are distinguished from each other. For example,
an individual level of system can be defined as "all that is me
is me and all that is not me, is not me." What is included inside the boundary is what distinguishes *me* from *not me*. It
is what distinguishes self and, thereby, determines the relationship of self to other. At an interpersonal level, one may
see another as intimate, friend, enemy, or unknown. The relationship is determined by where the boundary is drawn; for
example, is the "other" seen as being inside or outside the
boundary? At the group level, members of the group—for example, family members—are distinct and separate from non-
members. Those considered as part of the community are dis-

tinct from those not included within the boundary called community. In terms of the world, where boundaries are drawn determines relationships called allies and enemies.

THE NATURE OF INTERDEPENDENCE

This chapter begins with boundaries because the key to understanding the nature of interdependence is to first understand separateness, and boundaries create separation. It may sound paradoxical, but the concept of interdependence is based on separateness. Interdependence means at least two separate entities are involved in a relationship of mutuality. Without distinction between them, everyone and everything becomes the same; therefore we are only able to distinguish separateness by defining one person or thing in relation to someone or something else. Examples include defining an infant in relation to a parent, members of a family in relation to one another, people in relation to places, an employee in relation to a place of work, an organization in relation to an industry, and "things" in relation to their origins and uses. Thus we define separateness by defining relationship.

Understanding interdependence involves being able to see that the whole is made up of its parts. The Tao, which means "the one," is made up of yin and yang. So within "the one" there is a duality. A marriage is an example of oneness or a single entity that is formed by two individuals. A family is another example of a whole that is comprised of separate individuals who are related by birth or choice. An organization is a composite of people, geography, processes, equipment, and edifice, all of which are distinct and all of which are in an interdependent relationship.

Another key to understanding interdependence lies in polarities, or opposites. Two seemingly polar concepts exist in relation to one another—for example, synonyms and antonyms. Sweet exists in relation to bitter, pleasure in relation to pain. And yet, even with polarities, there is that extreme point where different things become the same. Sweetness can be so cloying as to become bitter. Pleasure can feel so good it hurts. Fear can be so acute as to create excitement, and vice versa.

Concepts and complex conceptual frameworks are also capable of interdependence. For example, the six frameworks of inventive organizations are interdependent. All six parts are needed to create the whole, and each is a characteristic of the whole; each principle exists in relation to every other principle. Within any system are entities that exist in relation to one another—the company exists in relation to its external operating environment, employees in relation to their work associates, leaders in relation to followers, and individuals in relation to the means by which they produce. In each of these examples, multiple aspects constitute the whole, and each aspect exists in relation to the others.

INDIVIDUALISM:
A DISCARDED DREAM
OR A REVISED BOUNDARY?

In American society, it is easier for us to see our separateness than to find our common cause. This is so because we think of the individual first and the community of individuals second. We have a strong affinity for separateness, which plays out in our organizations. Separation characterizes organizational hierarchy—a few lead and many follow—as well as our early assumptions about the division of labor—some plan and think and some do the work. Separateness is mirrored in how we draw organizational boundaries: we draw boundaries around functions, then divisions, and finally strategic business units. These boundaries divide our enterprises into a series of distinct and separate entities. Most often, these entities do not form relationships with one another. Frequently, they view each other as enemies. When I asked about organizational relationships, a young man in one company reported, "We circle the wagons and shoot in."

Our wake-up call came from Japan's assault on our industrial base. In the past twenty years, we in the United States have become good students of Japanese production methods, most of which are team-based. Teamwork is a natural outgrowth of the Japanese philosophy that "the group is more important than the individual." In an effort to match Japan's effectiveness and compete in global markets, many of our organizations have adopted team-based structures. In so doing, most of these organizations have not only made undue course correction, they have also created a dichotomy between espoused beliefs and organizational practices. Our cultural tendency toward individualism conflicts with Japan's cultural tendency toward "group." This conflict is evident in our attempts to create teams while we continue to reward individual performance.

In the rush to embrace a team concept, we have gone from one extreme—a focus on the individual—to another extreme—a focus on the collective. This change has brought about desires to move from steep hierarchies that favor individual contributors to flatter organizations with team-based structures, from an exaltation of managers to an exaltation of "self-managed" teams.

The tendency to go to extremes is common. All too often our organizational marching orders shift from centralization to decentralization or vice versa, from manually operated to automated, from short term to long term or vice versa, from power in staff functions to power in line functions or vice versa, and the list goes on. But systems are not that flexible. The imbalance that triggered the change to begin with is transferred to the other side of the spectrum, and is often more exaggerated. Teams are launched, hatched, designed, or concocted almost overnight, with little or no concern for the method. More important, other aspects of the system—the support mechanisms—are rarely if ever put in place ahead of time to support the new structure. Such mechanisms include knowledge of group dynamics and skills for leading and following in the context of a self-regulating group. When too much change is imposed too fast, the parts that make up the system become misaligned.

In seeking to foster interdependence, which is what is required to operate successfully in the Information Era, we need to take care not to try to discard individualism. We do not have to choose between the individual and the team. We must embrace both; however, we cannot mandate interdependence. We can only move toward the practice of interdependence as quickly as the whole system can move; all the parts of the system, including reward mechanisms and structure, need to change together and remain in alignment. Further, we must beware of overcorrection. The most agile organizations are those that understand interdependence as alignment among those entities that make up the whole. We do not need to draw boundaries to include only individual contributors or team-based operations. What we need is to ensure that our organizational boundaries include both the individual and the team—the "I" and the "We"—whether these boundaries are found in how we think, in how we design our organizational structures, or in our operating policies.

THE NEED TO ALIGN "I" AND "WE"

We will continue to err if we continue to shift from one extreme to another—from the idea of the individual as king to the idea of group as more important than the individual. These ideas need not be mutually exclusive. We can simultaneously focus on the group and the individual if we align the interests of "I" and "We." In essence, "I" exists only in relation to all else. And "We" is a collection of "I's." (See Figure 8.1.) Further, if we see ourselves as part of a greater whole—us—we understand our interdependence with other entities in the system.

Figure 8.1. I, We, and Us: Interdependent System.

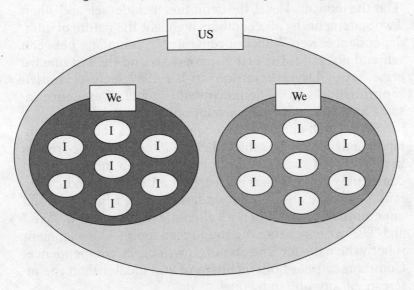

In Table 8.1, the definition of "I" can clearly be seen to depend on the context. At each successive system level, the definition of "I" is more inclusive because the boundary drawn around that level of system is more inclusive. The boundary that is drawn determines the nature of the relationship. In

Table 8.1. Interdependent Relationships
Between Levels of Systems.

Level of System	Interdependent Relationships		
	I	WE	US
Individual	Intrapersonal	Husband and Wife	Couple
Interpersonal	Partner	Partnership	Business
Group	Relatives	Family	Extended family
Organization	Occupation	Profession	Professional organization
Society	Neighbor	Neighborhood	Community

an interdependent relationship, which is anything other than "I" at the individual level, the definition includes self and other. Two statements by other authors highlight the nature of interdependence. Ken Wilber once wrote, "A boundary between self and not self is the first one we draw and the last one we erase." And David Berenson, in his 1989 lecture entitled "Spirituality," said, "The individual is a fact of existence insofar as it is a unit built of relationships."

When self and other are experienced as equals, true interdependence can be achieved. Such interdependence results in a "We" that simultaneously includes each individual and constitutes a whole that is greater than each individual. Interdependence also is the foundation upon which we build our common cause. When we align the interests of "I," "We," and "Us," we experience our interdependence. This alignment is both the basis for, and an outgrowth of, interdependence. Common cause is both inclusive of and greater than the interests of any one individual.

In Chapter Seven, a distinction is made between dependence, independence, and interdependence. When we see our source of support as in ourselves only, we act independently — we act in service and support of our *self*. When we see our source of support only in others, we act dependently — we act in service and support of *everyone but ourselves*. To be self-regulating is to see our source of support in ourselves and others. When we recognize the reality of shared support, we can act in service and support of everyone, including ourselves.

THE COCREATIONIST VIEW
OF ORGANIZATIONS

A wonderful metaphor for interdependence exists in the cocreationist theory of literature. This fancy term refers to a theory that until an author has written and a reader has read, there is no book. An author often intends for the reader to get certain meaning from his work that the reader does not get. And, conversely, the reader often reads into the work something the author did not intend. Thus neither creates the book. The book is created out of the interaction between the author and the reader and out of the individual experience of each.

Organizations are created out of relationships—relationships between customers and suppliers, leaders and followers, and between individuals and the means by which they produce. These relationships cocreate the enterprise. In Chapter Two, organizational strategy is depicted as driven by customer requirements. If we see our organizations existing in relationship to our customer requirements, we will see our "selves" existing in relationship to our customers. This relationship is one of interdependence. It can be one of partnership if we expand our concept of our organization—extend the boundary we have drawn around the organizational system so that the customer is included in our definition of the enterprise (see Figure 8.2).

Figure 8.2. Customer as Partner.

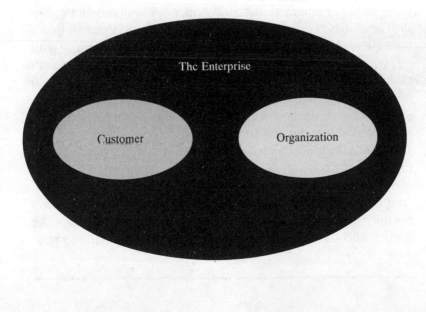

This story is well known; however, the philosophy that under-lines the story—the philosophy of partnership with one's end user—may be not readily apparent as one of interdependence.

In 1986, the Tylenol scare occurred. One person tampered with some capsules in a bottle of Tylenol and one of these capsules ultimately poisoned and killed another person. Although the tampering had occurred after the manufacturer, Johnson & Johnson, had sold the product to a retailer, the company held itself responsible for what had occurred. Rather than seeing itself only in relation to its retailers, the company saw itself in a health partnership with the entire customer chain, which includes the end user. The company immediately recalled all capsules from the area where the poisoning occurred for testing and disposal; all capsules in production also were discarded. The FDA was also testing capsules from the area, and their tests turned up a second bottle containing poison. The company immediately issued a nationwide recall of the product.

Within a week, James Burke, then chairman of Johnson & Johnson, declared that the company would no longer make capsules. Further, stronger bottle caps, seals, and shrink wrap were to be used in manufacturing all products. A new product called the Gel-Cap was developed, which was a "caplet" that combined the ease and comfort associated with swallowing a capsule with less vulnerability to product tampering—a virtue associated with tablets. All of these actions indicated that the company saw each of its tablets as a microcosm of the whole. If one capsule had been tampered with, the potential existed for every capsule to be contaminated. It was not good enough to recall one shipment. Every shipment of capsules had to be recalled. It was not good enough to throw out all capsules in the contaminated shipment. Every shipment had to be discarded. As a result of seeing the whole of the company in one capsule it produced, the whole of the company not only survived the Tylenol scare, but the reformulated product thrived and continued to increase the company's market share.

Organizations that see themselves in partnership with their customers cocreate their products and services with their customers. This cocreation can occur in the process of research and development, wherein customer usage is integral to the design. It can occur in market research, in which customer feedback is solicited to understand customer requirements. And it can occur in the design phase, in which organizations invite their customers' ideas and reactions to the product or service being developed. Where this occurs matters little. The issue is that partnership occurs only within a boundary that encompasses equals in a relationship of interdependence.

ALIGNING THE SEGMENTS OF OUR ORGANIZATIONAL COMMUNITY

At the same time our globe is "shrinking," our mobility is putting greater distance between us and our parents or grown children, between the places where we grew up and the places we now live, between ourselves and our friends from school. As these separations multiply, our hunger for community grows. So, too, does the time we devote to work. It is no wonder then that our organization becomes our second family—or at least the part of the organization in which we work. (People tend to experience the family nature of this relationship most intensely when it is about to end.)

An organization is not only a form of family, it is a form of community—a work community. While we may relate especially deeply to those with whom we work regularly and consider them our organizational family, that group exists within a greater whole—in a community comprised of many work "families." The organizational unit we call "family" is usually our function, department, or section. This unit is commonly referred to as "We." The organizational relationship that often is referred to as "Us" (or "our") includes the whole of the enterprise. It becomes "Us" when we acknowledge our interdependence and each "I" and "We" acts in service and support of the whole—the entire system—the total work community we call "Us."

Organizational size affects our ability to experience a sense of organizational community. As size increases, so do the complexities of creating a place where an individual is known and knows. Steep hierarchies that include more than a few hundred people make it harder for everyone to know and be known—to see the picture and to be seen as part of the big picture. Nonetheless, we need to find new ways to build and celebrate our organizational relationships—our work community—if we are to thrive at every level of system. It is not enough to focus on the parts of our enterprise and not on the whole, or to focus on the whole and not on the parts. We need to focus simultaneously on both. And to do this, we must focus on new ways to align the "I," the "We," and the "Us."

INTERDEPENDENCE OF COMPETITORS

In Chapter Two, mention was made of an engineer at Kodak who saw Fuji, a direct competitor, as the reason Kodak's products are as good as they are today. This notion of interdependence with one's competitor is a function of where the boundary is drawn. In this case, the engineer drew a boundary around the industry, and the nature of the relationship within the boundary was characterized as interdependent. Fuji was seen as a force that helped Kodak get better, rather than as an enemy that needed to be destroyed.

The interdependence of those within a given industry may or may not be appreciated, depending on how boundaries are drawn. In some cases, competitors become partners. This occurs when a high value is placed on interdependence—on aligning with a competitor in pursuit of a goal that is in the best interest of both organizations. In 1991, Johnson & Johnson/Merck Consumer Products (JJ/MCP) was founded on a relationship of interdependence. Although both companies produce drugs and could ultimately be called competitors, there was a significant area where Johnson & Johnson and Merck could achieve far greater results as partners than either company could attain alone. This contribution of each to the other created the common ground that aligned their interests, commitment, and efforts.

Merck produces prescription drugs that have limited patents. The company had no means to distribute these drugs once they came off patent and became nonprescription drugs. Johnson & Johnson produces and distributes nonprescription drugs. They have a distribution system and need more product for that system. It is less costly to increase market share if a company acquires a prescription drug that is about to come off patent, rather than creating a nonprescription duplication of that drug. In partnership, Johnson & Johnson and Merck each offers the other a part of a whole. Johnson & Johnson has the distribution system and Merck has the products. The alignment of these previously separate interests also involved alignment of interests within the corporate functions, once the new joint venture was launched.

Dave Vassar, Director of Operations, had a vision of the functions that constituted the new joint venture—the supply side and the demand side—acting as a team instead of remaining separate entities. Dave's function was Manufacturing. His counterparts were accountable for Sales, Marketing, Engineering, Finance, Human Resources, Product Development, and Quality Assurance. He invited his colleagues to a two-day off-site meeting in which they discussed company strategy, mission, and values. At the end of the two days, the entire group agreed to work together as the Business Team. Rather than each function writing its own mission statement, the Business Team wrote one statement, which then guided each member of the team's efforts in their respective areas of responsibility. In effect, they removed a layer of the organization. Rather than having one mission for the joint venture and one mission for each of the corporate functions within the joint venture, the Business Team's mission covered the whole of the joint venture as well as each corporate function included in the whole. When the Lancaster plant wrote its mission, it aligned itself with the whole of the corporation, not just with Operations.

This is an example of balancing "I" (which in this example could be viewed as the Lancaster plant), "We" (which could be viewed as the Operations function), and "Us" (which is viewed as the entire corporation). Whether we see our interdependence and seek to support it will depend on how and where we draw the boundary.

Another example of potential competitors as partners emerged in my work with JJ/MCP. During the start-up of the corporation, several consultants were hired. I had been hired by the director of operations to work with him and the Business Team. One of my colleagues joined me and worked with the Lancaster plant. Eventually, I recommended that the plant hire another firm, which creates distributed learning tools that enable employees to learn required skills just in time, in real time, on the job. Human Resources hired three consultants: one to help with testing procedures for new hires, another to recruit and screen new hires, and a third to develop a pay-for-knowledge system. The Finance function hired a firm that specialized in activities-based accounting. The Engineering function hired two firms to design and build the Lancaster plant. Early on, it became apparent that unless the consultants managed their boundaries and saw themselves as parts of a greater whole, the various clients within the system would not be able to manage their own boundaries or see themselves as parts of a greater whole.

I suggested to Dave Vassar that all the consultants meet. He told me his budget could not cover the fees of all the con-

sultants. Several firms had more than one consultant involved at the plant, and we needed everyone to attend. I believed that each consulting firm would come for expenses only, and everyone did. We agreed ahead of time not to discuss our fees and to honor the proprietary nature of each of our firms' materials and processes.

We used our joint meeting to present to one another our understandings of our respective assignments and our data-collection needs. At the end of the day, we agreed to use one firm to collect the data that all of us needed. We chose the firm whose data requirements were the most detailed. I acted as a conduit of information among the various firms. Ultimately, four of us joined for a three-day off-site meeting with the plant's management team. The time was used to develop the new plant's process flow, skills requirements, pay-for-knowledge blocks, critical success factors, and activities upon which accounting procedures would be based.

This joint cooperation extracted a price and created a benefit for all the consultants. Because data were collected by one firm for use by all firms, each of our respective contracts was for less time, and therefore fewer dollars, than had originally been anticipated. The benefits for us were that we were able to model for the client system the meaning of interdependence and, in our relationships with one another, learn a great deal more about the client system and each other's areas of expertise. Our client system benefitted because its time was efficiently used in providing the necessary data for all the consultants and, at the same time, it minimized its costs in those areas where different firms' needs overlapped. All of this occurred because of how boundaries were drawn and because each consulting firm balanced the "I," "We," and "Us." In this case, the "I" was each consulting firm; the "We" included all of the consulting firms; and the "Us" encompassed all of the consultants and the client system.

SEEING POWER AS "RELATIONSHIP WITH" RATHER THAN AS "POWER OVER"

To achieve interdependence, we need to see power as "relationship with" rather than as "power over" another. In the Industrial Era of steep hierarchies, power was a zero-sum game, something finite and scarce. Coupled with a belief in "command and control" or "command, predict, and control," and our underlying monotheistic philosophy, which exalts the individual above the group and one above all others, power was construed as power over others. In the Information Era of human and electronic networks, power is capacity. The more power each person has the greater the ability to act on behalf of something greater than oneself, the greater the capacity of the enterprise as a whole. Our ability to empower ourselves to act in service and support of the entire system of which we are a part depends on the nature of our relationships. When we see ourselves as interdependent and joined by common cause, we increase our capacity to attain our highest potential—as individuals and as those collectives we call organizations.

SEEING LEARNING AS RELATIONSHIP

Much has been written lately about the "learning organization," which, for me, is a result of organizational relationships. In her book *Making Our Lives Our Own*, Marilyn Mason writes, "The self that is growing through relatedness is the interdependent self" (1991, p. 105). Relationships contribute immensely to our learning. We learn in a context, and within that context are a series of relationships—a customer to a supplier, a leader to a follower, and so on. We learn from our transactions with others and our environment. The transactions that create learning are characterized by openness, which is a function of our interdependence, our recognition that the whole is reflected in each of its parts. To learn is to be affected by our relationships and to struggle within ourselves as a result of our relationships. We learn to soar and reach our fullest potential through our relationships with others and our environment.

Good organizational consultants create conditions for learning at all levels of the system. The consultant's role is to help those in the arena to stay in the arena — to not run away from the task at hand nor fight to the point of debilitating the system. The consultant's role is to facilitate learning, which, in the words of my colleague Marvin Weisbord often means moving "toward our anxiety." We learn when:

1. Our actions create changes in behavior or changes in boundaries

2. Meaning is consciously extrapolated from our experience, which means we feel closure

3. We have assimilated *what* we have learned into *our being*

Learning is both easy and hard. It is easy when we feel we have the *support* we need, which means we have the alliances and relatedness we seek. It is hard when we struggle with *control*, which involves our need for certainty and our fear of loss. The greatest learning comes when we experience enough support to stay engaged and struggle with our need for control. Our need for control is what creates our struggle in our search for interdependence. Our struggle is to see others as sources of relatedness, alliance, and certainty, not as sources of potential loss.

RELATIONSHIPS: HOLDING ON AND LETTING GO

Relationships are dynamic. So is interdependence. We define relationships by drawing boundaries around ourselves and others. When boundaries are impermeable or rigid, we lose the potential of what is inside the boundary as well as what is outside it.

We hold on to a boundary because we want to keep what is within it. But when we act as if the boundary is impermeable, the relationships within it suffer. How often do we find that when we try to hold on to a group, the group breaks apart. Some group members leave and others are not invited in. The result is atrophy. Boundaries, like the boxes of our current thinking, need to be examined with the understanding that our need to hold on will ultimately create the necessity to let go.

In our organizations today, we are redrawing boundaries as we redefine our relationships — our interdependence — with others, be they our work associates, our customers, our competitors, or others in the environment in which our enterprise exists.

REDEFINING BOUNDARIES: THE ROAD TO INTERDEPENDENCE

When organizations move from individual contributors and one-on-one, boss-subordinate relationships, to team-based structures that are self-regulating, they are creating boundaries that require interdependence. We learn about and appreciate interdependence best when we are inside boundaries that require us to practice interdependence.

After a work redesign, re-engineering, or restructuring project that results in team-based operations, it is essential to move people into the new structure, the new way of operating, as quickly as possible. Their struggle, then, will not be about whether or not "I" want to be in the structure; rather, their struggle will be about "self" in relation to "others." This is the struggle to balance "I" and "We." It leads us away from independence, dependence, and counter-dependence. It leads us toward interdependence, a critical component of inventive organizations.

The practice of interdependence is not only essential for inventive organizations, but it is also crucial for the Information Era. In this Era, our focus needs to be on critical linkages by which organizations achieve success. These linkages include human and electronic networks that enable us to share information, knowledge, and know-how across boundaries so that the whole of the enterprise is as strong as its strongest part. This new era of interdependence contrasts with the Industrial Era in which boundaries were drawn that created independence or dependence, and in which the whole of the enterprise was only as strong as its weakest part.

PART THREE

DARING: BOLD ACTS OF LEADING AND FOLLOWING THAT REDEFINE OUR ROLES, RELATIONSHIPS, AND POWER

This part of the book is about daring. It is about the bold acts of leading and following that sustain inventive organizations. It is about the nature of our relationships and interactions with others and about the intention, behavior, and impact associated with our actions. These acts of leading and following result from putting into practice — acting on — the underlying frameworks for inventive organizations that were presented in Part Two. These *acts* are distinguished from the *roles* of leader and follower. This distinction is important because our underlying assumption has been that "leader" and "follower" are labels that derive from roles rather than terms that describe actions. In inventive organizations, everyone dares to lead and everyone dares to follow in an environment of self-regulation, interdependence, and partnership.

In many ways, our organizations are illusionary. We act as if organizations are concrete entities that exist as something separate from the relationships between their constituents. We talk about them as inorganic. Just as we have made organizations things, we also have made behaviors or ways of being the prerogative of certain boxes on a chart. When we speak of these boxes, we distinguish between managers and employees, bosses and subordinates, leaders and followers. Such distinctions are illusions. Our organizations are not boxes on charts. Rather, they are a series of relationships in action — a series of transactions between individuals. These relationships — our interactions and transactions across boundaries that define self and others — are in the process of becoming. The process of becoming is an invisible and continuous process of defining, structuring, and redefining relationships with self and others at successive moments in time. A person who is categorized as a nonexempt or hourly employee is also an adult who may be married, own a home, have children, or lead church or community activities. The roles we take arise out of the context we are in — out of our transactions or interactions with others or a particular environment. In the case of work, we call "others and the environment" an organization. Our organizations *are* these interactions — these relationships. To do other than illuminate and enhance these relationships is to perpetuate the illusion that organizations are boxes on charts.

Organizations are no more confined to boxes on a chart than behaviors are confined to roles. Sometimes we act as if we can divide workers into two camps — those who think and plan and those who do the work; however, in reality, everyone thinks, plans, and does the work. We may act as if some lead and others follow. The reality is that everyone leads and everyone follows. In successive levels of system, those who "lead" at one level of system become those who "follow" at another level of system. Think of a manager. In the context of her function, she may be perceived as a leader. In the context of her bosses' function, she is likely to be perceived as a follower. Both roles arise out of assumptions about the hierarchy of organizational control that confine leadership behaviors to a role instead of seeing behaviors as actions that are available regardless of role. Inventive organizations are based on partnerships of discovery in which both parties, regardless of job title or function, act interdependently:

1.   To uncover entrenched assumptions that give rise to the current reality
2.   To align self-interests with common cause
3.   To create a future of everyone's choosing
4.   To unleash the full potential of all constituents

An organizational relationship that is acted out on the basis of hierarchy takes on the characteristics of hierarchy. This means the relationship either becomes one of "one up, one down" or of "peers." In actuality, this is a projected relationship based on our own internal dialogue concerning whether we should lead or follow. It is a dialogue that takes place within the context of our assumptions. In traditional hierarchical organizations, we stifle this internal dialogue and perform according to the roles we believe we have been assigned. In an inventive organization, we recognize this dialogue as the basis of choice. In other words, in inventive organizations, leading and following are not roles, but choices we make. In inventive organizations, everyone leads and follows, depending on the choice they make in that moment of the circumstances with which they are involved. In inventive organizations, organizational relationships arise out of what is appropriate in the moment, not out of the characteristics of the hierarchy.

Inventive organizations are based on relationships of mutuality, interdependence, and support and control at all levels of the system. Such relationships are not fragmented pieces linked together to make a whole. In inventive organizations relationships are based on wholeness, and each person is seen as a microcosm of the entire system. As such, each person leads and follows, thinks and does the work, and acts in service and support of the entire system.

We negate the acts of leading and following that are attendant on organizational life when we act as if those actions derive merely from titles. For years, I have watched executive secretaries act as sounding boards for, conveyors of information to, and key influences on CEOs and other "high level" individuals in organizations. Ask anyone about informal power—the power to persuade and influence—and they will tell you the executive secretary has it. Yet these acts of leading are made invisible. They are covert activities. In an inventive organization, they are overt. Secretaries and CEOs treat each other as partners, as do all others who are involved with the enterprise—employees, suppliers, customers, and stakeholders.

We also negate acts of leading and following when we make "one up, one down" distinctions between clerical and managerial work, exempt and nonexempt work, hourly and salaried work. During the Industrial Revolution, we created laws, known as the Fair Labor Standards Act, to enforce these distinctions. Our job titles, too, serve to reinforce these distinctions. Yet, in the last ten years, these boundaries have become blurred. The advent of personal computers has put the basis for the division of labor up for grabs.

Take, for example, secretarial work, which is categorized as nonexempt because it involves manual dexterity. Most secretaries spend no more than 25 percent of their time typing. On the other hand, managerial work has been categorized as exempt, or "professional" work, because it involves thinking and planning. In fact, most managers think and plan less than 25 percent of each day. Today, the primary skills for secretaries and managers are typing, thinking, planning, and doing, and their means of communication are the same—in person, by telephone, by voice, and by electronic mail. Each leads and each follows in different aspects of their relationship.

We need to formally recognize our current reality. We need to make visible all of our organizational relationships and those mechanisms that support these relationships—for example, policies, procedures, and role definitions. Leading and following are choices of behavior that are made within the context of serving self and others.

This section contains four chapters on what we must dare if we are to create and sustain inventive organizations.

In Chapter Nine, a model is introduced that captures the acts of leading and following in inventive organizations. The model contains three essential components: personal power, style, and expertise. Each of these components is treated in depth in Chapters Ten, Eleven, and Twelve. The model defines and illuminates power, style, and expertise—how each is learned and how it is used in the series of dynamic relationships we call the organization.

9

The Acts of Leading
and Following Versus the
Roles of Leader and Follower

In the Industrial Era, a manager was defined as one who plans, organizes, controls, staffs, communicates, delegates, disciplines, and rewards. The operative word was *control*, which stemmed from organizational size and the steep hierarchy of control that resulted from size. In this hierarchy, control was invested in roles—each with varying degrees of power over others. "Role power" is rooted in the dependent disposition of human beings, a dependence left over from infancy and fostered in our family and educational systems, both of which operate on the basis of caretaking and control.

As infants and children, we were dependent upon those who took care of us. They had power over us. They had control. Our early organizations evolved from family systems. In fact, in the early Industrial Era, organizations were "family" businesses. The father was sole proprietor. He had control over his sons, who were employees. The dependent nature of family relationships formed the dependent nature of early organizational relationships.

As organizations evolved from family businesses into ever more complex entities, they were modeled on the church and military hierarchies. Control became vested in roles, structures, procedures and policies, rules and norms. Those who have control over others have power by proxy. This means their power exists in their roles. As long as one is in a certain role, one has power over others in "lesser" roles—managers have power, subordinates do not. Subordinates accord managers power in exchange for their unstated dependence; namely, the expectation that managers will take care of them. This dependence is both a holdover from the conditioning of early childhood and a need for certainty and predictability.

As our organizations have evolved, those who have had role power have often abused it. This abuse led to the creation of intermediaries who intercede between those whose roles give them power over others and those whose roles are absent of power. These intermediaries take such forms as unions and government regulatory agencies. The myriad rules and laws prescribing our organizational relationships inhibit "creativity and imagination, causing organizations to degenerate into lumbering, politicized bureaucracies, vulnerable to attack" (Badaracco and Ellsworth, 1989, p. 42).

In addition to command and control, our Industrial Era mentality was one of compartmentalization. We drew tight boundaries around roles and functions, which fragmented responsibility, accountability, and authority. These boundaries led us to equate job roles with behavior—specifically, acts of leading were associated with managers and acts of following were associated with subordinates.

In the Information Era, organizational boundaries are fluid and flexible; they exist only to enhance learning, create competence, and ensure long-term viability. Roles are not fixed and job titles are less important than the skills and knowledge possessed by each person. Multiskilling, rotational assignments, and human and electronic networks have replaced fixed job descriptions, permanent assignments, and steep hierarchies. These changes require us to disassociate behaviors from specific job roles so that everyone's full spectrum of skills can be engaged to serve and support the entire system. No matter what our title or level in the system may be, we need to become proficient at leading *and* following. Moreover, we need to understand which behavior is required at what times and in what contexts if we are to create common cause, partnership, and interdependence.

Our old model for managers, which is based on having power over others, is giving way to a new model for leading. Our old model for subordinates, which is based on giving power up, is also giving way to a new model. Neither of these new models should be confused with the now popular notion that leaders and managers are different. That differentiation is one of semantics. The fact that we have engaged in a game of semantics is evidence enough that we are in a transition. This transition is not a matter of using new words to describe old roles; rather, it is a recognition that the locus of control is shifting from existing *in others* to existing *in self and others*. This shift signals that leading and following are acts based on an internal dialogue that results in our choice of how to interact with others. Once this shift is completed, the jargon of organizations will be about leading and following—acts that are not bound by roles but evolve out of deciding which behavior is appropriate, at any given time, in service and support of the entire system.

LEADING AND FOLLOWING IN RELATION TO SUPPORT AND CONTROL

Leadership is not the purview of a few nor is followership the purview of the many. To lead is to *guide* the development of the system. To follow is to *pursue* the common cause. These abilities reside in every person, in each dyad, in all groups, and in every dilineation of level of system. Leading and following are dormant or active depending on the nature of relationships between people or between people and their environment in the context we call "organization."

Leading and following are based on our needs for support

and control—for relatedness, alliance, certainty, and the avoidance of loss. In Figure 9.1, we revisit the transition continuums introduced in Chapter Two, adding support and control needs to these to understand more about how different acts of leading and following create fixed, adaptive, or inventive organizations.

A fixed state is a state of status quo and denial. It is directive and indicates a higher need for control than for support. This need for control is based on a *fear of loss* that is greater than the need for relatedness and support. An adaptive state is a state of confusion. It is political and, again, indicates a need for control that is higher than the need for support. This need for control is based on a *need for certainty* that is also greater than the need for relatedness and support.

An inventive state is a state of renewal. It is values driven and indicates an equal need for support and control. In an inventive organization, the *needs for alliance and relatedness* are *equal to the needs for certainty*. That is why inventive organizations are self-regulating. They are organizations in which individuals see their sources of support and control in themselves and others.

LEADING AND FOLLOWING IN A SELF-REGULATING SYSTEM

Our notions of a free enterprise system have resulted in control of the many by the few. They have spawned a way of operating that was effective in the Industrial Era but is insufficient for the Information Era. This era, with its attendant technology, obliterates the "cubbyholes" and "channels" described by Alvin Toffler, who writes "Any bureaucracy has two key features, 'cubbyholes' and 'channels.' Because of this, everyday power—routine control—is in the hands of two types of executives: specialists and managers. Specialized executives gain their power from control of information in departmental cubbyholes. Managers gain theirs through control of information

**Figure 9.1. Combined Transition Continuum
with Support and Control Needs.**

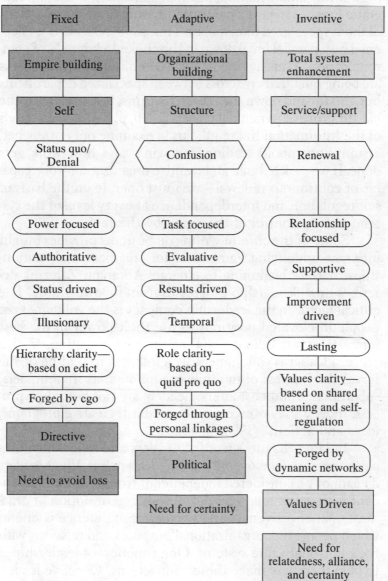

Source: Partially adapted from work by Peter Gibb.

flowing up through the channels. The breakup of the rigid little information monopolies that honeycomb the bureaucratic firm . . . means a painful shift away from the guardians of those specialized monopolies. This 'cubbyhole crisis' is deepened by a parallel breakdown in the choked 'channels' of communication. Thus nonhierarchical communications networks are being built that crisscross between specialized departments but also up and down the hierarchy. This, too, undercuts the old structure of pyramidal power" (1990, p. 88). The demands of the Information Era require us to examine our entrenched assumptions about leading, following, and how work gets done. If we seek to build an inventive organization—one capable of continuous renewal—we must operate on the basis of self-regulation and interdependence at every level of the system, not on control of the many by the few.

Some of the current writing on business provides insight into new underlying frameworks for organizational relationships that are beginning to emerge. Abraham Zaleznik describes how "leadership progresses from followership": "The critical factor in the leadership compact is the willingness of people in elevated positions to use their power in the best interests of subordinates and of their organization. In this sense, a leader is simultaneously a follower in that he or she serves the interest of multiple groups such as shareholders, subordinates and customers. Leaders are not bound by process. Indeed they overcome it to establish creative programs, ideas and actions" (1990, p. 13).

In James Krantz's words, "Leaders and followers mutually co-produce the overall system's leadership. What leaders do cannot be considered independent from, but interdependent with, what followers do. The emergent notion of organizational effectiveness and personal competence is one in which people link organizational purposes and missions with their personal value systems. One function of leadership is to help members make these connections. Effective leadership depends on a context of followership in which people are related meaningfully to their work" (1990, p. 60). And

Robert Kelley points out the essential qualities of effective followers: "(1) They manage themselves well. (2) They are committed to the organization and to a purpose, principle or person outside themselves. (3) They build their competence and focus efforts for maximum impact. (4) They are courageous, honest and credible. Followers see themselves as the equal of the leaders they follow. They are more apt to openly and unapologetically disagree with leadership and less likely to be intimidated by hierarchy and organizational structure. At the same time, they can see that the people they follow are, in turn, following the lead of others, and they try to appreciate the goals and needs of the team and the organization" (1988, p. 143).

TO LEAD OR FOLLOW— A DECISION BASED ON ENVIRONMENT AND CONTEXT

Throughout this work I refer to a system as a series of relationships in action. We choose to lead or follow based on how we wish to interact with others and our environment. Our environment may be defined by its quality; for example, a work environment may be creative, chaotic, frenzied, slow-paced, and so on. Context is defined as the set of circumstances or facts that result from a frame of reference. For example, the frame of reference for the product or service produced may be quality, value, low cost, or some other factor. The frame of reference for those who do the work may be one of stress, contentment, denial, confusion, invention, or renewal. Our actions do not have to be associated with our organizational role or position within the hierarchy. Rather, we choose to lead or follow based on how we wish to interact with others and our environment.

When we analyze a system in terms of relationships in action, we can begin to see the enormous complexities and subtleties inherent in our organizations. First, we must consider each level of the system—individual, interpersonal, group, and organizational—in terms of its environment and context. For example, an individual's work results from the interaction of oneself in relation to one's environment and in the context within which one operates. When two people work together, they relate within themselves, to each other, and to the environment in the context of their work. In team-based operations, several people relate within themselves, to one another, to the group as a whole, and to the environment in the context of their work. And an organizational act is based on (1) the entire series of internal relationships in action—including the individual, interpersonal, and group relationships; (2) the entire series of external relationships in action—including customer, supplier, regulator, economic/political/cultural influences, changing technology, the marketplace, competitors, and so on; and (3) the organizational context within which work is performed—whether it is fixed, adaptive, or inventive.

Second, we must consider how structure and roles, people and skills, tasks and technology, information flows and decision making, the built environment, and rewards and values affect each level of the system. Third, we must consider which part of the change cycle is associated with each level of system—status quo, denial, confusion, or invention/renewal. (See Figure 2.2.) These complexities exist whether we consider them or not; however, what we consider or look for will determine what we see. What we see and understand will affect how we decide to act—whether we choose to lead or follow.

NEW MODELS FOR LEADING AND FOLLOWING

Leading and following are actions we take based on our understanding of roles, relationships, context, and environment.

When job descriptions are fixed and organizational norms bind relationships and, thereby, behavior to organizational roles, we lead and follow according to the "rules." Conversely, when jobs are defined in terms of meeting or exceeding customer requirements, and organizational norms encourage participation regardless of one's level in the system, our choice to lead or follow is based on context (forces in me, forces in others, and forces in a particular situation) and environment (fixed, adaptive, or inventive). Roles, relationships, context, and environment form the background to our decision as to whether we lead or follow at any moment in time. Our choice has consequences for ourselves and our organizations. Our choice determines and reinforces behavioral patterns that result in the organization becoming fixed, adaptive, or inventive.

I was recently contacted by a very large bank because an executive vice president wanted to hold a two-day off-site meeting on leadership skills for the nineties for his direct reports and those one level below his direct reports. He had asked a vice president to create a list of skills requirements, which he had approved, and to find a consultant for the off-site meeting.

I met with the vice president and his training specialist. They had prepared a list of ten well-defined skills and outlined the time frames for teaching each of these, along with break and meal times for the off-site meeting. The list of skills included influence management, empowerment, and boundary management, among others, all aimed at helping management become less hierarchical, less focused on their particular "silos," and more able to develop employee involvement and participation in back-office operations for a major segment of the bank.

I asked what had caused the vice president to list these particular skills. He spoke about the command and control context in which the bank had been operating and the need to change, even though the bank's back-office operations were probably the best in the industry. When I asked what particular business goals would indicate that these were skills required to operate in the nineties, he told me that the executive vice president was about to "roll out his vision of the division" and he wanted people to be able to implement that vision.

Whenever I hear the words "roll out," I see a military tank moving to take over territory that is in another's domain. It was incongruous to me that the executive vice president would value the development of influence skills, empowerment, and boundary management in his subordinates if he intended to dictate a vision that they were to implement.

I suggested that training in these skills would not create the use of these skills if members of management were unable to influence the development of the division's vision. I recommended that, rather than conduct two days of training, the executive vice president hold a two-day off-site meeting in which he could present his vision for the division and engage the participants in discussion about the appropriateness of this vision and changes that would enhance it, given the bank's overall strategy and projected external operating environment. Time could be built in for reflecting on what kinds of influence skills were being used, how people were empowering themselves to create common cause, and in what ways people were operating on issues affecting more than their particular silos within the division. Such a meeting would accomplish both the real work of the division and create the context in which leadership skills for the nineties could be practiced and coached.

Both the vice president and the training specialist understood that training people in new skills would be of no value if those skills could not be utilized. They were, however, reluctant to do other than exactly what the executive vice president had directed them to do. Their reluctance to approach the senior officer with this idea was evidence enough that no amount of training would change the leadership norms in the organization. I concluded my comments in our meeting by saying that people already had much of the capability to lead in the manner indicated by the vice president's skills list. After all, the vice president had created the list. What was missing was the context in which these skills could be *applied, and training alone could not provide that. Context is created by the choices we make in how we work together.*

Figure 9.2 is a model that can be used to depict either acts of leading or acts of following. It works for both because whether we are leading or following, the same three components affect our success: personal power, style, and expertise. Expertise in this context refers to leading or following expertise, not the technical expertise associated with one's function, such as accounting, engineering, processing, packaging, marketing, customer service, and so on.

Figure 9.2 shows each component as a continuum. The

Figure 9.2. Model for Leading in Transition
and Following in Transition.

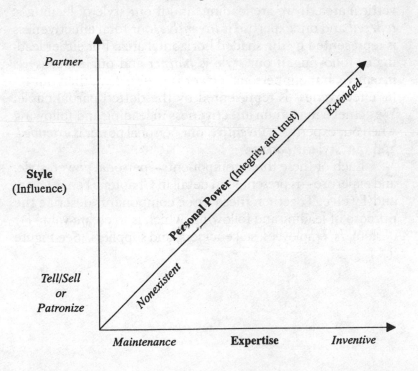

personal power continuum goes from *nonexistent* to *extended*; the *expertise* continuum goes from *maintenance* to *inventive*. Points of the *style* continuum are different for leading and for following. Briefly, the continuum for *styles of leading* starts with the *tell/sell* style and extends through *participate* to *facilitate* and finally to *partner*. The continuum for *styles of following* starts with *patronize* and moves through *comply* to *cooperate*, and finally to *partner*. (Each of these is identified and explored in the chapters that follow.)

Whether we are leading or following, this model assumes that our effectiveness is greatest when we push out on all three vectors, extending toward our maximum potential capability in all three directions. We can graphically plot our effectiveness by marking our position on the vector for each component (see Figure 9.3). For example, for either leading or following, if our style is *partner* and our expertise is *maintenance*, our total effectiveness is represented by the shaded vertical area. If we are leading, and if our style of leading is *tell/sell* and our expertise is *inventive*, our total effectiveness is represented by the shaded horizontal area. For either leading or following, if our style is *partner* and our expertise is *inventive*, but our personal power is *nonexistent*, then our total effectiveness is represented by the dotted partial circle. We achieve maximum effectiveness in leading and following when our expertise is *inventive*, our personal power is *extended*, and our style is *partner*.

Each of these three components — personal power, style, and expertise — is presented in detail in Chapters Ten, Eleven, and Twelve. Together, these three components describe the purpose of leading and following, which is to create value for customers, employees, stakeholders, and suppliers. (See Figure 9.4.)

Figure 9.3. How the Model for Leading and Following Works.

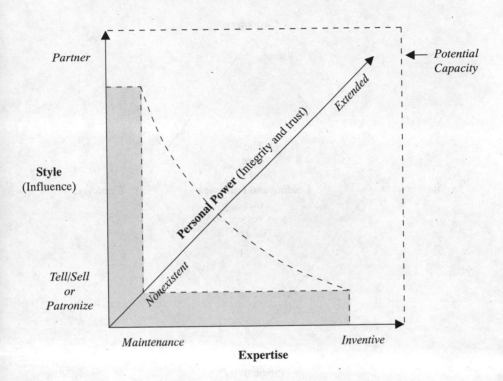

The essence of leading and following is to push out on all three vectors of this model because the outside dotted lines indicate potential capacity for greatness. In other words, leading and following effectiveness are greatest when our style is *partner,* expertise is *inventive,* and personal power is *extended.*

If our style is *partner* and our expertise is *maintenance,* our total effectiveness is the shaded vertical area on the model. If our expertise is *inventive* and our style is *patronize,* then our total effectiveness is the shaded horizontal area on the model.

If our style is *partner* and our expertise is *inventive,* but our personal power is *nonexistent,* then our total effectiveness is the dotted partial circle area on the model.

Figure 9.4. Acts of Leading and Following That Create Value.

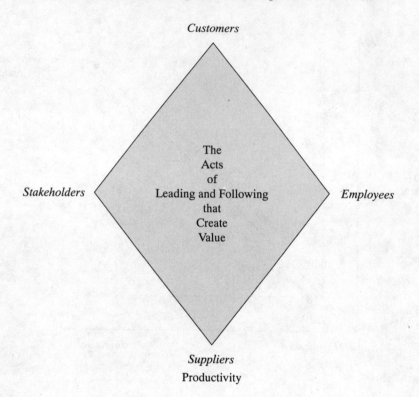

10

Personal Power:
The Source of
Lasting Relationships

We are best able to determine when to lead and when to follow when we see our power as residing in ourselves, not in a role. When we relate to one another based on roles, our behavior is prescribed by our roles. When we relate to one another as partners in pursuit of a common cause, our behavior is based on our knowledge of what we can contribute in the moment. Such knowledge is the basis for exercising our personal power—a power that is limited only by how we use it.

All forms of power have functional and dysfunctional uses. Our use of power is based on our underlying personal motivations and we use power differently in stable (as opposed to changing) environments. How we use power and which forms of power we use create our reputations. Our reputations are critical to our success. They are determined not only by our behavior but by the subtle and not so subtle strategies we use, including whether we present a nonthreatening image, align with powerful others, develop liaisons, use trade-offs, and diffuse opposition. Our reputations, more than anything else, determine the degree of personal power we have.

Such power can be seen as nonexistent or extended, depending on three attributes: credibility, integrity, and trust.

It is hard for us to exercise our personal power when we have been acculturated to honor role power in our institutions. In so many ways, who we are and what we contribute become circumscribed by our job title. We become so constricted by titles and by our interpretations of our job descriptions that rarely, if ever, do we give ourselves permission to execute fully even the circumscribed role that we have been "assigned."

If we look at the origins and development of our relationships, it is easy to understand our readiness to look to others for definitions of who we are and how we should act. As children, we looked up to our parents and our role was to obey them. In school, we looked up to our teachers and our role was to mind them. In our organizations, we have looked up to those to whom we report and our role is to do what is assigned to us. In each case, we see ourselves as subordinate to others. When we believe we are subordinate to others, rather than in partnership with them, we constrain our ability to fully recognize and realize our potential in our workplaces. We see our contributions as designated by the title of the role we are in and we tend to act according to our interpretation of this role.

One of the best examples of this phenomenon occurred while I was consulting to the Pacific Stock Exchange. In 1987, the Exchange had to close its clearing and depository function, which had been losing money for more than five years. More than three hundred people worked in that function, most of them in jobs categorized as "clerical." The majority of these employees were from the Philippines, Vietnam, and other Asian countries. While they understood English well enough to work in jobs where communication skills were of little importance, they did not speak English well enough to be readily understood. The chairman of the Exchange understood only too well how much these people valued their employment and how difficult it would be for them to find other work. In closing the clearing and depository function, he authorized outplacement support for every employee, not just members of management. As part of this support, a one-day class was offered on career search skills in which participants learned to identify their contributions and achievements, as opposed to their task and duties. They used this information to build their resumés and, at the same time, developed skills in how to interview for other jobs.

Victoria Emerson of Corporate Resource Group, a firm that was retained to provide outplacement support, conducted a series of one-day career search sessions for those who worked in the clearing and depository function. In the first class, Victoria asked a young woman, who was five months pregnant and single, to describe her job. She responded that she was a clerk. When Victoria asked her what she did, she replied that she counted stock certificates. Victoria asked her what she did on a typical day. The young woman indicated that she checked the serial numbers on the actual certificates and matched these against a sheet that indicated the number of stocks involved in a particular trade. She noted that sometimes certificates were missing. Victoria asked her what she did when certificates were missing. The woman described an incident that had happened two days before, when $250,000 worth of certificates were missing. She talked about the various steps she had taken to find the certificates, which she was able to locate. When she finished her story, Victoria looked at her and said, "Then you know how to solve $250,000 problems."

In one second, this woman's definition of who she was and what she could do was irrevocably changed. Her downcast eyes opened wide and her expression changed from one of subjugation to exhaltation. Until that moment, she had defined herself by the title of the role she had occupied—clerk. She had described her capabilities as the tasks listed in her job description. When she recognized that the delineation of her tasks did not indicate her contributions, she became aware of her own personal power— power that supersedes the circumscribed power associated with a particular role. Her awareness served her well. She interviewed with other firms on the basis that she knew how to solve $250,000 *problems and she readily found higher paying work than she had had as a clerk at the Stock Exchange.*

A more recent example of this phenomenon of defining ourselves by our job titles rather than by the contributions we make occurred in a recent conversation with my son, Ted. He recently joined a privately held company in which the CEO and owner is worth over four hundred million dollars. When I spoke with Ted a few days after he started his new job, I asked him how he liked the company and the people with whom he worked. He replied, "This is a very interesting place. The CEO has 350 people managing his investments." In twenty-seven years of corporate experience, I have never heard anyone describe a company in this way. Rather than delineate the corporate hierarchy and how many officers, managers, and "employees" work in the company, Ted sees everyone's role as managing the CEO's investments. I wonder how many of his work associates define their contributions similarly. I also wonder if this definition has anything to do with the enormous success of this organization, which grew from $100,000 twenty years ago to its present value.

When we talk about empowerment in business today, we are talking about creating greater awareness of our personal power and how we choose to use this power—this capacity—to make our work a meaningful contribution to our lives and to the organizations of which we are a part.

THE ATTRIBUTES OF PERSONAL POWER: CREDIBILITY, INTEGRITY, AND TRUST

Personal power is derived from three attributes: credibility, integrity, and trust. Each of these is an outcome of our words and deeds. Each is earned in the moment, each is created over a lifetime, and each is a hallmark of our character insofar as we are consistent in our actions. Our reputation can be obliterated in the blink of an eye. We bank our credibility, integrity, and trust in successive interactions and transactions with others. For many the account is low. For some it does not exist. For others, the account has been emptied. Whether the account is depleted or building, it is only as full as the last transaction.

Credibility is believability. It is derived from our reputation, from the esteem in which we are held. Our credibility comes from much more than what we know and do. It is the degree to which we are worthy of confidence, the degree to which we are trustworthy and reliable. We create credibility when, in successive interactions, we act in the interest of self and others, not simply self alone. We may be seen as true to ourself, but that is not credibility. That is consistency. To be credible is to be of good repute, held in high esteem by others. To be esteemed, we must act in ways that not only serve self but serve others as well.

Integrity is soundness, adherence to principle, uprightness. It is consistency in belief, action, and aspiration for oneself and one's organization. It is our ability to "walk our talk," to live by the truth we know, regardless of the setting we are in. As with credibility, integrity is enhanced or diminished by the quality of our interactions with others. We do not act with integrity when we are quick to point out our disadvantage and quick to take advantage whenever we can. We do not act with integrity when we convince ourselves that "nothing else could be done," that any sacrifice required is required of others as a means to "save ourselves." Integrity is assured when we see the same self in others as we see in ourself. That perspective enables us to act in accordance with the golden rule: "Do unto others as you would have them do unto you." It involves understanding our relatedness with others and the importance of acting in ways that serve and support self and others.

Trust is confidence, reliability, and certainty. Trust derives from our ability to tell the truth, no matter the setting, regardless of the risk; to leave nothing out, no matter the consequence; to express how we feel with concern for self and others. We trust ourselves when we do not hedge our bets. And we trust others when they do not cross their word.

Trust is a process, not a thing. It develops out of interactions with others that are best captured in a series of steps adapted from a couples communication program that was created by Sherod Miller and Daniel Wackman. The first step is *straight talk*, which involves our ability to tell the truth, actively listen, manage our differences and agreements, and support and confront. To tell the truth is to say what is so for us, without deceit, and at the same time, to recognize that truth is personal. It is not saying what we think others want to hear. It is saying what is true for us in ways that others can hear it. To talk straight is to pay as much attention to, and be as clear about, what we say when we are in agreement with others as to what we say when we disagree with others. To talk straight is to speak out for that which we support and to confront our own fears and the objections of others in speaking out about that which we do not and cannot support.

The second step is to make *commitments*. Commitments are a network of actions, not words. They are the consequences of promises and requests. When we make a promise or agree to a request, we create our priorities. When we make a commitment, we give ourself over to that which we promised or to that request we accepted.

The third step is *follow-through*. To make a promise or to commit is to give our word. Words without actions are hollow. Words that are inconsistent with our beliefs rob us of our integrity. To make good on our word—on our commitment—is to follow through, to act on our promise. To do otherwise is to "not walk our talk." When we do not walk our talk, our words are worthless.

The fourth step is *reliability*. We create reliability when we consistently follow through. We create reliability when our actions are consistent with our words. We create reliability when we consistently act in accordance with the unassailable linkage between saying what is so, making a promise or accepting a request, and walking our talk.

The fifth step is *trust*. It results from reliability, which is an outcome of consistently following through. Trust begins with talking straight. But to tell the truth and do nothing about it is not enough. We must make commitments — agreements as to what we will do about the truth. But to make commitments is not enough. We must follow through on our promises, for words without actions are devoid of meaning. When we follow through consistently, we create reliability. Reliability leads to trust. In the middle of the word "trust" is "us." That "us" is the heart of personal power. Personal power derives from the honoring, in words and deeds, the relationships among people that make up the system (see Figure 10.1).

Figure 10.1. Personal Power.

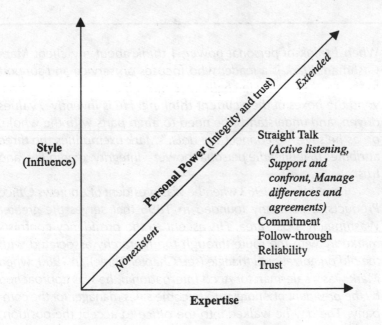

Note: The Straight Talk steps are attributable to the Minnesota Couples Training.

If we consider power as capacity, and we look at the power of credibility, integrity, and trust, we begin to see a new paradigm for power. It is not role power—power over others. It is not a box on an organizational chart that indicates turf, perquisites, and the resources one is entitled to. It is not formal (although it can be so). The new paradigm for power is informal, personal power. It is the willingness that empowers self and, in so doing, can serve as a model for others. It comes from consistency between our words and actions, between our values and deeds. It reflects our need to act on our own behalf and in the service of something greater than ourselves. Personal power is available to us in every action we take. It underlies our choice to lead or to follow and animates whatever we do. Personal power is the power of partnership for it is available in unlimited quantity and in equal measure to all.

When I think of personal power, I think about my client Mark Cashman. Mark is a leader who focuses on service and support to the total system. He challenges himself and others to go beyond the boxes of their current thinking. He is inventive, values driven, and understands the need to align parts with the whole, or, as he says, "to connect the dots." Mark exemplifies the three attributes that underlie personal power—integrity, credibility, and trust.

I met Mark in 1983 when he was president of Andrews Office Products, a company founded in 1896 that serves the greater Washington, D.C., area. His ascent to the presidency contrasts markedly with the route through the hierarchy associated with the old organizational triangle (see Chapter Three). In 1980, when Mark was a salesman for Acco International, he was approached by the president of Andrews to become sales manager for the company. The day he walked into the office to accept the position, he learned that the president had died the night before.

Having made the decision to join Andrews, Mark decided

to call the owner to find out if the position offered to him was still his. The owner interviewed Mark and asked him if he wanted to be president. He accepted. Mark was twenty-eight years old.

During the five years of Mark's leadership, Andrews quadrupled its sales, the staff grew from 35 to more than 120 employees, a new headquarters site was secured, and new corporate offices were built. The new offices were designed to be a showcase for Andrews products, which exemplifies the belief that you cannot treat your customers any better than you treat your employees. The company focused on developing the full potential of every employee as a means of developing its business. Mark's actions exemplified what James Lincoln, the founder of Lincoln Electric Company, observed: "A strong leader knows that if he develops his associates, he will be even stronger" (Badaracco and Ellsworth, 1989, p. 87).

In 1985, Mark was recruited to become president of Harper Brothers, a company he led back to profitability, navigating through a change in corporate ownership and the acquisition of two subsidiary companies. He spurred the innovation of new services, established and developed a senior management team, and managed a new relationship with Harper Brothers' new parent company. All of these accomplishments occurred at a time when the distribution channel for office products, which has changed more in the past five years than in all of its history, is squeezing profit margins and competition is greater than ever. Today, Mark is president of Hanson Office Products Mid Atlantic Region. He is forty-one years old.

What is the secret to this man's belief in himself and others? What is it that causes anyone who has ever worked in an organization he has led to revere him? How has he effected his remarkable achievements and left his indelible imprint wherever he has been?

In my view, two things stand out. First, Mark has a deep sense of values that have remained strong and uncompromised. He is a man of principles. He did not have to climb the corporate ladder, as do so many CEO's. Rather, he got there by a leap, and in that leap his values came through unscathed. In the preface *to this book, I write about my son, Ted, and the corrupting effects rites of passage often have on our ability to stick to our values. Mark, in his ascension to CEO, did not go through an equivalent to the paddling my son endured when he joined the boy's club in Piedmont. And because Mark did not undergo any injurious initiations, he never sought to put others through such a thing.*

Second, Mark sees power as capacity, not as "power over." He is empowered, and he provides the foundations for others to empower themselves. He believed in the power of teamwork long before it was in vogue. And he subscribed to and supported employee involvement long before the team became popular in management jargon. Mark talks straight. He knows no other way. He makes commitments and he follows through. He is reliable and trustworthy. For Mark Cashman, integrity and trust are the bases for all relationships.

PERSONAL POWER: THE POWER OF UNDERSTANDING SELF

Personal power, which is derived from our ability to act in the interest of ourselves and others, is developed from our ability to first clearly see and understand ourselves. Such understanding involves exploring and knowing the multiple aspects of self—the differentiation, integration, and interdependence of our various aspects—that in their totality make up who we are. As Marilyn Mason puts it, "Personal power grows out of our integration; it is our expressed integrity. Personal power begins with our relationship with the self and then extends to our relationships with others (interpersonal power)" (1991, p. 162).

Within each of us are drives, conflicts, assumptions, strengths, weaknesses, interests, expertise, fears, aspirations, experiences, beliefs, and values that, taken together, create our uniqueness and define our character. When we begin to explore ourselves, we become aware of which aspects are underdeveloped, overutilized, balanced, inaccessible, readily accessible, consistent, and inconsistent.

Our behavior results from interplay among various aspects of self at any moment in time. For example, if I am lonely and want to be part of a group, my drive to join may be weakened by my feeling of shyness. I may find myself reading about groups that are forming and marking dates on my calendar when the groups meet, but never going to a meeting. My behavior is a result of the interplay between various aspects of myself at any moment in time. Further, who I am at any given moment collides with the person I have been through successive moments in time. I may have tried to join a group at one time and felt marginal — an experience that may affect whether I try again. For each of us, a legacy of behavioral themes — traits — is created and enacted out of the interplay between various aspects of self in successive moments of time.

Traits are the characterological underpinnings of behaviors. They are what cause us to act in particular ways. Often we develop opposing traits. In one moment we may act unassuming and at another moment we may act egotistically. These opposite tendencies, or traits, are polarities. "The relationship between these opposing qualities is frequently out of balance . . . with one element winning and the other losing," writes Robert Kaplan (1991, p. 41). To discover and understand one's use of self is to reconcile valued and devalued personal traits and to integrate different aspects of self. Kaplan continues: "Growth can come in the form of escalating the internal conflict or . . . reversing the splitting and thereby making oneself whole. 'People enter a stage in which they integrate their once split awareness.' As we accept ourselves, we take back the misattributed bad parts and then become able to experience both ourselves and others as both good and bad, as whole" (pp. 44–45).

In his book *The Content of Our Character,* Shelby Steele

writes about two aspects of self that are fundamental to our ability to be self-regulating and to our use of personal power. He defines these aspects as the "believing self and the anti-self." The believing self is the part of us that aspires. The anti-self is that part of us that doubts. "The anti-self can only be contained by the strength of the believing self and this is where one's early environment becomes crucial. If the childhood environment is stable and positive, the family whole and loving, the schools good and the community safe, then the believing self will be reinforced and made strong. If the family is shattered, the schools indifferent, the neighborhood a mine field of dangers, the anti-self will find evidence everywhere to deflate the believing self." Steele believes that the capacity for belief and doubt are roughly the same from childhood on, "so that years later when the believing self may have strengthened enough to control the anti-self, one will still have the same capacity for doubt whether or not one has the actual doubt." Steele makes a strong case for doubt being an outgrowth of feelings of unworthiness. He writes that the "struggle between our capacities for doubt and belief gives our personalities one of their peculiar tensions and, in this way, marks our character" (1990, pp. 41–42). The tension between the self and what Steele calls the anti-self is most evident in our need for self-regulation—a need for freedom—which is a need for both control and support (discussed at length in Chapter Seven). Our understanding of our needs for control—for certainty and support, relatedness and alliance—is basic to our self-awareness. More important, our needs for support and control underlie how we see and use our personal power.

Our personal power is unlimited. How we use it determines the extent to which we and others experience our power as nonexistent or extended. When we do not act consistently with integrity and trust, we negate our personal power. When we act consistently with integrity and trust, our power is extended. Our use of this power is the most critical component in our relationships with other individuals. These relationships constitute the organization. We can choose to use our power or not. When we do so in service of self and others, we are on our way to creating inventive organizations.

TYPES OF POWER ASSOCIATED WITH FIXED AND ADAPTIVE ORGANIZATIONS

Power other than personal power is based on a belief that power is finite—that the amount of available power is limited. When limited power is distributed, the amount held by any one person will determine the amount available to others. The idea of power as finite is reflected in fixed and adaptive organizations, where the focus is on one's self and one's empire or on the clarity of structure and roles.

In inventive organizations, power is not a zero-sum game (which means if you have some, others will have less). Rather, power is seen as capacity. (The definition of power as capacity is attributable to Rosabeth Moss Kanter, a well-known contributor to the field of organization development.) A simple analogy comes to mind. If there is one electrical outlet in a wall, it appears that power is available for one electrical appliance. However, if an adaptor is placed in this outlet, power is available for multiple appliances. When power is seen as capacity, it is not treated as something to hoard. The more power is created, the more capacity is available for everyone. In organizations, "when the empowering of subordinates works, the total power in the organization available to the CEO may well increase. More people find ways to use the personal kinds of power latent within them" (Stewart, 1989, p. 62). The creation of capacity is a hallmark of inventive organizations.

Personal power is differentiated from role power, position power, information power, expert power, access power, relationship power, assessed stature, and the power to reward and punish, all of which are types of power that are associated with fixed and adaptive organizations — organizations structured on the basis of "one up, one down."

Role power is a good example of a belief that power is finite. Role power is associated with title. It is the implicit or explicit identification of "self as position." Titles confer status. The more scarce the title, the more valued the role. For example, there is only one chief executive officer. If there were more, the title would be proportionally less potent. Some organizations, such as banks, have rewarded people with titles, often in lieu of pay. The proliferation of a title, such as vice president, diminishes the value of the title, sometimes to the point of meaninglessness. When a title is used sparingly, its meaning and, therefore, the power associated with it, are enhanced.

Holders of diminished titles generally recognize the situation, even though those with lesser titles do not. At one time, I consulted to a regional stock exchange, whose senior management included the CEO, four senior vice presidents, and eleven vice presidents. The senior vice president for technology, which is the driving force in a stock exchange, had responsibility for an annual budget of $6 million but had authority to approve only $2,500 in expenditures. Anything in excess of $2,500 had to be approved by the CEO, who could approve up to $50,000. Both of these approval authorities had been granted by the board of directors, the majority of whom were both members and customers of the exchange. Expenditures in excess of $50,000 required board approval. This ensured the board's control of the organization. To avoid having to involve the CEO in every expenditure for technology, the senior vice president had suppliers invoice component parts instead of machines. This created a ton of invoicing and accounts-payable paperwork, but it enabled the senior vice president to execute his responsibilities without involving the CEO. His subordinates complained that their budget responsibilities and authorities were out of sync. They did not know the senior vice president could not delegate the authority they required because he did not have it to delegate.

More often, a title confines the role holder: a person's abilities are confined to the title and tasks associated with a job description. This phenomenon is prevalent because in hierarchical structures status and abilities are equated. All too often those at the bottom of the hierarchy can contribute much more than their titles or job descriptions indicate. Conversely, those at the top are often not capable of excelling in all that is conveyed by their titles. In both cases, the role holder is confined — in the former case to staying inside the job description and in the latter to the hopeless task of fulfilling inflated expectations.

Position power is associated with where one's position is relative to another's. Position power is frequently associated with "informal," as opposed to "formal," organizations. For example, an executive secretary to the CEO has position power. In terms of salary and title, the job is relatively low in the organizational hierarchy. However, in terms of position, the executive secretary can facilitate or block others' access to the CEO. Further, if an executive secretary is highly regarded by the CEO, which most often is the case, she can positively or negatively impact the CEO's impressions of other employees.

Information power is that power associated with having access to information. Who has access to which database? What distribution lists is one on. How much of what one receives is "confidential"? How much of what one is considering can be accessed by others before the decision to distribute this information is made? Prior to personal computers, secretaries had as much access to "important information" as did their bosses. With the advent of personal computers and distributive technology, information power had diminished. Many now have access to what once was in the hands of a few. Also, distributive technologies have created data overload, which often makes it impossible for us to read and digest all the data that are distributed and impairs our ability to distinguish real information from what is simply "more data."

Expert power is associated with a particular expertise. Frequently consultants are accorded this power, even though the message they often bring to the organization is one "insiders" have been delivering for years. Organizations frequently become addicted to expert power. The wisdom in the system is constrained or disregarded, as one outside expert after another is sought to "help" the organization become what it might be. Reliance on outside expertise is common in the old organizational pyramid, with everyone looking up to someone else for the answers. When no answer is forthcoming, people look outside the organization. While the retention of someone outside the system is an acceptable form of obtaining support, it is often done to avoid having to expose what we do not know to those who have been conditioned to equate knowledge and answers with power.

Access is another form of power. Organizational secrets are inaccessible. Those whose jobs are higher up on the hierarchy are less accessible than those whose jobs are lower down. Access to the inaccessible is a form of power that is different from role or position power.

Relationship power can be achieved through both the formal and informal organization. Most frequently, it is associated with the informal organization. Statements such as "I played tennis this weekend with the CEO" or "I was invited for dinner at the senior vice president's home" are meant to convey power derived from having a relationship with someone who is seen as powerful.

Assessed stature is yet another form of power. If one is seen as favored or admired by someone who is powerful, one achieves a stature that may well exceed one's role power. Sometimes this is referred to as referent power. In one organization, the CEO frequently referred to one of his direct reports as "my son." This senior officer was considerably younger than his peers and being called "son" exacerbated his struggle to be accepted by his colleagues because it drew attention to his age and experience. For his colleagues, the CEO's use of "son" conveyed favoritism.

The *power to reward and punish* is associated with role power; however, there are many whose titles may seem unimportant but whose power to reward and punish is significant. When I worked for The Automobile Club of Southern California, I used pool cars for business travel. There were more than fifty cars in the pool, all of which were maintained by mechanics who worked in the club's garage. If the mechanics liked you, you got a low-mileage, mid-sized car. If they did not, you got a compact with high mileage — and sometimes one that broke down.

HOW PERSONAL POWER RELATES TO LEADING AND FOLLOWING

There is much in the literature today about leadership and the characteristics of those who lead effectively, even though there is very little on followership and the characteristics of those who follow effectively. Almost without exception, leading and following are described as roles, not as behaviors. Regardless, we are beginning to see the emergence of some new ways to think about and define good corporate citizenship, including these:

- Empowerment of self versus control by others
- A focus on open relationships versus position
- Consistency between values and actions
- An understanding that leadership derives from knowledge and not status
- An appreciation for what power is supposed to accomplish versus a desire for power as an end in itself
- Recognition of the relevance of creating commitments that override the immediacy of personal interests
- An awareness of the kind of commitment that is available when people choose to consent freely to their governance

- The ability to see real power as that which comes from following others who are in a position to do things better than yourself
- Recognition that the only real control is self-control
- The benefits of everyone having the ability to address valid self-interests without compromising others' rights or legitimate expectations

What is being written about are new behaviors, not new roles. The focus is on leading and following, often termed guiding and pursuing, and the attributes of integrity, credibility, and trust—and how the dynamic play between acts of leading and following can create the system I call an inventive organization.

BECOMING PERSONALLY POWERFUL

This chapter has focused on personal power as the most critical of the three essential components for leading inventive organizations. Our integration of personal power, style, and expertise distinguishes how we lead and follow in inventive organizations from how leaders and followers function in fixed and adaptive organizations. In an inventive organization, leading and following are behaviors that we choose according to how we wish to relate to others and our environment. We need to ask ourselves not *whether* we should lead or follow, but *when* we should lead and *when* we should follow. We can best answer these questions when we are aware of the many uses of personal power.

One way to confirm the level of trust and integrity we have achieved is to use the survey in Exhibit 10.1. Ask those you work with directly and those who provide support to your function to rate you on the following scale. Compare the

Exhibit 10.1. Survey on Trust and Integrity.

Use the following scale to indicate how you think [name of individual] handles the following issues in the workplace:

1 = rarely   2 = on occasion   3 = often   4 = very often   5 = consistently

1. Understands the environment in which change is occurring ____
2. Understands the context of relationships between:

 Individuals in our department ____

 Our department and our suppliers ____

 Our department and our customers ____

 Our department and our support functions ____

 Our department and the organization as a whole ____

3. Walks his/her talk; actions are consistent with stated beliefs, values, and aspirations ____

4. Talks straight; does not use language to mask reality ____

5. Makes commitments ____

6. Follows through on commitments made ____

7. Is reliable . . . can be counted on to do what is promised or agreed upon ____

8. Is someone I can trust ____

9. Can balance individual wants and group needs ____

---

results with your own self-assessment. Focus on alignments and gaps between your perceptions and the perceptions of others. Begin dialogues concerning behaviors or actions that will enhance and improve the levels of credibility, trust, and integrity that constitute your personal power and that you seek to use in support of the entire system.

11

Style:
Choosing Partnership
Over Dependency

Autonomy and dependency, rather than interdependence, have resulted from the way we organized ourselves during the late Industrial Era. Autonomy has been equated with climbing the corporate ladder—we call the shots and have power over others. Dependency has resulted when we view those to whom we report as having our survival in their hands. It has been difficult for us to act interdependently—to see ourselves as partners—because in the United States we are caught between the idea of "the individual as king and one above all others" and our acculturation process, which is one of dependence on others. On the one hand we believe strongly in individual autonomy—the right to live and believe as one sees fit. On the other hand, all of our systems—family, education, government, private enterprise—have been organized around principles of caretaking and control.

The subject of style is inextricably tied to our notions of the hierarchy. In a command-and-control hierarchy there is an underlying assumption that those who lead need to control and protect those who follow. When we believe we need to control and take care of others, we create a debilitating dependency that constrains individuals and groups from achieving their potential and contributing as fully as possible. Our behaviors are those of dictator and subject, caretaker and ward, enabler and enabled, all of which reinforce the old hierarchy of "one up, one down."

One of the best examples of how we fall into a caretaker role is found in a management training program that was developed a few years ago by Federal Express. Fifteen managers arrived at an empty training room and were told they would soon be joined by fifteen blind people. Each of the blind individuals was to select a manager with whom to work for the next two days. The blind participants arrived and were asked to slowly circulate around the room. The managers were asked to start talking about themselves so that the blind participants could make their selections.

After the initial awkwardness of being in a training environment without the usual training paraphernalia, and after some initial embarrassment about talking out loud about themselves, the managers did as they were asked and the selection process began. The blind participants moved slowly around the room and listened to the managers as they spoke about themselves. Then each participant picked a manager with whom to work.

Once pairs were established, the managers were given a series of tasks that they were to have their blind partners perform. The first two tasks involved Tinkertoys. Each manager was given diagrams of structures their blind partner was to build. One diagram involved shapes. The other involved shape and color. For the third task, the managers coached their blind partners in using a broom to sweep a ball through an obstacle course. The next task was a tire walk in which managers prompted their blind partners as they walked through a set of tires that had been laid out on the floor. The managers' final task was to direct their blind partners to walk on a balance beam that was a few inches above the ground.

Then the tables were turned. The managers were blindfolded and taken on a walk by their blind partners. The walk occurred on the training grounds. A series of spotters were positioned around the site. As the blind individuals led their blindfolded managers, they called out the word "federal." If they began to wander off the course, one of the spotters would call out "express."

At the end of two days, the managers and their blind partners were asked to talk about their experiences. All of the blind participants reported that their managers never took the time to get to know them as individuals. They were never asked about their capabilities or what was their best learning style. Rather, the managers had focused immediately on completing the tasks and giving instructions as to what to do and how to do it. The blind partners felt they could have done much better had they been consulted about their abilities and their ideas for completing the tasks. Some reported they had never understood the entire task; rather, they had been told what to do, step by step, without ever having a sense of the whole.

When asked what it felt like to be blindfolded and taken on a walk by their blind partners, the managers reported discomfort, fear, lack of trust, and a sense that they could not perform the task without a sighted partner.

Both the blind participants and the managers were asked to tell what they had learned over the two days. Most of the blind participants were seeking employment opportunities. As a result of participating in the training session, they felt they better understood how they could help sighted employment recruiters "see" how to successfully utilize a blind individual's talents and capabilities in a place of work. The managers' discoveries were profound. Their big "Aha" was the recognition that they treated their blind partners exactly the same way they treated their subordinates—as incapable and in need of help that was best prescribed by the manager. They realized that they operated out of a set of underlying assumptions, principally these:

1. Employees needed and wanted to be told not only what to do but how to do it.

2. *Employees could not do their jobs without the manager's assistance.*

3. *It was the manager's role to figure out the best policies and procedures to achieve a particular goal.*

The managers also realized they had not spent time learning who their employees were as individuals, what their preferred learning styles and unique capabilities were, or how much they needed or wanted to see the big picture so that they could realize their full potential and contribute as fully as possible to the organization.

What draws us to enact these roles of dictator and subject, caretaker and ward? Is it a need to feel powerful and powerless? Is it a romantic belief that only a heroic few are strong and wise, and it is their obligation to take care of the many who are weaker and less able? Or is it a result of role power, which creates expectations of behaviors for those whose roles are in the category of leader and those whose roles are in the category of follower? In *The Social Psychology of Organizations*, Daniel Katz and Robert Kahn describe some of the social forces that produce role expectations and role behavior. They are concerned with "motivations, cognitions, and behavior of the members of the role set" and "the cognitions, motivations and behavior of the focal person" (1978, pp. 203–204). Their idea is that we enact our roles based on a circuitous process that involves the expectations of both the members of the "role set" and the "role holder." Katz and Kahn identify the members of the role set as people who "depend on [the role holder's] performance in some fashion; they are rewarded by it, judged in terms of it, or require it to perform their own tasks." The role set's expectations of the role holder are mainly "preferences with respect to specific acts, personal characteristics or style" and "are by no means restricted to the job description. . . . Even in the least punitive organizations, the enactment of a role within the limits of tolerance of the role set is a condition for holding the associated office" (pp. 190–191).

Our caretaker and ward behaviors come from the acculturation processes of our family upbringing, schooling, traditional command-and-control organizational hierarchies, and the underlying tension in each of us—a tension between wanting to have our own way and wanting to be taken care of. On the one hand, we want our autonomy. On the other, we want safety and security. When having one means giving up another, most of us opt for the promise of security.

It is important for us to understand that we co-create each role in our organizations by repeatedly sending and receiving role expectations. Katz and Kahn call such sending/receiving exchanges "role episodes." These episodes often result in leaders leading and followers following in ways that hold each hostage to their most feared outcomes. For the leader, this means accountability for someone else's mistakes, and for followers it means accountability for failures over which they have no control. The paradox is that a "leader's" potential for organizational success is greatest when authority and responsibility are commensurate in everyone's job and when "followers" only accept accountability for results when their authority is commensurate with their responsibilities (see Chapter Seven).

At the end of 1990, CBS ran a television documentary that sheds some interesting light on the effects of different acculturation processes. The camera followed preschoolers in Japan, China, and the United States. In Japan, we see a four-year-old named Hiroki beating up his classmates during free time. The teacher is in the room and aware of the situation; yet, she continues to clean up the classroom. One boy, in an effort to win Hiroki's affection, makes a Ninja starship and presents it as a peace offering. Hiroki stomps on the child's wrist. A classmate goes to the hurt boy and asks him why he wants anything to do with Hiroki. A year later, the school is revisited. Hiroki sits at a table, all alone. The other children, who sit together at another table, say that they have nothing to do with him because he does not know how to behave. Hiroki has been ostracized by his classmates. Early on, the Japanese learn about the power of a group and self-regulation.

In the visit to the Chinese preschool, we see children being strictly regimented. Because each family is allowed only one child, the teachers believe children are being spoiled. When the children come to class on Monday, they are given physical examinations and asked how many sweets they ate over the weekend. They are trained to use the bathroom at a particular time so they can learn to control their bodily functions. At lunchtime, no one speaks. The silence of thirty four-year-olds is deafening. Early on the Chinese learn compliance and obedience to higher authority.

The final segment of the documentary shows an American preschool. Two four-year-olds sit in a sandbox arguing over a shovel. A teacher intervenes. Each child is asked to explain what he wants; in effect, each is asked to make a case for possession of the shovel. After much negotiation, facilitated by the teacher, they reach an agreement. One child allows the other child to use the shovel for five minutes. When Japanese viewers saw this tape, they said it explained why the United States was such a litigious society. Early on, Americans learn how to negotiate and that negotiations require a mediator.

When we are acculturated to function as a member of a group, we learn about interdependent relationships. When we are acculturated to follow obediently, we learn about dependency. When we are acculturated to mediation, we create the basis for both counterdependence and dependence. If we cannot rely on ourselves or on our adversary in a conflict to resolve the dispute, we both become dependent on a third party to mediate an outcome.

STYLES OF LEADING
AND FOLLOWING

In general terms, we can say that to lead is to guide the development of a system; to follow is to pursue common cause. There are several styles of leading and following, however, and each is tied to our needs for support and control. In addition, there are functional and dysfunctional aspects to each one. (See Figures 11.1 and 11.2.)

Styles of Leading

Tell/Sell. The tell/sell style is directive. It often creates dependency and a sense of restraint on the parts of those being

Figure 11.1. Leading in Transition.

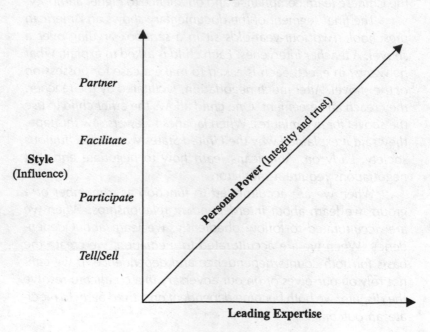

Note: Copyright © 1993, Jill E. Janov.

Figure 11.2. Following in Transition.

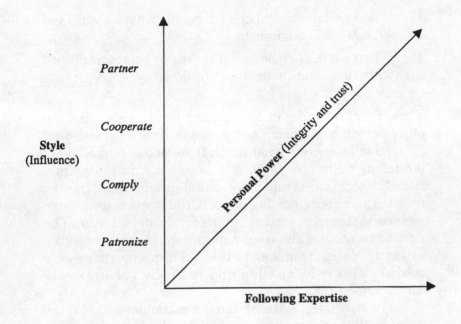

Note: Copyright © 1993, Jill E. Janov.

told/sold. To tell is to dictate. To dictate is to defend against the vulnerability of not having control. To sell is to persuade or co-erce. The tell/sell style derives from our underlying need to have others think that our way is their way. Dictators believe there is only one way to achieve certainty—their way. In terms of our needs for support, a tell/sell style indicates our desire to be in-dependent and have it our own way. One manager put it this way: "I learned I had to stop being a dictator. That I had to start listening to people. That I had to take action based on the things they were *telling* me" (Reid, 1990, p. 76).

The tell style can be *functional*

1. In an emergency, such as when we tell others to vacate a building that is on fire

2.   When customers have the opportunity to tell us about their requirements

3.   When we talk straight and tell people what we want and what we will commit to

4.   When we tell people "what" needs to be accomplished without telling them "how" to do it

These functional uses of *telling* come from a belief that the other person is an equal, not someone who is "one down."

To tell someone what needs to be accomplished without telling them how to do it is based on a previously presented concept called minimum critical specifications. In work redesign and re-engineering projects, the steering committee sets specifications or success criteria for the design team. The steering committee also communicates the boundaries within which the design team must work. Such specifications were used in a work redesign effort undertaken by a pharmaceutical manufacturer.

The design teams were given five minimum critical specifications that encompassed cycle time, the cost of nonconformance, safety, quality, and quality of work life for employees. One boundary was given: the aromatic machines that mix the compounds that become two over-the-counter analgesics could not be replaced or relocated. These machines were huge, multimillion-dollar pieces of equipment that mixed many batches of product at one time. But the succeeding steps—compressing, coating, and stamping—were carried out one batch at a time. This created an unbalanced line; however, the cost of this equipment was so great that changing it could not even be considered until the savings achieved through the plant's redesign could make replacement feasible. Within this constraint, the design teams redesigned the plant and achieved significant increases in productivity and job satisfaction. Successful leadership in this case depended on starting out with a clear statement of minimum critical specifications and boundaries.

The sell style can be *functional* when one (1) is providing needed information and the opportunity for choice and (2) wants to serve the best interests of both parties. Again, these ways of selling indicate that we see others as equals. The tell/sell leading style is *dysfunctional* when (1) others feel constrained or coerced into doing as they are told (that is, to "leave their brains at the door") and (2) others become dependent, and instead of asking questions or offering suggestions that could provide service and support to the entire system, they ask "how high" when told to "jump." In these cases, human potential is constrained. Rather than being treated as valuable assets, people are treated as extensions of machines. Rather than becoming resources, people become costs to be contained.

Participate.   The style of leading called "participate" is both reactive and directive. To participate is to take part in. In organizational terms, "to take part in" often means to do another's job. We participate in another's responsibilities when we see that person as incapable or when we withhold the authority they need to get the job done. This forces others to ask permission to do what they are responsible for doing. Worse, we create resentment when we hold others accountable for results when they lack the authority to execute their responsibilities.

To lead is to ensure that responsibility and authority are commensurate. The story of the senior vice president of technology who had a $6 million budget but authority to sign for only $2,500 is an example of an individual whose responsibilities and authorities were not commensurate. That imbalance created the need for the chairman of the exchange to participate in executing his subordinate's role. Only when authority and responsibility are balanced is accountability possible. (See Chapter Eight for a full discussion of this concept.)

It can be *functional* to participate when (1) an employee is new to a position and is being oriented to the work and the environment; (2) others are learning skills through on-the-job training; (3) someone has asked for help; and (4) the job takes more than one person. These kinds of participation result from an underlying belief in equality, not a belief in "one up, one down."

When we participate by performing another's job, we create dependency. Such participation often occurs when we are newly promoted. Most often, we are promoted on the basis of our technical expertise. When faced with the new responsibilities of leading, we often feel more responsible for results than we feel accountable for them. Because our best skill is our technical expertise, we are prone to act as an expert, an extra pair of hands—a "doer of the work" that got us promoted in the first place.

It is *dysfunctional* to participate when (1) assistance has not been requested; (2) participation does not enable others to learn; and (3) participation is a subterfuge for proper delegation of authority. In these cases, participation is based on an underlying belief that another person needs help. Such participation sends a mixed signal. It is perceived as a need for *control* that is hidden under the guise of support. (The Federal Express story at the beginning of this chapter is an example of a dysfunctional participative style.)

Facilitate.   The style called "facilitate" also is directive. To facilitate is to ease or to make less difficult. Facilitation can be viewed as coordination, in which case, the facilitator may be seen as a conductor—someone who can get different people with diverse skills to play harmoniously off the same sheet of music. To facilitate is to *foster*. We facilitate when we provide a foundation for another's progress. Doing so indicates an underlying belief that without our support, others are not able. In effect, to facilitate is to prepare the ground so others may walk on it.

It can be *functional* to facilitate when:

1.   A new group is forming and the form stage needs facilitation

2. An individual is having difficulty in asking for what he or she needs

3. A third party is required—someone who can be objective in facilitating interactions between individuals and groups who are having difficulties relating to one another

4. A meeting is being held and requires facilitation from someone not involved with or affected by the content of the meeting

5. An organizational boundary is to be crossed—whether that boundary is between people, people and technology, or levels or functions within the organization—and the crossing can be eased

6. Different people or entities need to be brought together to create a new alliance or enterprise and someone can serve as the link

These kinds of facilitation are chosen and are based on a belief that others are more able when they are enabled.

It is *dysfunctional* to facilitate when (1) facilitation has not been requested or agreed to; (2) the person facilitating is working his or her own agenda; and (3) facilitation creates or exacerbates dependent behavior. In these situations, facilitation is imposed and can create dependency or counterdependency. When groups are told to be self-managing and they are trying to decide how to govern themselves, they often remain leaderless and dysfunctional for a long time because every time one member tries to facilitate, the effort is seen by others as a bid to take over. Two extremes can result: people may want someone to take over so the impasse can end or people may not want anyone to lead. The former desire can lead to dependency, the latter to counterdependence.

Styles of Following

Patronize. The patronize style is both supportive and condescending. Because this style is based on an underlying belief in "one up, one down," it can be misleading. On the one hand, when we patronize from the position of being "one up," we may be seen as providing support. On the other hand, when we patronize from the position of being "one down," we are acting out our hostility and counterdependence.

The patronize style can be *functional* when we wish to (1) model encouragement and support; (2) influence an outcome in an arena in which we otherwise have no influence; and (3) protect that which cannot protect itself.

To patronize is *dysfunctional* when we (1) try to endear ourselves to those we seek to manipulate; (2) want to create IOUs that can be cashed in at a later time; and (3) want others to believe we admire and respect them as a means of protecting ourselves from their abuse.

Comply.   The style called "comply" is one of conforming, acquiescing, or yielding. It is to act in accordance with others' wishes, requests, demands, requirements, and conditions. We comply when we see ourselves as "one down." Willing compliance can lead to dependence. Malicious compliance, which occurs when we conform because we feel we have no other choice, leads to counterdependence.

To comply is *functional* when (1) our needs and wishes are in alignment with requests and requirements stated by others; (2) an emergency occurs and others have to take control of the situation; and (3) consensus is the operative mode of decision making and what others desire is not our preference but we can live it.

To comply is *dysfunctional* when we (1) feel confined by circumstances or the status quo; (2) fear the consequences (real or imagined) of not complying; (3) feel we have no choice but to do as we are told; and (4) have a choice but are afraid of being held to account for doing other than what was requested.

When we comply in exchange for some unstated want or desire, we act as if we and others are equals when, in fact, we are depending on them to take care of us in exchange for our submission.

Cooperate.   The cooperate style is one of providing active assistance to another. Often we cooperate with others to achieve a common goal. To cooperate is to act out of an underlying assumption of mutuality. Whether we see others as "one up" or "one down," we believe our cooperation will result in mutual benefit.

To cooperate is *functional* when (1) we experience common cause and (2) our actions result in mutual benefit.

It is *dysfunctional* to cooperate when (1) we go along to get along; (2) the potential risks far outweigh the potential benefits; and (3) what we want in exchange for our cooperation is unspoken.

To cooperate does not imply enthusiasm, although we may be enthusiastic in our cooperation. Rather, to cooperate is to work with others in ways that serve each of our own self-interests but not interests greater than ourselves.

Partnership — The Style for Leading and Following in Inventive Organizations

To partner is to act on our awareness of our interdependence. To partner is to serve, support, and inspire the unleashing of everyone's full potential. It is based on a belief that others are inherently able and that we serve each other best when we view ourselves as partners in the discovery of both our abilities. In so doing, we foster our own and others' growth and development. To partner is to act on our awareness of mutuality, to learn from each other and learn together. To partner is to work together to serve self and others in pursuit of something greater than ourselves.

Partnership is based on trust and integrity.* Partnership recognizes the "Us"; the "I" and the "We." To partner is to know we are safe enough to experiment so we can discover more. If

---

*"The key to non-dependent trust is that—as an individual and as a professional—you must care for yourself and assume responsibility for your future. Non-dependent trust thrives on honesty. Perhaps the most important aspect of non-dependent trust from the corporation's point of view is the understanding that companies are in a partnership with employees" (Morin, 1990, pp. 47, 51).

we are to discover together, we need to view trial and error as the road to invention. Years ago, Franklin Roosevelt said, "This country needs bold, persistent experimentation. Take a method, try it; if it fails, admit it and try another. But above all, try something."

To partner is to honor the wisdom in the system, to learn from what works and what does not work. To partner is to have the courage in the face of accountability, to risk being wrong as well as being right. To partner is to know that often it is from our mistakes that we understand and achieve success. To partner is to have so compelling a belief in ourselves and others that we can abandon the "hands on" control that comes from our fear of being accountable — accountable for success and accountable for learning how to succeed.

In leading or following, to act as a partner is to exhibit a bold indifference to traditional management norms. It is to create support to "challenge entrenched systems that work against collaborative effort" (Ohmae, 1990, p. 85). To partner is to build personal power and to value relationships more than structure. To partner is to hope and to dare.

Mark Cashman, who was introduced in Chapter Ten, is a person who leads in partnership with others. He believes everyone is eager to learn and capable of creating and thus capable of committing to standards and values that create organizational competence and effectiveness.

When I met Mark he was president of Andrews Office Products in Washington, D.C. He was interested in developing an employee handbook for the company, which, at that time, had about 120 employees, 30 of whom were members of the Teamsters Union. Like most small companies, Andrews did not have a human resources function; however, with 120 employees, the company was in need of programs and policies that would support staff development. My two suggestions were to create an employee advisory committee (EAC) to act as the human resources function,

*and to train Mark's administrative assistant, Stephanie Claros,
to administer the HR function, which would be filled by the
committee.*

*Mark invited employees to volunteer for the EAC. He sought
a diagonal slice of the system, which meant a committee comprised of employees who represented all functions and levels
within the company, including a mixture of short- and long-tenured
individuals, older and younger, male and female, minority and
nonminority, union and non-union. Nine employees came forward. They structured themselves and decided to rotate leadership of the committee in nine-month cycles. They determined
membership qualifications for others who would volunteer to
serve, and established staggered terms so the whole of the committee would not turn over at one time. Stephanie served as liai-
son between the committee and Mark. The EAC's first responsibility was to create, advise on, and make suggestions about
programs and policies that would affect employees' working lives.*

*With initial consultant support and Stephanie's facilitation,
the committee created a salary administration program, a performance planning and review process, a code of conduct, a job
posting system, an employee handbook, and policies on absen-
teeism, holidays, vacation, educational assistance, advancement
opportunities, and third-party consultation for job-related problems, to name a few. One unexpected outcome resulted from having two union members serve on the committee. Once the EAC
had developed and recommended policies and procedures, which
were approved for implementation by management, all the union
members within the company asked to stay with their union
but be governed by the company policies that two of their members had helped to create. The EAC is still in existence today, years
after Mark Cashman left Andrews to head another company. Andrews is an excellent example of what is possible when leaders
believe employees are competent and of how such beliefs lead
to actions that create learning, organizational competence, and
employee commitment.*

Much of today's business jargon seems to indicate that managers are no longer needed. The terms "self-managed" or "self-directed" teams, "autonomous work groups," and "team-based management" have many believing that success rests on eliminating middle managers. But the distinction between leaderlessness and leadership is important. Someone needs to lead. Leadership can be, but does not have to be, associated with role. Leadership can rotate, as it often does in self-regulating teams. Leaderless groups do not function; rather, they breed anxiety, create chaos, and suffer a lack of shared meaning. Often feelings of fear result in efforts to thwart or eliminate anyone who tries to lead.

When an activity involves more than one person, we need a context for cohesion. And the context needs to be one of freedom, not license. The significance of this idea for the nation as a whole is noted by John Donahue of the Kennedy School of Government at Harvard, who says, "'The U.S. suffers from the flip side of the social boon of choice.' Economic, cultural and political divisions threaten to rend what Justice Felix Frankfurter called 'the binding tie of cohesive sentiment that is the ultimate foundation of a free society.'" ("Why Nobody Can Lead America," 1991, p. 44). When the context for cohesion is one of freedom, leadership recognizes the interdependence of those who guide and those who pursue. This interdependency is best honored when the underlying belief is in partnership.

It is *functional* to partner when we want to:

1. Develop organizational capacity to invent and execute systemically

2. Build alliances that serve individuals, groups, and organizations simultaneously

3. Create futures and organizations worthy of everyone's commitment

4. Strengthen the "I" and the "We"

5. Differentiate and integrate the richness and power of diversity

6. Promote interdependence and self-regulation within and across boundaries

7. Develop organizational competence, learning, and community

It is *dysfunctional* to partner (1) without trust and integrity as the foundation for the partnership and (2) when the context of the interaction indicates that other styles could be functional.

Functional and Dysfunctional Uses of Style

If we look at the functional and dysfunctional uses of leading and following styles, we find some interesting correlations. For example, when the leading style is *tell/sell*, it usually engenders the following style of *patronize* or *comply*. If the use of *tell/sell* is functional, it will engage the functional use of *patronize* or *comply*. If the use of *tell/sell* is dysfunctional, likewise it will engage the dysfunctional use of *patronize* or *comply*.

When the leading style is *participate*, it usually engenders the following style of *comply* or *cooperate*. When the leading style is *facilitate*, it usually engenders the following style of *cooperate*. When the leading style is *partner*, it inspires the followers to partner as well.

It is important to note that while particular leading styles engender certain following styles, the reverse is not so. When leading takes the form of guidance and following that of pursuit, and when both are well executed, the result can be the creation of value for customers, suppliers, stakeholders, and employees. However, followers' responses can definitely affect the success or failure of leadership's efforts. A manager at Harley-Davidson had this to say: "We retained one of the Big Eight accounting firms and spent $6 million to install a new corporate system on a crash basis. Nothing came out of this effort because no attempt was made to involve the people who really understood how the place worked. From that, we learned a key lesson: Don't try to put systems in from the top down" (Reid, 1990, p. 31). This comment points up the extra dimension that leadership can provide.

Context, Style, and Situational Leading and Following

In the best of all worlds, leading and following can be shared, rotated, and chosen. Both behaviors are required if individuals and groups are to work in ways that allow them to fulfill their potential. In the best of teams, everyone leads and everyone follows—and everyone knows when to do which without being told. All that is required is experience in working together and adherence to mutually developed and accepted guidelines that honor the dignity and worth of each human being. When I work with design teams, a moment usually arrives when the team is called upon to do the extraordinary. The time is insufficient for the task and the materials at hand may not be the exact or best materials for what is required. With perfect awareness of themselves and one other, each member moves toward what he or she does best and what will support the whole. At this moment, everyone is leading and everyone is following. This results in a superb execution of tasks and deep satisfaction at both the individual and group levels of system. When leading and following are choices, we are better able to serve others. When leading and following are roles, our choice often becomes one of service to self or others.

I am reminded that everyone leads and everyone follows whenever I see design teams creating the presentation of their proposal. It is a time when everyone has learned to optimize the "I" and the

"We." Everyone on the team knows what they do best. The group has learned about diversity, uniqueness, and how to integrate what it learned to differentiate. Individuals have done battle. Nagging suspicions have been superseded with honor for differences of opinion. Bothersome individual traits have turned into good-humored barbs of affection. And the attitude that "nothing changes" is replaced with "we can make it happen."

At one plant that produces household cleaning products the speed record was broken when it came to presenting their redesign proposal. On the afternoon of June 4, 1990, the design team presented their proposal to the steering committee, which deliberated on the recommendations the following morning. That afternoon, the steering committee informed the design team about what was immediately acceptable, what required more study, and the one change required in the proposed structure. The design team presented their original proposal and the steering committee's reactions to it to the entire plant the next afternoon. Usually this process takes weeks and sometimes months. The delay is debilitating to everyone and usually results from old-pyramid thinking—the "trickle down theory of communication."

This timely dissemination of the proposed and accepted redesign plan put a lot of pressure on the design team. They had six hours to gather more data and revise their presentation to incorporate the steering committee's response. The nine-member team arrived early on June 6. Energy was high. With little discussion and perfect awareness of themselves and one another, each person moved to the place where he or she could make the greatest contribution to the whole. Some worked alone, some in pairs. They staked out the space they needed to complete their work. One member moved to a separate room to make several large charts. He kept in communication with those who worked in the main work room by popping in from time to time. His team mates checked with him frequently to see if he needed any help.

Food is always a necessity for design teams. The name of the game is feed the mind and feed the body. When lunchtime approached, one team member began taking sandwich orders. He quickly returned with food from a delicatessen. As the team worked on, members spontaneously decided to buy a gift for the plant manager. Quickly a decision was made as to what to buy and one member left to go shopping.

As I assisted anyone who wanted help, I watched a kind of miracle in the making. It was as if one body had eighteen arms and eighteen legs. The group moved as one, yet each member contributed where he or she could contribute best. They all led and they all followed. The rotation of roles was seamless and unspoken. They had control and support, as individuals and as a group. They were interdependent and self-regulating. And at 2:00 P.M. they delivered to the entire plant one of the finest design proposal presentations I have seen. This was leadership and followership in their purest forms, without hierarchy, without competition, and without factionalism. In the words of Lao-tzu, "when the . . . work is done, the people will say it happened naturally."

THE CONSULTANT AS PARTNER: A MIRROR FOR ORGANIZATIONAL RELATIONSHIPS

Interdependence, partnership, personal power . . . for me, all of these beliefs and values underlie the client/consultant relationship. Client dependence on consultants is always mirrored in employee dependence on the organization. It is imperative for consultants to develop relationships with clients without creating dependency. This requires consultants to act out the value of interdependence and the belief that the wisdom already is in the system. The consultant's role is to work as a partner with the client so together they discover how to unleash that wisdom.

Toward the end of 1990, I was asked to consult to an electronics division of one of the big three auto manufacturers. Although much of the division's work was done overseas, where labor rates were considerably lower than those in the United States, one of the division's plants, which was forty years old, was still operating in the United States. The plant had been ordered to close because it contained asbestos. To save some 3,000 jobs, management promised to build a new plant in the United States if the union would agree to a new work group strategy in which individuals would become multiskilled and work in self-managed teams. The union, which wanted assurance that jobs would remain in the United States, agreed to the concept on the basis that multiskilling would also allow employees to earn more money.

A work group committee was formed, consisting of the plant's senior management and the union's leadership. A consultant was hired to redesign the plant's structure based on a "product stream" that married Engineering and Manufacturing. Teams called work groups were designated based on three major product streams, each of which would produce multiple electronic components. Simultaneously, the company built a new plant, designed entirely by engineers who had not and would not work on the "shop floor," and began to move 3,000 employees into the facility, which contained new equipment, technology, and business systems. Compounding all of this change were several changes in key management personnel who had fulfilled their two-to-four-year assignments at the plant and were transferred back to corporate headquarters in the Midwest.

Halfway through the launch of work groups and the movement of 3,000 employees from the old facility to the new plant, the work group committee decided to take a time out. Such a decision is rare and laudable. The committee wanted to assess what was going well, what could be going better, and what midcourse corrections, if any, would enhance the implementation of the work group strategy.

I was one of several consultants who were invited to meet with the work group committee. Prior to this meeting, I spent two-thirds of a day meeting with the plant manager, the union leadership, and the head of Employee Relations—the woman responsible for work group–employee involvement, training, and communications. What stood out for me from these conversations was that employee involvement, a hallmark of plant philosophy, had been overlooked. The people who did the work had not been involved in the redesign of the plant. In effect, the work group strategy had been envisioned, negotiated, designed, and implemented by senior management and the union leadership.

During my interview with the work group committee, I said that if I was retained I could not do an "expert" assessment of the work group strategy. Rather, to conduct the assessment, I would partner with a team of employees who represented a microcosm of the system. My underlying assumption was that the assessment needed to provide a model for employee involvement by including those who did the work. I believed the employees were capable of doing the assessment with some training and coaching on methodology. I was also operating on the belief that sound consultation is based on a partnership wherein both client and consultant are committed to a common cause, the client retains ownership of the change target, and the consultant supports the organization in becoming more skilled rather than more dependent on outside support.

I was asked to facilitate the assessment. The assessment was announced to everyone in the plant and employees were invited to volunteer to be members of the assessment team. Forty people volunteered to participate and eight were selected to achieve a maximum mix; every level and job function was represented on the assessment team and the group included younger and older, short- and long-tenured, male and female, minority and non-minority employees, some of whom believed in the work group strategy and some of whom did not.

After two days of preparation that included a team-building exercise, training in how to interview, brainstorming forty-eight questions and selecting eight to be asked of all interviewees, and selecting a stratified random sample of 290 employees who represented 10 percent of the plant, the team, working in four pairs, began to gather data. Every interviewee was promised and received a complete, unedited copy of the final report; thus they were involved with providing information and were also fully engaged by receiving the final report. During many of the interview sessions, I sat in the room, took my own notes, and gave feed-back to the interviewing team on what they were doing well and other choices they had for probing particular answers they received to certain questions.

Once the data were collected, I prepared a draft of the findings and recommendations. The assessment team reviewed and made changes to the draft, and then we all prepared the final presentation. Team members were to present the findings and I was to present the recommendations. We had a tight timeframe in which to pull all the pieces together. While I worked on prepar-ing the final written report, team members prepared their indi-vidual presentations. There was no time for a "dress rehearsal." The team assured me they were prepared. From the work they had already done, I knew they were as good as their word.

The next morning, thirty people gathered to hear the report, including the work group committee and several invited guests. Each team member presented a portion of the findings. Many had never made a formal presentation before. From my seat, I could see each speaker, in profile, at the podium as well as the audience. Members of the team spoke in clear voices even though some-times their hands shook or a foot tapped. As each member com-pleted his or her segment, the others on the team gave thumbs up signs or nodded their heads in approval. When the entire presentation was completed, the plant manager stood up and said, "I now know beyond any doubt that work groups can work. I have just seen an example of this, here, today."

The team held a spontaneous luncheon celebration after the presentation. They had discovered individually and together ta-lents and skills they had not had a chance to use before. Each of them now knows how to conduct an assessment. The plant, rather than being dependent on an outside consultant for future assessments of strategies in progress, can now rely on skills, knowl-edge, and competence developed by a team of interdependent individuals. My relationship with the client was one of partner-ship. It is a style that was mirrored in the assessment team.

CREATING PARTNERSHIP IN OUR ORGANIZATIONS

The ways we see ourselves and the ways others see us can differ greatly. Much of the discrepancy is due to what can be seen and what is often invisible. Intention drives behavior. Intent is often invisible. Our behavior impacts others. Frequently our intent, behavior, and impact on others are not aligned. When this occurs, how we see ourselves differs from how we are seen by others.

One way to assess our own intentions to partner and our exhibited behaviors and their resulting impact is to ask ourselves some questions about our styles of leading. Look at the description for each of the four styles and ask yourself:

1.   What is my intention?
2.   What is my behavior?
3.   What is my impact?
4.   If my intentions and behaviors are not aligned, how do I stop myself from acting on my intention?

To delve deeper, ask yourself these questions:

5.   What is my felt need?
6.   What is my expressed need?
7.   What environment enables me to align my felt and expressed needs?

Intention results from our underlying assumptions, beliefs, and values. What is your answer to this question?

Is the figure already in the stone and is the sculpture
the one who sets it free, or
does the sculptor create the figure?

Your answer is an insight into the assumptions, beliefs, and values that underlie your leadership style.

Often our intentions vary with the situation, particularly when the situation feels productive rather than conflicted. We can better understand how our intentions may vary when we look at the functional and dysfunctional uses of each of the four styles of leading and following that are described in this chapter. Given these descriptions, what style do you use in productive environments and which style do you use when there is conflict? Do these style preferences differ?

Look at the Models for Control and Support in Chapter Seven.

- Where on each scale and within which quadrant would you place your behavior?

- Where on the scale and within which quadrant would your work associates—the person to whom you report, your peers, subordinates, and internal suppliers and customers—place your impact?

- What actions can you take—what can you change or strengthen—and what support do you need to enable you to align your intention, behavior, and impact in the style of your choice?

- In terms of *control*, is your placement in a particular quadrant due to a need for certainty or a fear of loss (resistance)?

- Where on the following continuum would you place yourself?

Have it my way	Help others learn my way	Learn by myself	Help others learn	Learn with others

- Where would your work associates place you?

- Where do you want to be? What support do you need to be there?

12

Expertise:
Choosing Invention
Over Maintenance

Expertise in leading and following is not the technical know-how that qualified us for our first job or led to our first promotion, nor is it knowledge about the service or product we help produce. Leading in inventive organizations requires *inventive expertise—expertise in guiding the development of systems and managing systems.* Following in inventive organizations also requires inventive expertise—*expertise in managing self and interactions with others in pursuit of common cause.* Such expertise includes:

Leading	*Following*
Managing boundaries—intervening to challenge norms and test assumptions underlying beliefs and actions	Planning
Providing resources	Organizing, controlling
Managing interdependence, change, and invention—	Staffing, informing

developing agendas of issues, aspirations, strategic challenges, and individual intentions	
Coordinating hope and the creation of organizational meaning—building learning communities	Solving
Developing individuals, groups, and community—creating the means for discovery, choice, and action	Measuring, appraising, evaluating
Ensuring conditions for continuous improvement, involvement, self-regulation, learning, and renewal	Rewarding
Creating customer-supplier partnerships	Developing customer-supplier partnerships
Developing capacity	Building knowledge

The foregoing ideas on leading expertise are not new. In fact, many of the ideas presented in this chapter can be found in bits and pieces all over the literature on change, leadership, manufacturing, and total quality management. Almost every organization has conducted or is considering conducting a training program that deals with at least one of these areas of expertise. All too often, these programs are implemented within existing structures, roles, and operating frameworks that are incompatible with the leadership behaviors described here.

This chapter offers three new perspectives that address these common difficulties. First, leading and managing are differentiated on the basis that leading has to do with managing systems and following has to do with managing self and interactions with others. Second, the role traditionally associated with managing in a command-and-control hierarchy is now translated into behaviors for following in a self-regulating environment. Third, leading and following expertise are presented as interdependent and neither is associated with a particular role. Expertise in leading and following allows us to choose the behavior (contribution) appropriate to a given context so that self and others are served in pursuit of common cause.

Inventive leading and following expertise is based on whole-systems thinking. Just as one aspect of a system is linked to every other aspect, each aspect of inventive expertise is linked to every other aspect and all are tied to a focus on customer requirements, core work, and the values the organization wants to live out. Inventive expertise impacts underlying assumptions about structure, roles, people, skills, tasks, technology, information flows, decision-making processes, policies and procedures, the built environment, and reward mechanisms. As we develop inventive expertise, we change our focus from one of controlling and being controlled by others to one of managing self and strengthening relationships between individuals, groups, customers, suppliers, and people and the technology by which they produce.

LEADING EXPERTISE: EXPERTISE IN MANAGING SYSTEMS

If we think of leading as guiding others, rather than controlling them, we can begin to more closely examine behaviors associated with managing systems, as opposed to managing others. There are eight primary behaviors required to manage systems. Each of these is described in this section. (See Figure 12.1.)

Figure 12.1. Leading in Transition: Expertise.

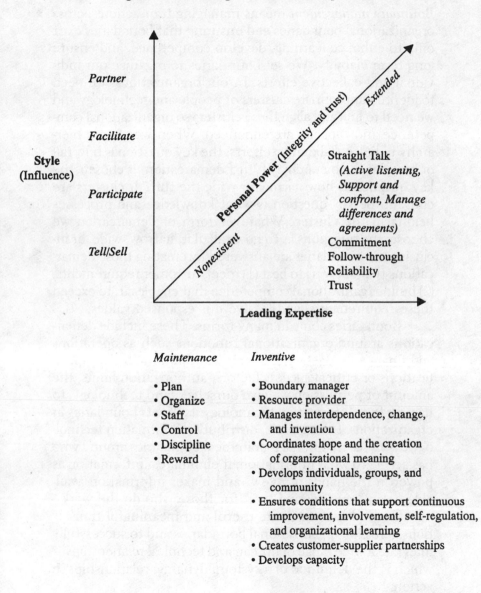

Notes: This figure copyright © 1993, Jill E. Janov. The Straight Talk steps are attributable to the Minnesota Couples Training.

Boundary Management

Boundary management means managing transactions across organizational boundaries and ensuring that boundaries exist only to enhance learning, develop competence, and ensure long-term viability. We set boundaries to organize our individual and collective efforts. In our organizations, we need to identify appropriate clusters of people and technology and we need to link and align these clusters so organizational competence and capacity are enhanced. When we choose hierarchy to link collaborative efforts, the key question is how tall or how flat the hierarchy? If "turf demarcation" is chosen, the key question is how narrow or wide the turf? If clusters are chosen, the key question is what knowledge and processes belong in the cluster? Whatever form of demarcation we choose, the questions as to how tall, flat, narrow, wide, or inclusive the boundaries are answered by creating those demarcations that allow us to best (1) meet customer requirements, (2) build organizational competence that enables us to exceed these requirements, and (3) live our espoused values.

Boundaries come in many forms. These include demarcations around organizational functions such as operations and finance, budgetary constraints, minimum critical specifications or critical success factors, authorization limits, the amount of permission we give ourselves, and technology, to name a few. Information technology itself sets boundaries in organizations. For example, distributive information technology by-passes traditional hierarchical boundaries around who has access to what information; it eliminates "information as power in the hands of a few" and makes information available as an "empowering tool" for those who do the work.

To lead is to facilitate useful and meaningful transactions across all organizational boundaries and to successfully integrate a wide range of human and technical relationships — which is the definition of a system: dynamic relationships in action.

Boundary management means that we manage systems

rather than control others. To lead means we shift our focus from looking down and within a specific area to looking out, across, and up. This means that we lead when we see our accountability for the system's well-being, not simply the well-being of certain people or of a particular function or department. To manage systems is to focus on boundaries — where they are set and what purpose they serve — because the system's well-being is dependent on transactions that occur at and across organizational boundaries.

Resource Provider

The provision and control of resources is critical in any organization. To lead is to provide and ensure required resources exist. To follow is to communicate resource requirements and control those provided. Resources include people, the built environment, budgets, information, training, policies, procedures, and operating practices, methods, measurements, and rewards, to name several.

It is impossible to hold people accountable for the results they achieve when they do not have any control over the means by which they produce. Therefore, in inventive organizations, to lead is to hold ourselves accountable for providing resources and to follow is to hold ourselves accountable for controlling the resources provided.

People are the most valuable resource in any organization. They are the critical element in developing organizational competence. They are the repository and conveyors of organizational know-how. What they do with what they know how to do will determine organizational success. We can tell how much we value people by how we treat those individuals who are lowest on the hierarchy. Whatever we overlook in honoring the dignity and worth of every individual within our organizations, we also overlook in honoring the dignity and worth of our customers and suppliers. We cannot develop relationships with our stakeholders that are any better than those we develop as work associates.

To lead in an inventive organization is to engage those who do the work in managing themselves and their interactions with others. This means that those who do the work decide who to hire, how to integrate new members, how to constructively manage differences and agreements, and how to terminate failed relationships. To lead inventively is to coach and develop individuals and groups so that whatever the workforce configuration — intact teams, project task forces, or individual contributors — everyone acts in service to self and others.

Next to people, the most critical resource is *the built environment*, which includes layout, facilities, furniture, equipment, the electronic infrastructure, aesthetics (decor, artwork, signage), furniture, grounds, parking, and all the other structural and hardware elements that constitute the place in which we do our work. In most companies, the majority of employees are treated as renters rather than owners of their work space. Their space is designed and furnished by people who do not work in it, and those who occupy the space rarely have any power to change it.

The concept of employers as "renters" of their work space always comes to mind whenever I check into a hotel. It is obvious that the check-in area does not work — for the customer or for the person who serves the customer. Inevitably, those behind the counter are required to perform a mad dance. They consult a monitor and use a computer to check my reservation. I have never seen one of these computers placed at eye level; rather, to use them an individual must hunch over the machine from a standing position. Next, they take my credit card and dash to an imprint machine that is several yards away. They lean down to grab a folder to house my room key and confirmation slip. They take off in another direction to get a key to the room or to pull open a drawer filled with small plastic rectangles that are fed into another machine that programs a new lock combination.

Often the front desk phone rings while I am being served. And very often the phone is out of reach or behind a panel that conceals the hotel's back-room operation. If I ask for change, another "run" is made to a cash drawer. Luggage assistance requires yet another move down the seemingly endless counter to punch the bellhop call button.

Check-in staffs do their jobs standing on their feet, eight hours or more a day. Usually they stand on beautiful marble floors that provide no cushion for the leg work that is part of their job. Their uniform requirements include dress shoes, which are least conducive to comfortably navigating the endless corridor designated as their work space. I often wonder what this space would look like if the people who worked in it and those they served had a say in how it should be designed.

Dick Hayworth, president of Hayworth Office Systems, has a vision that one day larger companies will have company stores where non-manufacturing employees can purchase what they need to do quality work. The size of their work space might be specified and the budget for equipping it might be fixed; however, within these constraints, people would design and furnish the space in which they work. Even smaller companies could take advantage of this concept if their office products dealer provided a similar "employee store." New employees would go to the wholesaler with a set budget to select and purchase what they need for their work space.

In manufacturing environments, the built environment supports quality outputs when it is designed by a consortium of architects, engineers, equipment manufacturers, production specialists, maintenance and skilled-trade personnel, staff support functions that ensure compliance with regulatory requirements, and machine operators, all of whom understand customer requirements, core work processes, financial and space limitations, and time requirements to redesign existing facilities or build new ones, and all of whom work in partnership to ensure that the built environment enables execution of the company's strategy. *Reinventing the Factory*, by Roy Harmon and Leroy Peterson (1990), illuminates many of the "decidedly low-tech" techniques—such as materials management, layout, objectives, constraints, compromises, aisle systems that avoid gridlock, big gains from small containers, cooperative recovery, cells, focused storage, one-touch set-ups—that can result in labor savings of 40 percent, space reductions of 50 to 80 percent, productivity gains of 10 to 12 percent, reductions in set-up and change-over costs of 75 percent, and reduction of quality defects 75 to 100 percent. These ideas have been tested at Harley-Davidson, 3M, Johnson & Johnson, and the Inland Division of General Motors. And these ideas can be generated and tested anywhere that leaders think systemically and involve the people who "live" in these environments in the design of the environment.

Budgets are a critical component of every work decision. Yet somehow we have come to believe that the majority of adults we employ cannot understand or will be frightened by the realities of the corporate checkbook. Everyone can understand and support the whole system when everyone knows the economics of the situation, the technical and human requirements, and the built environment. Only then can everyone manage the bottom line.

Budgets are constraints, and constraints can spawn invention. Vaughn Beals, chairman of the board for Harley-Davidson, hypothesizes that Japanese manufacturing methods have their origin in the scarcity and high price of land in Japan. Economic necessity means Japanese factories must be small, with machines placed close together, so there is no room for excess inventory" (Reid, 1990, p. 66).

Providing resources also includes ensuring *access to information*. Today organizations are faced with both a dearth and a glut of information. In fixed and adaptive organizations, a dearth of information flows results from the "trickle down" theory. Those at the top disseminate information through the hierarchy. Each level holds on to some of this information and passes down some, until what could have been a river becomes a trickle by the time the information reaches those at the bottom of the hierarchy. The underlying assumption that information is power and power is finite chokes needed information flows. To make matters worse, information does not flow upstream any better than it flows downstream. Peters and Waterman, in their book *In Search of Excellence,* coined the phrase "management by walking around." Why is there a need to manage by walking around? In fixed and adaptive organizations, the boundaries are so numerous that senior managers often do not know what is going on in their own organizations and the "troops" rarely have contact with "upper management." This results in complicated communication channels, increased report writing and record keeping, and fewer people having the ability to see the big picture, all of which result from unnecessary boundaries across which partnership is required but not easily obtained. (Often I am asked to consult to an organization because "we have a communication problem." Ralph Strayer of Johnsonville Foods says, "I have come to believe that there isn't such a thing as a communication problem; it's a responsibility-is-in-the-wrong-spot problem.")

Authors Badaracco and Ellsworth coined a metaphor for the glut of inessential boundaries when they called organizations "hierarchies of wastebaskets" (1989, p. 128). They believe that as information moves up the hierarchy, more and more of it is thrown away. Senior executives are asked to make decisions on the basis of a few paragraphs that condense several pages of careful analyses that took months or even years to complete.

At the same time that organizational practices constrict necessary information, advances in technology increase the options for information flows and the creation of data. On the plus side, distributive (as opposed to centralized) computer operations, open architectures, and relational databases can help to broaden (and/or circumvent) many of the old information channels. On the minus side, technology has led to the rapid creation and dissemination of previously impossible volumes of data. Unfortunately, in too many instances, our organizations are becoming glutted data mills. Data are not synonymous with information. Data are facts. Information is knowledge pertinent to the context and environment. Information is "know-how" or "know-what" that we communicate and receive because it is of use, not simply because it is available. When we abuse technology, we create too much rather than too little data and spend too much rather than too little time ferreting out what needs to be read and what needs to be tossed.

Information flows are irrevocably tied to boundary management. When boundaries are set and managed in ways that clog the flow of information, we impede the development of the very competence that ensures organizational success. The key to inventive organizations is to have the right people at the right place at the right time with the right skills and information, ready to act. Without the right information, it does not matter if the right people are at the right place at the right time, ready to act. When information is hoarded as power, quality outputs are thwarted. When people are "saved" from disturbing or confidential information, rumor mills are fueled because information voids are filled in with guesswork. When work associates are treated as children who need protection from the workplace they were hired to make thrive, our organizations merely survive.

Training is one of our most time-consuming and costly resources. Much as "communication" has become the "catch all" for what ails our organizations, training has become a "cure all." Inventive organizations are learning organizations. Some learning can be acquired through training. All too often, however, training is poorly planned, inappropriately delivered, inadequately evaluated, and constrained or rendered useless by organizational structure, policies, procedures, reward mechanisms, roles, and norms that are not aligned to support the implementation of what is being learned. To be effective, training needs to be

1. Learner centered, rather than teacher centered, which means the intended audience needs to be involved in the design of the training
2. Designed to appeal to various learning styles
3. Relevant to "real time" and "real work"
4. "Just-in-time"
5. Seen as aligned with organizational policies, practices, operating norms, and prior training initiatives

Policies, procedures, and practices are resources that can inhibit or facilitate invention. When our policies are based on controlling people and processes, our organizations become fixed and adaptive. To lead in an inventive organization is to ensure that policies, procedures, and practices are devised for guidance and that they do not become a substitute for the often painstaking search to find and expand our common cause.

Measurements are a kind of resource when what is measured is meaningful to those who consume our products and services.

Rewards are resources that result from meeting and exceeding customer requirements. They enable us to recognize individual and collective human achievement and to invest in the future of the enterprise.

Manages Interdependence, Guides Change and Invention

To manage systems is to manage boundaries in ways that acknowledge *interdependence* and create partnership. Interdependence is evident when accountability for the entire enterprise is shared by individuals, groups, and functions, regardless of their respective roles or expertise. Partnership occurs when we make a practice of *developing and working agendas of organizational issues, individual aspirations, and strategic challenges* within and across organizational boundaries.

Change.   To lead is to guide change. Guiding change is not a matter of forcing different options and directions; rather it is creating ways to anticipate what changes will be needed and when change should occur so that people and resources are aligned to move in an agreed-upon direction. This requires the development of informed and integrated human networks — loosely coupled or tightly linked — that have line of sight to the customer and can see the big picture. To guide change is to guide others in looking back and looking forward, looking inwardly and outwardly, so that both the enterprise and its operating environment are considered simultaneously with the possibilities at hand.

Invention.   To lead is to guide the invention of processes and practices as well as new products and services. It is to encourage discussions about how formal policies and procedures are being circumvented and how people are working outside the limits of their formal job descriptions to make work more efficient without sacrificing quality. Such practices go on all the time, yet people do not discuss them because they fear reprimand and reprisal. To lead is to help the system learn more about what is not being done that is required to be done — such as the steps that are eliminated when a crisis occurs — so that obstructions to work process and productivity can be eliminated.

Invention occurs out of the tension between what is and what can be envisioned, regardless of the level of system. At an individual level, invention occurs when we discover ways to synthesize opposing ideas. Invention also occurs when we apply an idea or process that was developed in one context to a different context. At the interpersonal or group level, invention develops out of synergies and conflicts between people or between individuals and their interactions with their environments. At an organizational level, invention is spawned out of impatience with the status quo, an honoring of history, and an urgency to break new ground.

Coordinates Hope and
the Creation of Organizational Meaning—
Builds Learning Communities

To lead is to *coordinate hope and the creation of organizational meaning*. Hope is a feeling that what is desired is also possible. In our workplaces, we call our hopes our vision. A touching example of a hope that is also a vision comes from Herman Miller, a furniture and office systems manufacturer, which strives to be "a gift to the human spirit." When we talk about our hopes, we discover our aspirations for the deeper meaning of what we do.

Organizational meaning is being created all the time. Meaning is discerned from actions, artifacts, policies, norms, structure, rewards, values, technology, workflows, roles, tools, equipment, environment, information flows, attitudes, practices, and every other aspect of the system. Meaning also is discovered, explored, ignored, shared, argued, eradicated, and reinvented. Individual meaning is created out of the collisions between fresh and cumulative organizational experience and how we interpret these experiences. Organizational meaning is created out of our interactions with others and with our work environment; it reflects a common interpretation of what has been, what is, and what can be.

The making of meaning should be a conscious act, explicit and not implicit, purposeful and not accidental. Without the conscious extraction of meaning, we cannot apprehend our organizations. To lead is to guide and coordinate this apprehension—this conscious grasping of meaning.

Develops Individuals, Groups, and Community

To lead is to *develop individuals and groups by creating the means for discovery, choice, and action*. Development occurs when enough support is provided to challenge underlying assumptions that result in personal or organizational constraints. Whether constraints are real or imagined, individually or organizationally imposed, they must be explored before it is possible to create options for moving beyond what was previously possible. To lead is to change the context—manage the system—that gives rise to constraints so that individuals and groups can develop enhanced capacities for making choices and taking action.

Group dynamics are an evolving science. To lead groups is an art. Groups evolve through stages of development that have been described in various models. Some models focus on performance, such as those developed by Mills (1964), Gibb (1964), Tuckman (1965), Young (1976), Tuckman and Jensen (1977), Lacoursiere (1980), Moosbrucker (1988), and Osborn, Moran, Musselwhite, and Zenter (1990). All of these include at least four and often five stages. The first stage is an introductory stage that is variously referred to as "the encounter," "forming," "orientation," "possibilities," "start-up" or "why am I here?" The second stage is a testing stage, where consciously or unconsciously individuals are testing the development or loss of their individual identity—"I"—within the context of the group—"We." This stage includes conflict over control among group members and with the leader. It is variously referred to as "testing boundaries and modeling roles," "storming," "confusion," "dissatisfaction," "who are you," and "movement—joins other forces." The third stage is focused on formation, solidarity, and developing process. It is referred to as "negotiating norms," "norming," "resolution," "what do we do," and "finds identity." The fourth stage is one of differentiation and production. It is referred to as "performing," "production," "tightly formed," "how," "self-directed," and "units become systems." The fifth stage is one of disengagement, "separation," "termination," or "adjournment."

Another way to view these stages is to look at boundaries. In the first stage, individual boundaries solidify and the challenge is to have these boundaries recognized by others. In the second stage, data about "give-up" and "get" are gathered and analyzed while boundaries are tested and sometimes assaulted. In the third stage, new boundaries are drawn that create a unit or group. Dual boundaries now exist—the "I" and the "We." In the fourth stage, the group boundary is solidified and controlled. Very often, this boundary becomes impermeable as opposed to fluid. The group, in its formation, takes on a "we/they" mentality, with the underlying assumption being adversarial. When groups are strong enough to be fluid, their boundaries are permeable. The formation of fluid boundaries creates inventive organizations.

Other models for group development are focused either on emotional climate—such as those devised by Schultz (1958), Dunphy (1968), Kaplan (1974), Bennis and Shepard (1974), Osborn and others (1990)—or on revolt—such as those by Slater (1966), Hartman and Gibbard (1974), and Osborn and others (1990). The models based on emotional climate track our needs for inclusion, affection, control, dependency, power, intimacy, fight, flight, enchantment, cooperative self-management, and consensual validation. Revolt models track our needs to see leaders as gods or as fallible. Revolt models also track needs for certainty, optimism, utopia, competition, intimacy, loyalty to the team, and termination.

All of these models are frameworks for assessing when and how to intervene at the group level of a system. A group goes through a sequence of stages. When members leave and new members join, these sequences are repeated. Each stage of the sequence builds on the former stage. Each stage has unique symptoms, and each stage requires different kinds of interventions. Changes from one stage to another may not be continuous. Development within each stage represents a process of clarifying the individual within the group and the group within the external environment or context in which it operates (see Gillette and McCollom, 1990, pp. 137–138). To lead inventively is to understand group development. To lead is to stay at the boundary and intervene to support the group's development of capacity, rather than to create dependency or ensure control.

The development of work groups and team concepts has become synonymous with flattening hierarchy and making

first-line and middle managers endangered species. Teams are
not ends. Teams are a form of structure, and structure should
be based on strategy. Self-regulating environments can be
team-based or individual contributor–based. Self-regulation
occurs if support and control exist where the work is done
and there is linkage to the larger system and the context in
which work is performed. To lead inventively is to ensure that
support and control exist at all levels of the system and that
individual efforts are aligned with the larger system and its
operating environment.

To lead is also to *develop organizational community.* We
need a sense of community—of inclusion and belonging—if
we are to create and pursue common cause. Community occurs when individuals feel recognized as a part of that which
is larger than a role or department. Community is the "Us"
of organizations. We have no sense of community when we
feel invisible in the larger organization. Sometimes people
seem to be little more than a collection of titles, each with
its attendant state of privilege or lack thereof. In manufacturing environments, for example, people in uniform often
feel they are treated as a faceless category called hourly employees. People in management are similarly lumped together
in the epithet "white shirts." To lead is to develop the context for feeling known and knowing, for coming together as
partners in pursuit of common cause, and for managing the
system so that every member identifies with the whole of the
enterprise and not simply a part of the organization.

---

*Recently, I was invited to speak at Old St. Patrick's Church, the
oldest Catholic church in Chicago, which is housed in the oldest
building in downtown Chicago. The church parishioners had dwin-
dled to a handful when a dynamic pastor, Father Jack Wall, came
to Old St. Patrick's in 1983. In 1987 Father Wall hired John Fontana, executive director of the Crossroads Center for Faith and
Work. John's belief is that God is where people spend their time,*

and today people spend their time at work. John created a speakers
series, underwritten by Johnson & Higgins, Inc., on creating health
in the workplace. Once a week several hundred people leave their
offices after work and go to a half-hour service that precedes a
simple but hearty meal in the church auditorium. After breaking
bread together, those gathered listen to a speaker. My topic was
"Creating Individual and Organizational Satisfaction."

I arrived at 5:30 to join in the worship. As I sat in the last
pew, I saw that the audience was made up of people who would
be strangers if not for the church program that draws them together.
They meet and share a common experience. A bond is formed.
A place of belonging is created. And out of that sense of community and the strength derived from the bond of common experience, each person goes forth with the living of his life.

Witnessing this sense of community around me, I thought
of the many weeks I had spent in Spain and my great love for
the plazas that are part of every city and pueblo. The plaza is
a gathering place. It is in the center of the town. During the day,
the entire community passes through it. The young girls will walk
in one direction while the young boys walk in the opposite direction so they can coyly flirt with one another. Old men walk with
their hands clasped behind their backs. Mothers push babies in
carriages. Businessmen nod in acquaintance. Some people sit at
small tables having drinks and eating tapas. To be in the plaza
is to see the community—the whole of the community and the
individuals who make up the community. It is to mingle, to nod,
to acknowledge, to see and be seen. I realized that John Fontana
has created a plaza in Chicago.

In organizational terms, a plaza is not the company cafeteria
where people gather by rank or eat in separate dining rooms according to their rank on the hierarchy. A plaza is where people
of all ranks meet and mingle. Recently many of our organizations
created "almost accidental plazas." They are accidental because
they have arisen out of necessity rather than intention. They are
"almost" plazas because they are visited only by those who smoke.
They are the places outside our office and factory buildings where
people gather to have a cigarette. Sometimes you will see execu-

*tives and hourly employees nodding and talking to one another
as they brave the elements to feed their habit. Even though these
two individuals work within the same organization, without the
almost accidental plaza, they would never meet.*

Ensures Conditions That Support Continuous Improvement, Self-Regulation, Learning, and Renewal

The idea of *continuous improvement* attracts us because it
connotes the possibilities of perfection—for ourselves, our institutions, and our world. It also can be demoralizing because
it connotes an unachievable state. In some work environments, continuous improvement is seen as a whip that creates "management by stress." As employees strive to continuously become more effective and efficient, a mentality takes
hold that "enough is never enough," which fuels resentment
and stress. Further, many see continuous improvement resulting in strict stipulations for work processes, the proliferation
of exacting procedures, and a prescriptive environment that
inhibits discretion, experimentation, and self-regulation.

As I use it in this book, "continuous improvement" means
a framework for creating conditions for invention. Where continuous improvement is valued, both process and results are
valued equally. To lead is to focus on continuous improvement
as a journey, not a destination; it is to evoke experimentation—
the creation of safe emergencies to test the existing boundaries within an organization, whether these boundaries are between people, groups, customers and suppliers, or individuals
and technology. And it is to guide the setting and celebrating
of milestones so that progress can be noted and time-outs can
be taken for making meaning of our experience. Continuous
improvement is inevitably linked to what we measure and
whether our underlying assumptions cause us to define improvement as evolutionary or revolutionary.

To lead is to *ensure conditions for self-regulation*. Leading is guiding the examination of everyone's needs for support and control. When support and control are balanced in every organizational role, partnerships are possible between individuals and groups—partnerships based on service to self and others in pursuit of common cause. Self-regulation is critical to inventive organizations and is the determinant of the nature of internal organizational relationships. These internal relationships are reflected in the relationships created with external customers and suppliers.

To lead is to enhance the possibilities for invention by *ensuring optimal conditions for learning*. When we are encouraged to learn from what works as well as from what did not work, conditions exist for experimentation. If all we reward is what works, and if all that does not work is punished, we become risk aversive and the possibilities for invention are lost to our need to play it safe. Paradoxically, the only way we can play it safe in our organizations is to continue to push our boundaries—to be inventive.

Whenever I work with project teams, I always insist that we celebrate their efforts before they present their recommendations and results. At first, the teams are perplexed because they believe they only have the right to celebrate success, and they define success as acceptance of their findings and recommendations. Therefore, in their minds, there is nothing to celebrate. When I ask what they have learned as a result of their endeavors, they uniformly tell me they have learned a great deal. They also know they can apply what they have learned to do to other situations. This knowledge is "second-loop" learning, which creates organizational competence—learning about how we learn—and this needs to be honored and celebrated as much as if not more than "an accepted finished product."

Invention is not simply envisioning and creating something that has not existed before. Invention is more than applying a process developed for one use to some other use. Inventive organizations often miss their intended mark, take what initially could be described as a mistake, determine whether the outcome has other applications, use what they learn, and pass on the knowledge to other parts of the organization. August Jacacci of Metamatrix Associates calls this process "gather, repeat, share, and integrate." Inventive organizations see the wisdom in their "mistakes" and treat failure and success with equal respect. James Burke, chairman of Johnson & Johnson during the Tylenol incident that resulted in the company abandoning capsules and inventing tamper-resistant gelcaps, learned this lesson early in his career. The story goes that Burke's first product idea failed miserably. He was summoned to Chairman General Robert Wood Johnson's office and asked, "Are you the one who just cost us all that money?" Burke nodded. The General said, "Well, I just want to congratulate you. If you are making mistakes, that means you are making decisions and taking risks. And we won't grow unless you take risks" (Senge, 1990, p. 300).

Learning is the basis for building competence. Competence is knowledge and skill, and it creates organizational capacity for continued invention and renewal. We build competence when we learn about how we learn. Organizational competence is created when such learning is shared across boundaries. It is not enough to think in terms of inventing products and services. To lead is to create conditions that develop competence. These include:

1. Fidelity to the spirit of inquiry and dialogue
2. Designating time to think about how we think and how we learn
3. Experimentation—valuing mistakes and successes
4. Viewing the processes of production and service as systemic rather than discreet—which means seeing the link-

ages between idea generation, production methods, and consumption

Creates Customer and Supplier Partnerships

Over and over again, a system has been defined in this book as a series of relationships in action. An open system, by its very nature, is part of a larger context that includes external customers and suppliers. To lead is to develop an awareness of our interdependence with our customers and suppliers — *to create customer and supplier partnerships.*

Many people in large organizations have no contact with customers and suppliers. Much of what the customer wants is relayed through layers of the organization that filter and reframe customer requirements and customer satisfaction. Much of what is done with incoming supplies is unknown to those who create the supplies. Those at the top of the hierarchy often have as little customer and supplier contact as do those who are isolated on factory floors. In both cases, partnership is more rhetoric than reality because we do not experience interdependence without contact. To lead is to ensure regular contact between organizational members and external customers and suppliers so that we have firsthand experience of our interdependence and are able to act accountably for the whole system at every level of the system.

Develops Capacity

To manage systems is to develop capacity, which is to attend to circumstances conducive to the growth and development of the individual and the organization. We do not attend to these circumstances by focusing on quarterly share price. Such a focus sacrifices the long-term viability of the organization for short-term results.

Recently, I was informed that a chief executive officer of a worldwide organization would retire in two and a half years. The company's stock is currently $42 per share, and he wants it to be $60 when he retires. The only way to create this increase is to cut operating costs. Thousands of people are being laid off—people whose competence could be applied to new organizational endeavors. Even if these cost-cutting measures result in a share price of $60, it is questionable whether the organization will have the capacity to exceed that price, let alone sustain it.

To build organizational capacity we must reconsider what we invest in and how we use all of our resources. Short-term measures, such as layoffs, ultimately result in a long-term loss of potential customers for our products and services as well as the loss of stockholders, whose investment capabilities support the development of our capacity. Worse, layoffs have a domino effect. They erode the tax base of our communities and, thereby, our ability to generate funds for the rebuilding of our infrastructure. Without investment in roads, bridges, waste management, electronic highways, we will not create the means to support the further development of capacity. The building of capacity is critical to leading, and particularly to guiding the development of that level of system we call organization.

EXPERTISE IN FOLLOWING: MANAGING SELF AND INTERACTIONS WITH OTHERS

In our old command-and-control hierarchies, we think of followers as those who need to be told what to do and how to do it. This way of thinking has resulted in the "act of following" being an act of maintaining the status quo; we focus only on what we need to do to survive in the organization we are supposed to serve. Survival skills include knowing how to make the boss look good, not raising standards, controlling expectations, working the rules to our own advantage, not making waves, asking and not informing. Such skills constrain contribution, result in dependent or counterdependent relationships with those who command and control, and reinforce the status quo. (See Figure 12.2.)

Figure 12.2. Following in Transition: Expertise.

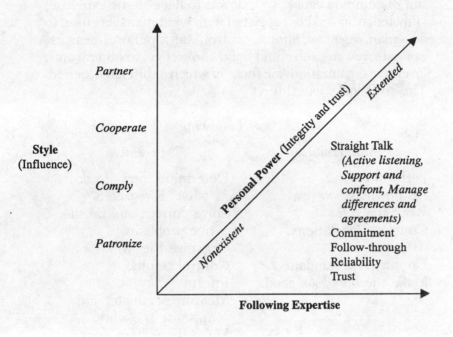

Notes: This figure copyright © 1993, Jill E. Janov. The Straight Talk
steps are attributable to the Minnesota Couples Training.

In inventive organizations, to follow is to pursue. It is to manage oneself and one's relationships with others in pursuit of common cause. To follow is to have all the expertise, knowledge, and skills associated with what managers used to do—plan, organize, inform, control, staff, appraise, measure, evaluate, reward, solve, and build knowledge. In other words, inventive organizations are those in which a shift has occurred. The shift looks like this:

Acts of Following

Maintenance	Inventive
Perform as told.	Determine "how" to do "what" is required.
Do not make waves.	
Work the rules.	Solve current and prospective problems.
Control expectations.	
Ask.	Organize the work.
Do not raise standards.	Control results.
Make the boss look good.	Inform.
	Measure, evaluate, and appraise the work.
	Make the system work.

This shift creates a partnership wherein to lead is to guide and to follow is to pursue—a relationship of interdependence, not dependence, counterdependence, or independence. This shift re-creates leading as guiding and managing systems, and re-creates following as managing self and relationships with others in pursuit of common cause. When to lead means to give up planning, organizing, and controlling work and work schedules, and to shift one's focus to the boundary of a function, those within the boundary do the planning, organizing, and controlling of what is in the boundary—and a new partnership is created. This partnership leads to the co-creation of means and accountability for meeting and exceeding customer requirements.

The way in which new members are brought into an organization creates the norms—the unwritten rules—that

guide acts of following. When new members come into prescribed situations, where job descriptions and performance
specifications are fixed and determined by others than those
who do the work, their focus is on staying within prescribed
and often rigid boundaries that limit potential contribution.
Conversely, new members in inventive organizations are invited to define their contributions after gaining familiarity with
the organization and the work required to meet customer requirements; they are able to fulfill their potential. Such inventive environments are not valued by everyone because
many have learned too well to depend on others to tell them
what to do. Dependence constrains those who are depended
upon as well as those who are dependent. To build satisfying and productive work environments, everyone must work
interdependently — in partnership — with others. This requires
that we pay particular attention to how new members come
into the organization and make sure that the process of joining is based on partnership.

Plan

To follow is to plan — to arrange how work is to be done and
to develop the best means possible to do what is required to
meet and exceed customer requirements. When those who
do core work have line of sight, they are best able to plan work
flows, work processes, and production schedules. The old adage "Leave your brains at the door and do as you are told"
is replaced by "We will plan *how* best to do and control *what*
needs to be done."

   To plan is also to set priorities. In actuality, a priority
is nothing less than a promise or commitment; therefore, to
plan is to be accountable for the outcomes of set priorities —
for the results achieved, and not simply the tasks performed.

Organize

To follow is to organize work by focusing on outcomes and
results, not tasks and activities. To organize is to arrange
which people will do what in which order to achieve organi-

zational goals. To organize is to arrange space, schedules, tasks, forums, coalitions, skills development, start-ups, scale-ups, implementation of enhancements, and all other aspects of the work we do.

Inform

To follow is to provide information as to what is, what can be, and what should be eliminated or changed. It means we understand that it is not only what we do that determines our future, it is what we do not do. When we fail to inform, when we fail to participate, that which we fail to do determines our future as much, if not more, than all that we do. When we fail to inform, we reinforce what is rather than what can and should be — we reinforce rather than create organizational renewal, for who better than those closest to the work have the wisdom and knowledge to reinvent "how we do things around here."

Control

To follow is to control the provided resources and the processes by which work is done and, thereby, control the work itself. It is to focus on consistency — certainty — and the avoidance of loss by ensuring and exercising authority commensurate with responsibilities. It is to be accountable for that which is controlled — resources and results.

Staff

To follow is to manage oneself and one's interactions with others. This includes responsibility for hiring peers, integrating new work associates, managing working relationships among peers, and terminating relationships that fail. When such responsibility is considered part of leading, individuals avoid accountability for developing partnerships in which everyone can act in service to self and others.

Solve

To follow is to develop knowledge and resources to solve existing problems and anticipate prospective problems. It means to isolate obstacles that thwart achievement of desired results and recommend solutions that rid the system of these obstacles.

When we believe it is not our responsibility to solve problems, when we "throw it over the fence" to another function (which may or may not have the knowledge to enhance processes, the equipment, and all the other means by which we produce), we abandon the potential for renewal and reinforce the status quo. In essence, we forfeit our hopes for more satisfying work and a better organization. When we take responsibility for solving problems that plague us and our organizations, we increase our own and the organization's competence. I will always remember an employee on a production line who fashioned a part out of tin foil to enhance machine capability and reliability. The part was later fabricated by the equipment manufacturer and added to all of its machines. This same individual could have accepted the status quo because he was "not being paid" to enhance the equipment and make his job more satisfying. He chose to serve himself and, in so doing, to serve others. We make it better for ourselves when we are also willing to make it better for others.

Measure

To follow is to measure processes and results. Appropriate measurement criteria are based on customer requirements and the strategy by which the organization wishes to compete. These criteria are not fixed; rather, they are continuously examined in terms of reliability and appropriateness. Measurement criteria should not result in a paper trail aimed at reducing accountability. Measurement criteria should be based on an understanding of the economics of the business and its goals.

In inventive organizations, to follow is to seek *methods and measurements* that support achievement of goals and provide control in ways that serve the entire system. Most important, inventive organizations seek alignment between methods, measurements, and customer requirements. Such alignment is achieved when the introduction and use of methods and measurements are experienced as integrative and supportive of multiple levels of system.

To frame methods and measurement is to reframe "critical success factors" into "critical linkage factors." This means we know:

- How— Skill, competence, secrets, processes
- Who— Which people bring information and which people need information; networks, internal and external
- When— Development of new products, lead times, pacing market, closing out old products
- What— Mastery of consistent set of meanings, ability to see patterns, trends, applications, and new frameworks for thinking and doing
- Where—Market niche
- Why— Context (vision) and how efforts relate to context

All of this makes it possible for us to think systemically and achieve desired results.

Any method needs to be designed by those whose work is most affected by the method. To do otherwise means we cannot be sure new methods will be implemented correctly or that they will produce intended results. For example, "just-in-time" (JIT), which is a method for inventory control, can be a valuable resource. However, if those on the production line experience JIT as eliminating needed inventory buffers, regimenting work flows, and, thereby, creating workforce tension, they experience JIT as a method of driving a financial agenda with little or no concern for employee stress levels. The method is now seen as a "flavor-of-the month" technique that serves short-term financial goals at the expense of customers and employees.

In many important respects, our measurement criteria have not kept pace with our business operations or our need to create inventive organizations. The origins of these measurement criteria can be found in double-entry bookkeeping, which was invented in the fifteenth century. These criteria continue to be reinforced by CEOs who have been promoted predominantly from staff support functions, such as finance, marketing, and legal—a phenomenon of the past fifteen to twenty years. The loss of CEOs with production backgrounds has led to an obsession with "management by the numbers," and particularly management by the wrong numbers or incomplete numbers. For example, we are obsessed with the cost of labor and overlook the cost of equity as it pertains to processes such as paperwork that are no longer needed. We have proliferated staff functions to create and manage measurements and measurement criteria when such control belongs to line operations. This fragments core work and creates too many "hands in the pot"; it increases unnecessary boundary management and results in a lag in response time because where something occurs, where it is observed, and where it is controlled are in multiple functions. Further, many staff functions become customers of, instead of support to, line operations. How many reports for the finance and human resources functions serve the line functions required to produce the reports? And how many of these reports are driven by customer requirements?

Management by the numbers shows up everywhere. During my early tenure as director of human resources for the Federal National Mortgage Association (FNMA), I heard numerous complaints about the organization's Performance Review System. The system was designed so Human Resources could track and report the efficacy of a bell-shaped curve, which dictated that 5 percent of the workforce would be rated 1 for "unsatisfactory performance," 20 percent would be rated 2 for "does not meet performance standards," 40 percent would be rated 3 for "satisfactory," 20 percent would be rated 4 for "exceeds requirements," and 5 percent would be rated 5 for "outstanding." Interestingly enough, most managers never gave a 5. In their minds, it was not only unachievable, to give it meant you could never again rate the employee lower than that. Their faulty logic had everything to do with a half-baked system. The company had a performance review program; however, it did not have a performance planning program. It was impossible for managers to review what had not been planned.

There is no logic to support use of a bell-shaped curve. First, equal employment statutes argue for the comparison of individuals to standards, not to one another. Second, if a company's values are to hire, develop, and retain the best people, it is illogical to predetermine that many of the best hires will be unsatisfactory or need improvement in their performance. Third, if there are no plans against which to compare individual performance, any process that purports to be a legitimate performance review is an illusion. Most important, if plans and reviews are not linked at an individual level, annual unit plans and forecasted results cannot be linked at the group or organizational level. Success factors cannot be achieved if critical linkages are overlooked.

At FNMA, financial projections for salary expenditures drove performance percentages. At the beginning of each year, managers designated performance ratings for their subordinates and then filled in the forms according to their designations as people came up for review each month. Some managers were quite honest about their dilemma. Rather than try to convince subordinates that their performance warranted the overall ratings they received, the manager would say, "This is your year for a 3 rating. Next year it will be Sue's turn."

At an organizational level of system, a company cannot track its own performance properly when it sabotages the tracking of individual or group contributions. Most performance review processes, which should be designed to ensure a meaningful dialogue between boss and subordinate, are corrupted by numbers and *curves that make a mockery of such dialogue. One of my first efforts at FNMA was to appoint a joint Human Resources/Manager/Employee Task Force to create a process that would support an open and ongoing dialogue, about performance goals and results, between managers and their employees.*

The task force developed a Performance Planning and Review Process that made explicit the linkages between employee contributions, managerial expectations, and departmental success criteria. The planning and appraisal processes were the joint responsibility of the manager and the employee. This eliminated the "teacher/student," "one up, one down" context of the past and created an adult-to-adult discussion of expectations, contributions, and results.

The employees drove the process. They set performance goals, negotiated these with their managers, negotiated changes to these plans as business requirements changed, and sent their managers self-appraisals to indicate that it was time for a "formal" review. Employees on the task force proposed and got company agreement on the designations for ratings categories, which were changed from "1 to 5" to "Unacceptable," "Requires Improvement," "Good," "Commendable," and "Distinguished." The overall rating triggered the amount of the "merit increase." I put "merit increase" in quotations because we were not successful in getting the company to rethink and revise either the bell-shaped curve or the Hay System that drove this curve. Ultimately we failed because the critical linkage between rewards and reviews was overlooked.

CEOs and staff functions are not solely to blame for our archaic measurement criteria or for the overproduction of meaningless reports that clog the vital organizational arteries that could fuel invention. Financial analysts, who upgrade and downgrade corporate stocks and bonds, are largely responsible for the prevalent preoccupation with quarterly profits — with the creation of shareholder wealth — at the expense of our long-term investments in R&D, technology, plant and equipment — all of which support invention and lead to the creation of shareholder value.

Who should drive measurement factors and criteria? We need to start from scratch and let customer requirements dictate criteria that are sanctioned by those who serve the customer. All of this needs to occur in concert with the provision of resources that make desired success possible.

Sometimes a measurement factor is correct but the criteria for the factor need rethinking. Xerox measures customer satisfaction, which is important to measure. In an effort to regain market share and beat the competition, Corporate Customer Service established a four-hour response time as a measurement of customer satisfaction. This meant that from the time a service call was received until the time service was successfully rendered, no more than four hours could elapse. A longer response time adversely impacted a work group's customer satisfaction rating. A shorter response time had no impact. One work group decided its customers should determine the satisfaction ratings. They interviewed their customers and asked what response time was needed. The customers said it depended on circumstances. Sometimes they needed a two-hour response, sometimes four hours, and sometimes eight was just fine. Together, this work group and their customers wrote up three codes that they called code 1, code 2, and code 3. The customers set the criteria for each code and then used the appropriate code when they called for service. The work group promised to meet each code's response time, which they tracked. In four months, their customer satisfaction rating went from 65 percent to 100 percent, where it has remained for over three years. What they learned is that at least 50 percent of their calls are code 3, which requires an eight-hour response time. This gives them the ability to meet the code 1 and code 2 calls in the timeframes required.

Appraise

In inventive organizations, there is no need for elaborate feedback mechanisms and channels of communication. Corporate results accrue from whether or not customer requirements are met, and work is designed so that customer requirements are the critical success factors in every function performed. In this way, the work itself becomes the feedback mechanism — it meets specifications or it does not. And because everyone has line of sight, everyone can see their contribution to the whole.

Evaluate

To follow is to evaluate actions and results as a means of creating learning and developing greater competence and capacity. Inventive organizations evaluate what goes well and what does not go according to plan, because both outcomes contain the potential to learn more about how we learn.

Reward

To follow is to create ways to recognize individual and team efforts. In inventive organizations, the well-being of organizational members rises and falls with the well-being of the organization, and peers decide how to measure contribution and disperse rewards.

The issue of rewards is a loaded one; it is based on subjective assessments of the relationship between what people contribute and what they earn. During the Industrial Era, wages and compensation were driven by a labor market theory of value. Salary surveys indicated average compensation for particular jobs and a pseudoscience was made of evaluating the worth of work, creating job descriptions and salary grades, and determining timeframes for performance reviews. This "science" has been compromised by notions of cost-of-living-adjustments, availability of required skills (which drives rates up or down), and underlying assumptions that a four-year degree is worth more than twenty-five years of experience. At issue is how we value and evaluate contribution.

Employee abuses during the Depression, union and management divisiveness over compensation philosophies and practices, the continuing and exacerbated discrepancies between executive pay and organizational performance all have contributed to the real and perceived discrepancies between what people contribute and what they earn.

Today many organizations are replacing compensation systems based on time and task with new systems based on pay-for-knowledge, pay-for-skills, and gainsharing. Pay-for-skills is a difficult and bold revamping of current reward mechanisms because it flies in the face of the labor market theory of value. When we implement pay-for-skills, we value the creation of individual learning, organizational competence, and workforce flexibility over competitive regional labor rates. Unfortunately, pay-for-skills is a stopgap measure. As this system matures, people will "max" out— reach the upper limits of pay rates and stay there.

The next step is some form of gainsharing, which attacks deeply held values and underlying assumptions about who creates and who is entitled to share in organizational profits. To develop a gainsharing program, we must undertake an often painful assessment of our measurement criteria, accounting practices, and belief systems about the worth of individuals. This effort is best guided by an outside consultant who is a recognized expert in reward mechanisms, understands systems thinking, and has no axe to grind in helping the organization to examine its assumptions about the creation of wealth.

Ultimately, gainsharing and skills acquisition need to be combined so that the amount of gainsharing one receives is related to the skilled contribution one makes. Decisions as to how to distribute gainsharing dollars should be made by the unit receiving these dollars. The unit could be a team whose members decide how to distribute the reward, with or without participation and approval from their formal leader. A unit also could be a group of individual contributors who regularly work together but report separately to one individual.

Another challenge on the horizon has to do with state and federal statutes regarding pay. The Fair Labor Standards Act (FLSA) became law after the Great Depression. It makes a distinction between exempt (not eligible for overtime pay) and nonexempt (eligible for overtime pay) individuals. State laws that are more stringent than the FLSA supersede the federal statute. Union rules contain three workforce designations: hourly, salaried, and exempt. We need to revisit all of these designations and statutes as self-regulation at all levels of the workforce becomes reality. Those who do the work can best decide which work schedules balance personal needs and professional commitments.

Further, we need to revisit the FLSA definitions of clerical, professional, and management skill, which separate (1) work that involves manual dexterity from work that requires us to think, (2) work that requires decision making from routine work, and (3) work that is clerical in nature from work that is managerial. These distinctions were made prior to the advent of personal computers and our need to create inventive organizations. The distinctions no longer apply; worse, they impede the creation of partnerships and result in inequities in pay between people using the same skills—for example, typing—in performing their jobs.

Rewards are resources that can support (1) individual learning, (2) the development of organizational competence, (3) team spirit and a sense of organizational community, and (4) good customer and supplier relationships. Much more than other resources, rewards reflect practiced, as opposed to, espoused, organizational values. Today, organizations emphasize teams yet continue to reward individual performance. This disconnect between "talk" and "walk" creates a focus on "self," not a focus on service and support to the entire system.

Build Knowledge

To follow is to build knowledge. Parker Palmer, in his book *To Know as We Are Known: A Spirituality of Education* (1983), describes what is, for me, the most useful definition of knowledge within the context of this book. To paraphrase his work, to build knowledge is to search for truth, not just facts, theory, and objective reality. "To know in truth is to engage the known with one's whole self . . . to enter into a relationship with someone or something genuinely other than us but with whom we are bound. What will change is our relation to the facts or to the world the facts make. Truth requires the knower to become interdependent with the known . . . a co-participant in a community of relationships with other persons and things, with whatever our knowledge makes known" (p. 31).

We build knowledge by interacting with the system—customers, suppliers, stakeholders, and work associates—not by viewing the system from afar, hearing others' impressions of it, or doing as we are told. This interactive way of building knowledge is communal in nature and is based on differentiating and integrating I and other, subject and object. It is a way of knowing, a way that is born not only from our curiosity or need for control, but from our compassion. It is less individualistic and competitive and more cooperative, supporting interdependence, partnership, and pursuit of common cause. "Knowledge arises from the commitment of communities for a mutual, interactive quest to know and be known" (p. 37).

In the final analysis, if we are to build knowledge, "We must [perpetually] try to understand more about the knowledge we possess; for that knowledge also possesses us" (p. 6).

DEVELOPING CUSTOMER-SUPPLIER RELATIONSHIPS

To follow is to focus on external customers as a means of determining what is required to serve internal customers. Inventive organizations are designed from the customer requirements "in" and from the core work "out." This means that external customer requirements determine core work, and within all internal organizational relationships, each internal supplier serves each internal customer based on meeting external customer requirements.

RELATIONSHIP OF LEADING AND FOLLOWING EXPERTISE

To thrive in today's global economy, our organizations must master the complexities and dynamics of change — changing customer requirements, changing competitive environments, and changing markets. Our organizational strategies must be aligned with these changes and our organizational structures must be aligned with our strategies. We need to create dynamic flexible structures based on self-regulation and interdependence at all levels of system. Such structures require new models for leading and following. (See Chapter Nine.) Just like people and relationships, the models for leading and following are "in the process of becoming." They are not static. Leading and following are actions that evolve within the context of systems thinking and invention. The leading and following models are based on five assumptions:

1. Systems are relationships in action.
2. To think systemically is to understand boundaries and critical linkages.
3. To create an inventive organization is to coordinate hope and build organizational competence and community.
4. To perpetuate an inventive system is to manage interdependence and develop organizational meaning and learning.
5. To preserve an inventive system is to ensure conditions for continuous improvement, self-regulation, and renewal.

If we consider leading and following as behaviors rather than as fixed roles, we can more readily see the interdependence between expertise associated with guiding the development of systems and expertise required for individuals to serve self and others in pursuit of common cause. One supports the development of the other. Put another way, the ability to manage self and interactions with others arises out of the ability to manage the context in which relationships are developed. It is the interdependence between these acts and the fact that these acts can and should occur regardless of role or level in an organization that enables us to create inventive organizations capable of meeting and exceeding customer requirements.

In her book, *The Hero Within*, Carol Pearson writes:

There are no true hierarchies in soulmaking. The evolution of the collective human soul depends equally on each of us, and none of us is more important than anyone else. With knowledge comes the responsibility for creating environments that encourage growth and development. Those of us who are organizational leaders easily can see that we are responsible for the environment in our organization. However, everyone helps create environments. No leader does it alone. People need environments that are safe and supportive, in which they feel valued as unique individuals, in which their souls are honored and they are not seen as objects to be used and tossed aside. These environments also must provide a realistic level of challenge—enough so that people will not be bored or stay stuck in their ways but not too much so that success is impossible. Furthermore, people grow in places where honesty can be counted on and where integrity and appropriate assertiveness are expected and rewarded. And people need to be cared about enough that they will not be allowed to get away with being dishonest, manipulative, irresponsible or passive/aggressive. Healthy environments include caring but firm confrontation and consequences for behavior that is harmful

to others or to the group. Finally, people need environments characterized by a shared commitment to personal growth and that provide ongoing education and
discussion [1986, p. 161].

This is a poignant summation not only of inventive expertise but also of personal power and style—the three components of inventive acts of leading and following.

PART FOUR

MAKING THE TRANSITION: THE START OF THE RECONSTRUCTION

This section of the book is about making the transition. A better way to think of this is as the start of the reconstruction. We are having to reexamine and change our assumptions about organizations because we are in a transition from the late Industrial Era to the Information Era. As we make this transition, it feels as if everything is up for grabs—how we organize work, design processes, and manage ourselves and our organizations—and that there is not much to hold onto. In fact, we can hold onto three axioms that will support us as we rediscover such old ideas as quality, as we experiment with such new ways of operating as empowerment and self-managing teams, and as we rethink how we think. The three axioms are these:

1. Build a mile of road, drive a mile of road.
2. Make visible what is invisible.
3. The wisdom is in the system.

    The notion "Build a mile of road" comes from a belief that when we chart a new course, we are never certain we will arrive at our destination. We build the way in increments, one mile at a time. And we must drive the mile we have built to reach the place where we can begin to build the next mile. When we honor the journey as well as the destination, we can learn about how to build the next section of road from our experience in building the preceding one. Sometimes we discover the next section has to be reconfigured or the direction rethought because of events that were unforeseen when we chose our destination. In our efforts to move beyond where we are it is essential to remember that we can best manage the unknowable when we manage incrementally—when we build a mile of road and drive a mile of road.

The second axiom—"Make visible the invisible"—reminds us that if we are to be inventive we must think anew about all we take for granted. We must recognize our work associates for who they are and what they can do, not by job titles and hierarchy. We must question all that has become familiar—rules, boundaries, procedures—because all too often these have become invisible constraints. And we must regularly revisit our assumptions about success and failure if we are to move beyond the current status quo. When we view our organizations as a series of relationships, it is more apparent that our actions and interactions are based on invisible connections between how we think, what we value, how we know, and what we assume and believe. These invisible connections create organizational strategies, structures, policies, and operating procedures, none of which is the essence of our organizations. The essence is in what we hope and what we fear, what we avoid and what we dare. The essence of our organizations and the means for organizational renewal are invisible unless we make visible the invisible.

The third axiom—"The wisdom is in the system"—means that what we seek exists within the series of relationships that are the system. There are numerous examples of untapped wisdom in our relationships with customers, suppliers, work associates, and stakeholders. Wisdom remains untapped when it is not recognized or supported. It is constrained by our beliefs about "how we get things done around here." It remains contained because of the boundaries we draw and the ways in which we define organizational roles. It is only when we illuminate our entrenched assumptions that we can redraw boundaries and redefine roles in ways that enhance the nature and results of our organizational relationships.

When I met David, he was a chauffeur for a publisher of educational materials for kindergarten through eighth grade. David is a very bright young man who grew up in Japan and is fluent in Japanese. He not only knew what it took for a company to be successful in Japan, he probably had more information about the company for which he worked, from driving its executives around, than anyone else in the system did. He could see the big picture and the little picture, but no one asked for his opinions. David was invisible, except to those who took the time to talk to him as he performed the duties of his role—that of being a chauffeur.

One day while David was driving me on one of my many trips from the airport to the company's headquarters, he told me he had an idea that could create a profit center for the company and simultaneously create a convenient and much needed service for employees. The company had several limousines that were serviced in a small garage that was located at the headquarters. David thought the garage could service employees' cars, which would give them access to the automotive maintenance they needed without their having to take time away from work. The service, which could be offered at better than competitive prices, would create company revenue. This would turn the garage, which was a cost center, into a profit center. In the process, the employees would be provided with the convenience of having their cars fixed or maintained at their place of work for less cost than that associated with a dealership.

David understood interdependence better than anyone I met at the company. He understood ways to align individual interests and company interests. He knew about common cause. I called the company recently and learned that David is no longer an employee. His idea never had a proper hearing, if any hearing at all, because he was invisible except within his narrowly defined role as chauffeur. And although many may have defined him by the role he performed, David can lead as well as follow. Unfortunately, the company only availed itself of part of his ability. His potential and desire to serve and support the entire system was squandered in the box called his "role" in the organization.

These three axioms also apply to the three components of the models of leading and following in Chapter Nine. *Expertise* is aligned with "build a mile of road, drive a mile of road." Inventive expertise is in the process of evolving. What we know about required expertise in leading and following will be enhanced by our experiences and experiments as we continue to build and develop our organizations. Therefore, as we progress down each mile of road, what we learn should determine the expertise we need to build the next mile of road.

Personal power is tied to "make the invisible visible." Personal power is the only power we have that is permanent and cannot be taken away. All other power is temporal and based on circumstances and conditions that often are out of our control. To make this power visible is to acknowledge what we already know; namely, it is who we are much more than what title we hold that will determine the final verdict on our influence.

Style is tied to "the wisdom is in the system." The *partner* style best describes leading and following in a partnership of discovery in which everyone is accountable for uncovering and utilizing the full potential in every level of system — intrapersonal, interpersonal, group, and organizational.

The final chapters of this book are about the start of the reconstruction. Chapter Thirteen is about the development of a program for Xerox Corporation and what was learned about how to manage the transition between "how it used to be" and "how it is" to "what is possible." Chapter Fourteen is about what we might expect, what we can hope, and what we must dare as we transition ourselves and our organizations into the twenty-first century. Our only safety net during times of organizational transition is the nature of our organizational relationships. What is called for today are partnerships. These partnerships are forged when we are able to differentiate between the traditional roles of leader and follower and the acts of leading and following that renew us and our organizations.

13

The Wisdom Is in the System: Start from Where You Are

Xerox is a name known to everyone. It is the company that developed the first plain paper copier and created a revolution in office documentation. My involvement with Xerox began with the U.S. Marketing Group's Customer Services Organization when field managers were struggling to lead newly formed work groups. The story of these managers' efforts to define new acts of leading and following is a story of how one company that was created out of inventive technology suddenly became fixed and adaptive before managing the transition to become inventive, not only in its technology but in the very partnerships that underlie the organization's current success.

The plain paper copy story began in 1939, when Haloid-Xerox began to develop the process called xerography. It took from 1946 to 1959 to complete the research and production of the first plain copier, the 914. Xerox expected to sell 5,000 of these machines in three years, but by year's end 1962, two years after the machine had been introduced, 10,000 had been shipped and the company was backlogged with orders.

During the next fifteen years, Xerox dominated the industry. At one point, their main U.S. competition was 3M and IBM, but the acceptance of the Xerox product was so high and success was so overwhelming, the company became fixed on its own technology. In effect, Xerox was addicted to its greatness. Efforts were focused on developing bigger and faster machines, with more and more options, all of which resulted in higher costs. Because the company believed customer acceptance was assured, it lost touch with the market. And the market was changing.

By the mid-1970s, large companies wanted to place duplicating equipment strategically throughout their operations. The Japanese entered the copier business and introduced high-quality small and mid-sized machines that cost far less than a Xerox product. These machines also proved a perfect complement to the enormous growth in the late seventies and early eighties of new, small businesses; these customers needed smaller, less expensive, low-maintenance equipment. Xerox missed these important market signals as it continued to focus its energies on bigger and more costly machines. To complicate matters, quality had become a problem for Xerox—so much so that Xerox was embarrassed to find the reject rate for its Japanese affiliate, Fuji Xerox, to be a fraction of the rate for American Xerox parts. The company's focus on its own "belly button"—on its own internal assessments of what to build and what to measure—led to unhappy customers and forced Xerox to own up to a critical truth. Markets, not manufacturers, dictate product requirements, and quality can only be measured against customer requirements, not internally devised standards.

After the debacle of the late-1970s, Xerox entered the 1980s with a corporate mandate: customer obsession and quality control. Under the leadership of David Kearns, who left IBM to join Xerox in 1971 and became CEO in May 1982, the company organized quality circles. As part of creating these circles, Xerox trained people on problem-solving techniques, group dynamics, and interpersonal skills so they could come up with recommendations for manufacturing improvements. In 1983, the Leadership Through Quality process was introduced, based on external and internal benchmarking. Line management's role was identified as being one of coach and expediter rather than dictator. And customer satisfaction became the number one priority, with quality defined as meeting customer requirements. Thus Xerox became adaptive. And it became adaptive in a big way.

The first step toward implementing Leadership Through Quality was to train first- and second-level manufacturing managers in the same interpersonal skills that had been taught to the quality circle teams that had preceded the Leadership Through Quality process. Additionally, these managers learned a six-step problem-solving process and a nine-step quality-improvement process.

The company undertook intensified and institutionalized analyses of its competitive posture. It turned to benchmarking—measuring itself against the products, services, and practices of its toughest competitors—not simply in its own industry, but in others as well. For example, L.L. Bean was selected for distribution procedures, Deere Company for central computer operations, Procter & Gamble for marketing, and Florida Power and Light for its quality process. Benchmarking proved so valuable that today more than 240 different functional areas of Xerox are benchmarked against comparable areas in other companies.

As part of Leadership Through Quality, employees on the assembly lines were given more control. They could stop the line when problems were identified. At one point, a multi-million-dollar assembly line was scrapped because its configuration made it impossible for operators to talk with one another. Union and manufacturing management joined together in these quality efforts, but making quality equipment was just part of the story. Selling that equipment and ensuring quality service after the sale were as integral to retrieving lost market share as making equipment that met customers' needs.

Prior to 1984, when Leadership Through Quality became a way of operating for Marketing as well as Manufacturing, Charles Ray, Vice President for Customer Services, had introduced the idea of work groups to the Customer Services function in the U.S. Marketing Group. The organizational challenge was to move from a focus on "results" to creating "enablers" so the company could focus on quality. This transition looked like this:

Results Focus →	*Enablers* →	*Quality Focus*
■ Activity driven	■ Participative management	■ Customer focus
■ Short-term focus	■ Employee involvement	■ Long-term goals and short-term objectives
■ Win/lose	■ Quality work groups	■ Problem solving
■ Competition and bottom-line results	■ Gainsharing	■ Continuous quality improvement
■ Individual focus		■ Cooperation and teamwork

As part of this transition, from a results orientation to an enabler and quality focus, the pros and cons of work group strategies were analyzed, the risks were evaluated for both the groups and managers, and the potential paybacks were assessed. At first, work groups were introduced as optional, not "have to." But by 1987, with continuing changes in customer requirements, increased pressure from global competition, and operating expenses increasing faster than revenue, work groups became mandatory in Customer Services, based on empirical data that showed high levels of empowerment and real customer satisfaction could be achieved in a team-based structure.

Xerox learned many valuable lessons as it moved toward a systemic approach to its manufacturing operations through its introduction of quality circles, problem solving, and quality processes. The company took these learnings and turned its attention to Sales, Administration, and Customer Services. Each of these entities had been a separate functional area, with different goals and reward systems, that reported through separate hierarchies to Rochester. However, in the customer's eyes, selling and servicing equipment were one process, not three. Structuring Sales, Administration, and Customer Services as separate entities made it easy for things to fall between the cracks. Salespeople sold machines with service warranties and maintenance contracts that were serviced by Customer Services technical representatives. Administration handled billing. At best, this structure created a relay of sorts. At worst, the baton was easily dropped between the handoff from Sales to Service.

Xerox changed its functional approach to a systems approach by integrating the selling and/or leasing and the servicing of its products. The company decided to link Sales, Administration, and Customer Services by creating district partnerships, with common goals and reward systems for each function. As part of this reorganization, changes were made in the span of control for first-level Customer Services managers. From 1984 to 1989, these field managers' span of control increased from twelve technical representatives to twenty. Most excess field managers were assigned to service or to other positions, and few decided to leave the business.

These changes in structure, roles, and people indicated changes in the company's underlying operating assumptions. The company was moving from independence to interdependence, which came about for four primary reasons. First, Xerox had learned the painful lesson that it did not have a captive audience. Second, the Leadership Through Quality process implicitly included steps to put more control at the point where work occurred—first on the manufacturing floor through training people in problem-solving and quality-assurance processes and second in district partnerships that could create a "seamless" process for customer sales and service. Third, to "circle the wagons and shoot in" was the debilitating outcome of too much internal competition and "not-invented-here syndrome," both of which occurred with the separation of sales, customer help requests — Administration — and technical service. Fourth, Xerox needed to stop the red ink and prevent further erosion of its customer base while simultaneously recapturing lost market share.

New structures can be announced, people can be redeployed, and roles can be rewritten in new job descriptions; however, old habits die hard, and old policies, procedures, reward mechanisms, controls, information flows, decision-making processes, and outmoded skills die even harder. True, there were new District Partnerships made up of highly skilled senior management people and those in Sales and Administration could delegate far more authority than had been the case when Sales, Administration, and Customer Services each had its own steep hierarchy that reported to Rochester. True, there was a manager of regional customer service operations in each of the five districts who was accountable for that region's district managers. The district managers were accountable for nine field managers, each of whom was accountable for between sixteen and twenty technical service representatives (known as tech reps). The increased span of control in a one-on-one, facilitator-subordinate hierarchy created an unworkable situation for field managers. Tech reps may have been assigned to an office, but their jobs were to move from one customer location to another to service requests deployed by Customer Support. How could one field manager manage as many as twenty subordinates whose jobs were "on the road"?

The answer was work groups. Why not create the idea of partnership between tech reps through work groups. Work groups would establish a more empowered environment, which would enable tech reps to find, use, and be accountable for better ways to meet and exceed customer requirements. The implicit value was interdependence at all levels, with a focus on customer satisfaction. The idea made sense. Its implementation was not easy.

Without any real understanding of what a work group might be, field managers configured these groups based on a continuation of normal territory assignments. For example, some field managers put all level 1 tech reps into a group. The levels represented the complexity of the machines people were trained to work on. A tech rep 1 worked on smaller, less complex machinery. A tech rep 5 worked on the largest and most complex equipment. The stress levels for the different tech reps were related to the complexity of the equipment. This was problematical when some field managers used geographic territory to create groups; for example, all representatives working in a rural or urban area were combined into a group that included level 1 to level 5 reps.

A tech rep 1's goal was to complete quality work quickly and move onto the next customer. Frequently these reps saw their customers once and never saw them again or saw them infrequently, which did not enable them to create strong customer-supplier relationships. When they saw the customer, the customer's machine was down and the customer was anxious and wanted a quick, quality repair. Because time was of the essence, there was little opportunity for relationship building. The real need was to move rapidly from one location to the next. Average repair time enabled level 1 reps to repair six to eight machines in one day. Little customer relationship and moving quickly created stress.

At the opposite end of the spectrum was the tech rep 5, who was frequently in one customer's location for several days at a time and on a regular basis. These reps worked on larger, more complex equipment that required skilled preventive maintenance. When repairs were needed, the complexity of the equipment resulted in longer service calls. These reps built stronger customer-supplier relationships. The stress in their jobs was from mastering the complexity of the equipment and being able to get the machine up and running as quickly as possible. Reps usually entered the hierarchy as a tech rep 1 and moved up to higher level

positions and more complex equipment as customer buying patterns—purchases of more complex and larger equipment—created demands for more highly skilled reps.

The newly configured work groups represented a pot-
pourri of success and chaos—chaos specifically related to
what occurs when familiar structures and underlying assumptions about how to work give way to new ideas about
how best to operate. In many cases, the concept of work
groups was foreign to reps who were accustomed to working alone. Suddenly they were part of a group, which had
more responsibility, accountability, and authority to make
group decisions. Many of the older and longer-tenured tech
rep 5s were openly against work groups. They preferred
the old tradition of being given a list of customer calls and
performing their jobs solo.

Even with work groups, the increased span of control
left many field managers experiencing enormous difficulty in
coaching, counseling, reviewing, and ensuring that all the business processes were adhered to and all the business goals
achieved. Xerox had a strong value on inspection for results
as measured by customer satisfaction, which is not surpris-
ing given its previous history of ignoring the customer. Inspection and self-regulation can easily be interpreted as clash-
ing values. In reality, they were experienced by field managers
as competing priorities. Given that field managers had come
up through the hierarchy, they knew about control and how
to control. They knew far less about how to create conditions
for self-regulation. It is no wonder that in feeling responsible
for results, field managers felt out of control trying to manage
sixteen to twenty direct reports, work group or no work group.
The problem of coordinating groups was solved with the creation of a customer services specialist—one person from each
group who was promoted to a higher level and assisted the work
groups in processes required for their growth. The customer
services specialist also became the link between the field manager and the work group in many locations. In effect, Xerox
put back more "management" than it had eliminated when

it increased the field manager's span of control. The difference was that this new level of "manager" was actually a lower level "coordinator."

Work groups received training on decision making, problem solving, the quality process, and interpersonal skills. The customer services specialists were trained to play a facilitator role in each group. And soon the field managers felt even more uncomfortable. They were now caught between directives that were coming from on high (to keep improving, measuring, and inspecting for results) and the counterdependent insurgence of work groups that either wanted to be left alone to do what they had been trained to do or were highly resentful that they had to take on "managerial responsibility." From tech reps to district managers, individuals factionalized into three groups: true believers, forced believers, and nonbelievers.

In late 1987, Bob Barstatis, who was part of Xerox's Organization Effectiveness Group, asked if I could spend an hour with him so he could learn more about work redesign. I could see that Bob was troubled about something. As he began to tell me the story of how Xerox created work groups, I recognized a familiar quandary. Here was a company that had gone from fixed to adaptive and had articulated the aspiration to become inventive, yet was still operating out of the old paradigm. Work groups had become an edict because managers had been reluctant to give up power that would enable employees to create customer satisfaction. The chaotic external environment, increased global competition, and significant loss of market share had driven Xerox's transition, yet at an individual level, people were operating out of *fear* of the unfamiliar, not service and support to the entire system, not *flow*, and the elimination of the old familiar organizational structure—form—was the cause.

I told Bob about an approach wherein the employees who do the work are the ones who redesign the way work is done, and their efforts are guided by a steering committee who provide minimum critical specifications that must be met in the proposed redesign. I took him through the steps of a customer analysis, a work flow analysis, an upset or noncon-formance analysis, a quality of work life analysis, and a values analysis, all of which create the material out of which a new structure is designed. Bob was grateful for my observations, but he seemed even more troubled than when we began our conversation. I knew I had validated many of his concerns and he was not sure what to do with his awareness. How can one person influence such a large system?

In March of 1988, I received a call from Bob. He invited me to meet with key members of Xerox's regional organi-zation effectiveness staff and with Bob Mann, who was man-ager of customer services training for all of Xerox's U.S. Mar-keting Group. Bob Mann presented his need to create a man-agement training program for field managers and roll it out by June. This program was intended for all 800 customer ser-vices field managers throughout the United States. Bob wanted to know if I could deliver their customer requirements in the timeframe they stipulated, what my approach would be, how much it would cost, and how Xerox would take over the run-ning of this program once the pilot was fine-tuned. All I kept thinking about was if training was the "solution," and if a suc-cessful program were to be designed, what implications would it have on other aspects of the system. I also was aware that this was Xerox—that magic company, so good at training that at one time they had a subsidiary called Xerox Learning Systems, a subsidiary whose training products I had used in the 1970s when I was at The Automobile Club of Southern California.

As a consultant, I always feel the tension between want-ing to be responsive to my client's needs and wanting to cre-ate awareness. It is so easy to "catch the client's disease" and move from *sensation* to *action* too fast. How could I get Xerox to understand that "to go slow is to go fast" when they were asking for a program—from design to implementation—in ten weeks? And how could I get up to speed on what they had already done in terms of training field managers so that what-ever was designed would integrate with previous training efforts (as opposed to being experienced as an "add on"). Xerox was on a quest to integrate its system, and I wanted to support that in the development of this program.

I asked my late colleague Kathleen Emery to work with me on this project. At that time, we both were senior associates for Block Petrella Weisbord, a firm that specializes in whole-systems improvement. We began to work on a preliminary design, which we would take to the organization effectiveness specialists, obtain their input on it, and continue to flesh it out. We requested and received all the materials Xerox had used to train field managers over the past ten years. We received a wheelbarrow full. We also asked to talk with several district managers and field managers around the country to get a better sense of their needs.

Our design was based on three underlying assumptions. The first was that we wanted to integrate this training effort with previous efforts and use the Xerox language and models to avoid adding new terms to the considerable vocabulary already learned by field managers. (David Kearns, CEO of Xerox, is quoted in the May 1990 *Training & Development Journal* as saying, "The key thing about training is that it should integrate. The strategy of the company, the direction of the company and the skills and behaviors that people need in order to get the job done should all be combined and integrated into training" [p. 42].) Second, we realized that every field manager and district manager had come into their roles from the traditional one-on-one boss-subordinate hierarchy. None had ever worked in a work group. Third, we were concerned that the philosophy of "the individual as king" was being replaced with the philosophy of "the group as king." (This dilemma is being experienced in every company that decides to move toward team-based management. It is a case of the pendulum swinging from one extreme to another. We wanted to balance the "I" and the "We.")

We believed it was important to use this training experience to bring district managers and field managers together and put both in their subordinates' roles. District managers would experience what it was like to be a field manager and how district managers could support field managers in transitioning to their new role. Field managers could experience what it was like to be a member of a work group and what the group needed in the way of leadership from field managers.

Because the purpose of the program was to support field managers in managing groups (rather than individuals), Kathleen and I used the Tuckman model, which was familiar to Xerox managers, as the basis of understanding group dynamics. This model—which describes group development as *form, storm, norm,* and *perform*—created the first four sections of the program. We believed it was important for field managers to experience each aspect of group development.

The whole of the pilot included not only *form, storm, norm,* and *perform,* but a section on how to maintain a high-performing group and a section on the leader's personal transition. On June 5, 1988, the pilot was conducted at the Embassy Suites in Ventura, California. Twenty participants—two family groups, that included two district managers and their respective family groups of eight field managers each, attended along with Bob Mann and four organization effectiveness specialists—Bob Barchevsky, Rich Thier, Pam Klobucher, and Dave Holmes.

Kathleen and I had our hands full. In addition to conducting the pilot and debriefing with the organization effectiveness specialists at the end of each day, we had numerous logistics to manage. We had arranged with the hotel to help us with an assignment we were going to ask each group to perform once they had formed into groups. The assignment was for each group to conduct a quality survey of the hotel. The hotel told us the Xerox participants could have access to any hotel employee; however, they could not approach paying guests other than members of our own group. In return for their cooperation, we invited the hotel management to sit in on the groups' quality assessment presentations once they had completed their assignments.

The logistics became the easy part. What was hard was that both the participants and the organization effectiveness specialists were going through the change cycle (see Figure 2.2) simultaneously. People arrived in "status quo." By the afternoon of the first day, they were into "denial." By the morning of the second day, everyone was into "confusion." We kept telling each other and the organization effectiveness specialists that this was to be expected, in fact welcomed. Confusion means you are getting closer to learning. But the anxiety was very high, and it took every ounce of our best consulting skills to keep the specialists in "awareness" at the end of each day (and not to catch their dis-ease, which had them wanting to redesign the pilot, point by point, day by day). The sections of the pilot were as follows:

Program Kickoff. Participants were told there are thirty-two hours of material and four days in which to work. They were asked to decide their own work schedule, which was the first of many experiences with self-regulation. They chose to work from 7:30 A.M. to 6:30 P.M. each day, with a one-hour lunch, so they could leave at 11:30 A.M. on Friday and beat the traffic home.

Participants received a brief history of the company's Leadership Through Quality strategy and how this program supported the strategy. People were asked to select a partner for the session, someone they could watch and provide feedback to at the end of the session.

Form Stage. Field managers were asked to form four groups, two per district manager. They were given sandwich boards and asked to write down their skills as members of a group, walk around and read each other's boards, and select work groups. The district managers, who were acting as field managers, were told they could intervene or not intervene; however, if they intervened, they were to write down the intent of their interventions and their outcomes.

Once groups were formed, the symptoms and antidotes for diagnosing and intervening into the Form Stage were developed by the participants. At this time, they moved out of their work group roles and into their back-home roles of managers as a means of bridging the classroom experience with back-home applications. They each recorded their learnings as preparation for a back-home exercise that was explained at the end of the session.

Norm/Storm. Each group was told it would be asked to perform a task. And each group was asked to write a mission statement (goals), determine roles members would play (facilitator, scribe, timekeeper, link to the district manager who was playing field manager, and so on), determine processes to be used (decision making by consensus or majority rule, for example), and what their relationships would be with one another (ground rules) and with their district manager who was acting as a field manager.

This part of the program created both norming and storming—managing differences and agreements. Again, field managers, played by district managers, had the option to intervene.

After norms were decided, the first video was made. Each member of a work group sat in front of a video recorder with his team mates and made the statements, "I want _____ and we, as a group, need _____." These wants and needs included their expectations of the district manager, who was acting as field manager and who made an "I want and we need" statement to each of his two work groups. Each person saw a playback of their portion of the tape. Each was asked to say what they liked about what they had said, and then his or her group members were invited to state what they liked. The emphasis was to build on strength. Video is a very powerful tool when used interactively in training.

The symptoms and antidotes for diagnosing and intervening into norm/storm stages were developed by the groups, along with learnings that would prepare participants for the end-of-session, back-home exercise.

Perform. The names of four areas of the hotel were written on a flipchart. Each was to be surveyed for quality using the Xerox nine-step quality process. Each work group selected an area to work on. This involved some negotiation between groups. At this point, the district managers, who were playing field managers, were given a whole packet of material that could be useful to their groups. They had the option of offering this material or waiting for the groups to ask for support. Whatever they did, they were asked to record the intent and outcome of their intervention.

Without exception, the four work groups became counterdependent. They relied on each other and never asked for assistance from the district manager who was acting as a field manager. This mirrored the behaviors of Xerox's real work groups; however, during this stage of the program, the participants were unaware that they were duplicating the behaviors of their subordinates.

Part of the instructions given to work groups included a request that they set a midpoint milestone in their task and that once they hit that milestone, they stop working.

When the groups hit their milestones, the district managers, acting as field managers, announced that some personnel changes were going to be made. They selected one person from each team and switched them with a person from another team. The purpose of this announcement was to allow groups to experience the addition of a new person and the loss of a work associate. The teams were shocked. They had bonded, and a certain amount of competition had arisen as to which team was going to be the best team. The orientation of the new member was up to the group and the new member. Again, the district managers acting as field managers could intervene if they chose to.

When their tasks were completed, the management of the hotel attended the presentations. They were so impressed with the findings and recommendations that they knocked $1,800 off the final bill for Xerox. I had occasion to revisit that hotel two months later and found they had implemented almost all of the recommendations.

At the end of the Perform Stage, symptoms and antidotes for diagnosing and intervening into the Perform Stage were developed by the participants. They also recorded their learnings for their back-home exercise.

Maintenance. Once teams become high performing, the question of how to maintain commitment and performance arises. At this point in the program, work groups were disbanded and field managers and district managers resumed their real roles.

This section included linkage of headquarters, regional, and work group strategic plans and goals, and positioned the field manager as a resource provider so that goals could be achieved. To be resource providers, field managers needed training in meeting management, managing differences and agreements, decision making, active listening, and in how to support and confront. Working in groups of four, participants were to develop a fifteen-minute module that would train other participants in a specific skill. The emphasis was on distinguishing between being a resource provider who was "directive" and one that was "facilitative" (meaning customer oriented, with the "back-home" customer being the work group). These modules were presented and feedback was given as to whether the development and presentation of the module had been directive or facilitative.

Personal Transition. In this section of the program, field managers paired up with the partners selected at the beginning of the program and each gave the other feedback as to behaviors that facilitated group development and those that inhibited group development. The purpose of this exercise was to create more awareness of the intent and impact of individual behavior on group behavior and to set the stage for some back-home partnering to coach and counsel each other as peers.

Field managers evaluated the stages of development for each of their respective, back-home work groups and assessed the group's developmental needs. They then focused on their own support requirements to ensure they would be able to support their work groups. Each selected another field manager who was geographically suited to be a peer coach and they discussed how as partners to support one another and celebrate success.

A second video was made with each family group. Each field manager made a commitment to his or her own transition, stating before the camera, "This is what I will let go of, this is what I will hold onto, and this is what I will move toward." Each one also asked for support from other field and district managers to make this transition. The district managers made the same statements. As with the first video, each person saw a playback of his or her statements, noted what he or she liked about what they had said, and then received feedback from family group members as to what others liked about what was said. Again, the emphasis was to build on strength.

Close. At the close of the program, participants were asked, if they had it to do over, what they would do differently in this program. The unanimous opinion was that they had been foolish to work from 7:30 A.M. to 6:30 P.M. everyday just to get out by 11:30 A.M. on Friday. If they had it to do over, they would have scheduled in some free time during the day so they could take advantage of being at the beach. Additionally, at the beginning of the program, Kathleen and I offered to hold rap sessions on any topic the participants wanted to spend extra time on. One morning, two-thirds of the class attended a 6:30 A.M. rap session.

We had been using a working title, and we wanted the pilot group to have the opportunity to name this program, so the participants were asked to name the program. They chose the name Manager as Work Group Developer, known as MAWGD.

Participants completed program evaluations, as did the organization effectiveness specialists and the data confirmed that everyone had passed out of the box called confusion. Most were into invention and some were still in discovery.

Follow-Up. Six months after completing the program, field managers and district managers reconvened to review their "Holding On and Letting Go" videotapes and to check their progress and state what additional support they needed to move forward. Responsibility Charts were introduced as a tool for supporting the continuing transition to self-regulation at all levels of the organization.

The end of the pilot signaled the beginning of another phase. It was obvious that the organization effectiveness specialists needed a Train the Trainer session because they were not accustomed to delivering experiential training of the nature of MAWGD. Most of their training skill was teacher-centered learning, where the presenter is the "show," next is the material, and last are the participants. Most of these specialists were highly skilled presenters, entertaining and good at teaching. They now had to make their own transitions. We described it as moving to a learner-centered focus wherein the participants were the "show," next was the material, and finally the facilitator.

The Train the Trainer session was given in August in San Francisco with about twenty organization effectiveness specialists in attendance. It was a tough three days, during which each had to facilitate the group in some portion of the program. Each specialist was offered an opportunity to be shadowed by either Kathleen or me when they conducted the program for the first time. Several accepted the offer. They worked in pairs. One pair evidenced all the counterdependency manifested by the work groups in the pilot. They decided to go it alone. On the second day of their first program, the participants walked out. They perceived no value from the program, which was designed to be highly experiential. The presenters, who were inexperienced with facilitating experiential learning, were using their familiar lecture mode. The revolt was an awakening. In one of the specialists' words, it was the "most sobering and learningful experience" of their lives. They had experimented, it had not worked, and they had learned. This pair later turned out to be one of the best teams of facilitators for MAWGD.

When it came to linking the learnings and outcomes of MAWGD to the Leadership Through Quality initiative, the organization effectiveness specialists knew the importance of creating firsthand knowledge of this program for those in the hierarchy who managed the district managers and field managers. I was asked to conduct a one-and-a-half-day version of the program for everyone in Regional Operations and all the headquarters Customer Service Staff in Rochester. Many of those invited were disgruntled to learn they were expected to take one-and-a-half days out of their hectic schedules to experience and understand MAWGD. And without exception, at the end of the program, every group said, "We should have experienced the entire program." In fact, this was not necessarily true. The program had been designed for managers of work groups, and the regional and headquarters managers were not managing groups.

Did MAWGD as part of the Leadership Through Quality strategy solve all the issues attendant on leading and following in inventive organizations? No. The program built a mile of road. There is still a ways to go. Only recently have people been evaluated based on work group performance, and not simply on individual contribution. Some of the old policies and procedures, measurement criteria, and inspection processes continue. It is a hard task to dismantle methods of caretaking and control that are ingrained not only in the Xerox culture but in the culture of most American organizations. This statement by Peter Kolesar sums up the situation neatly:

> Xerox has yet to resolve how to do all the "improvement stuff" and still make it possible to sell product. Xerox, its Baldrige Award notwithstanding, recognized the problem but never resolved it. It took Xerox senior managers years to recognize that major elements of its well-designed "Leadership Through Quality" program were not being effectively implemented, that it was not fulfill-

ing on its grand design. Under pressure for quarterly results, many business unit managers at Xerox had gone back to business as usual and quality management processes had been in effect shelved. Xerox was finding that, strenuous as they are, quality program design and quality training are the easy parts of total quality. The implementation is what is really difficult. Four years after the roll out, when Xerox did a rigorous self-assessment as part of its preparation for the Baldrige Award, it created an extensive list of required enhancements to its quality efforts. The deep culture, systems and technology changes that the highest levels of quality management require do not appear to yield to the "quick study" and rapid implementation that the American corporate culture seems to demand [Kolesar, 1993, pp. 163–164].

And yet, within the old paradigm, some have created a new paradigm. One regional manager, Theresa Myers, said, after she had been through the "roll up" of MAWGD, that she was "no longer inspecting for results," she was inspecting "for support."

Has progress been made? Yes, significant progress, and it continues. In 1989, Xerox won the Malcolm Baldrige Award for Quality. The company benchmarked its quality process against the Baldrige standards and confirmed its own progress through its Leadership Through Quality strategy. And change continues as Xerox continues to stand the pain of looking at itself through its customers' eyes. Recently, Xerox decided to reduce the regional staffs and reduce the number of levels between senior management and where the work gets done. Is this creating more transitions and more uncertainty? Of course. Xerox continues to invent its future and its organization, and this creates transitions — for individuals and for the organization. The company has learned and some of the lessons have been painful. Years ago it lost out on the idea of the Dynabook, which was developed at their Research Center in Palo Alto (PARC) and the technology later became Apple computer. Today, Xerox engages its customers in helping to identify what is needed before it is produced and they continue to obsolete existing advantages as they move toward creating the company as it is defined — not in the copier business, but in the document processing business.

Xerox may not be ahead of everyone in these endeavors, but they have approached the nineties with a systemic view of their operations — a view that is based on meeting and exceeding customer requirements; streamlining essential work that creates customer satisfaction; living out the values of partnership with customers, work associates, and the work itself; moving forward to create support and control — self-regulation — at every level of the system; continuously improving and continuously inventing; and taking steps toward creating an organization where everyone can act in support and service of the whole while honoring the "I," the "We," and the "Us."

LEARNINGS FROM XEROX

My own learnings from this assignment were numerous. First, *the acts of leading come from the acts of following.* Whether we choose to lead or to follow, a key influence on each of us is the expectations of those with whom we work. This means that in addition to the nature of tasks with which we are engaged; our previous experience of self and others with respect to leading and following; the behaviors required by the stage of the group's evolution, organizational norms, and reward systems; *a key influence on our behavior comes from those our actions impact.* In the case of a leader, a key influence is those who follow. To state this more clearly, I believe the acts of leading evolve from the needs of those who follow. In inventive organizations, these needs are met, partially met, or ignored, based on the three critical components of the models on leading and following: our personal power, style, and expertise.

The development of Xerox's Manager as Work Group Developer is a clear example of how *inventive organizations build relationships from the top down and the bottom up.* The managers were put in charge of work groups. They took on this responsibility without any previous experience or training in how to manage groups. While this was not a planned strategy, it was serendipitous. It was out of the needs of those who followed — the members of the work group — that the expected actions of the manager evolved. The training that was delivered to the managers was designed to support the needs of their followers.

This notion of leading developing from the needs of those who follow is grounded in the entire organization being focused on customer requirements, core work, and organizational values. And it is driven by what Lisa Faithorn, an anthropologist, ecologist, and consultant, calls "three ways of seeing — me or you, me and you, us" (1990, p. 13). It is the Us — the "Us" in self-regulation that is illuminated in Chapter Seven; the "Us" in interdependence that is illuminated in Chapter Eight; and the "Us" in the word *trust,* which underlies *personal power,* illuminated in Chapter Ten; the "Us" of partnership that is developed under *style* in Chapter Eleven; and the "Us" in developing *expertise* in managing systems and ourselves and interactions with others that was illuminated in Chapter Twelve — that makes possible what Lao-tzu wrote so long ago: "When the . . . work is done, the people will say it happened naturally."

Second, the acts of leading and following are acts of creating value — for customers, stakeholders, suppliers, and employees. By *value* I mean the ability to simultaneously create

- Superior value in the eyes of the customer
- Dynamic competitive advantage
- Long-term shareholder value
- Supplier partnerships that focus on benefit for both parties

■   Employees sharing in the gains they create in their organizations

Certainly there are programs and strategies that address competitive competence, competitive advantage, shareholder value, and gainsharing. What we need is to lead and follow in ways that simultaneously address all of these needs so the entire system is served.

One example of what I am describing is what has been espoused by Jack Welch, Chairman and CEO of General Electric. He embarked on a strategic redirection of GE in 1986 that on paper seems to embody the underlying worth of creating value for everyone. His aim is to make GE number one or two globally by "combining financial strength, market position, and technology leadership with an organizational focus on speed, agility, and simplicity." Welch goes on to say that "GE has achieved world market-share leadership in nearly all of its 14 businesses. In 1988, its 300,000 employees generated revenues of more than $50 billion and net income of $3.4 billion." GE's business leaders are charged with "creating and growing new global business. Each staff person has to ask, 'How do I add value? How do I help make people on the line more effective and more competitive?'" Welch is "championing a companywide drive to identify and eliminate unproductive work in order to energize GE's employees" (something called Work Out). He is seeking ways to "release emotional energy at all levels of the organization and encourage creativity and feelings of ownership and self-worth." He says, "Ten years from now, we want magazines to write about GE as a place where people have the freedom to be creative, a place that brings out the best in everybody. An open, fair place where people have a sense that what they do matters, and where that sense of accomplishment is rewarded in both the pocketbook and the soul" (Tichy and Charan, 1989, pp. 111–120).

Second, model what you teach. Kathleen and I partnered in the MAWGD program and organization effectiveness specialists partnered in delivering the final product, an example of partnership that is a strong value within Xerox. We provided opportunities for participants to experience self-regulation within the training program, and we modeled facilitative, rather than directive, styles.

Third, training should be just-in-time. Get the people in their roles and the structure in place and then train. This creates better potential for participants to apply their learnings to their jobs because they already are struggling with the challenges of these jobs.

Fourth, I learned that consultants, too, go through the cycle of change in every client assignment. What I most need to do as I go through this process is to avoid catching the client's dis-ease. The client's fears can be contagious; if I catch them, I help solidify the status quo instead of supporting and exploring the successive needs to hold on—denial—and then let go—confusion.

HOW TO INTEGRATE AND DIFFERENTIATE OUR DUAL NEEDS TO LEAD AND FOLLOW

The story of Xerox's Manager as Work Group Developer program tells how training was used as the context in which field managers and district managers differentiated and integrated their dual needs to lead and follow. They did this by viewing themselves as individual systems, and in so doing, they began to better understand how to create fit between their intentions, their actions, and the contribution they sought to make in the workplace.

We can use Xerox as an example of how to view ourselves as systems. In our working lives, each of us receives inputs that we convert into outputs. Our inputs come from suppliers—those who give us work. These suppliers may be in the chain of command to whom we report, they may be in staff support functions, or they may be external customers who give us direct inputs or requests. We may complete our conversion process alone or with others in the system. Regardless, our outputs are directed toward a customer—someone who may be internal but ultimately leads to the external customer of the organization.

Figure 13.1 is a schematic of the individual as an open system. As you look at it, ask yourself these questions:

1. When you picture yourself as a system, what are the forces that impact you? They may or may not be the same as external forces mentioned in the figure. They may also include your boss, time constraints, or demands on your attention and energy from myriad "others."

List these forces, and beside each one indicate how it impacts your ability to lead and follow.

2. What do you value in your relationships with customers, work associates, and your work itself? In what ways do the outside forces you have identified affect your ability to live out these values?

List your values and note the impact outside forces have on your living out each one. Put the two lists aside.

3. Think of the process by which your company creates and brings products and services to market. What words come to mind that describe this process?

Write these words down and then look at how you would describe the way your organization is managed. What are the similarities?

What are the similarities between your operating style, that of your organization in managing itself as an entity, and the process by which your company creates and brings product or service to market?

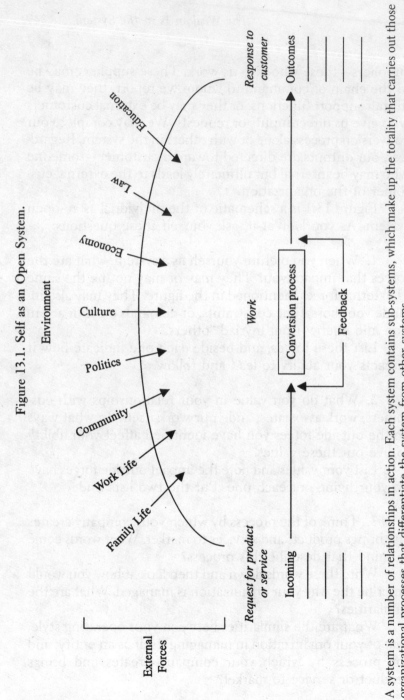

Figure 13.1. Self as an Open System.

A system is a number of relationships in action. Each system contains sub-systems, which make up the totality that carries out those organizational processes that differentiate the system from other systems.

DISCOVERING YOUR OWN DISCOVERY PROCESS

If you look back at the six frameworks for inventive organizations and the questions you answered about yourself as a system, you can begin to uncover your own needs for support and control. This discovery will enable you to transition into acts of leading and following that create inventive systems. First, each of us needs to forgive the context in which we have been working. It is easy for us to feel that we are at the mercy of a bureaucratic system that has choked off its own creativity and, perhaps, its ability to survive. It is not uncommon for us to feel overpowered by an awareness of how processes used to create and market products become processes used to manage and, very often, thwart organizational learning and the creation of competence and community. So, to forgive the context is also to forgive ourselves and whatever powerless feelings we may have with respect to our organizations. The question now is What kind of influence do we have on our organizations and what kind of influence do we seek?

To lead and follow is to create value for customers, shareholders, suppliers, and employees. (See Figure 13.2.) To create participation, productivity, and learning all at once, we must ensure that everyone understands the various aspects of the system: the economics (capital, budgets, resource constraints, and rewards), technical aspects (tasks, technology, information flows, decision-making processes, operational boundaries), social elements (structure, roles, people, skills, managerial boundaries), and the components of the built environment (layout, facilities, electronic infrastructure, ergonomics, and so forth). With this understanding, everyone has the ability to influence the organization. To know to what degree we use this ability we need to ask ourselves:

1. What is my impact on end-user requirements?

2. What is my impact on the core work that meets or exceeds these requirements?

Figure 13.2. Acts of Leading and Following.

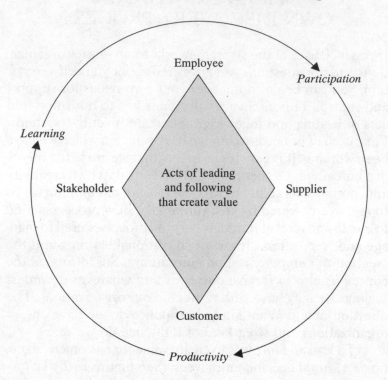

3.   What is my impact on the espoused values of this organization? Do I walk our talk when it comes to how we want to relate to customers, work associates, and the work itself?

4.   What is my impact on developing a systems perspective — on creating awareness and actions that strengthen the linkages necessary to support relationships in action?

5.   What is my impact on invention — on going beyond the unexpected by creating an environment that supports experimentation — *safe emergencies* — learning, and the development of core competence and capacity?

6.   What is my impact on self-regulation — on ensuring that

support and control exist to enable everyone to act in service to self and others?

The answers to these questions are intended to create awareness of *what is* as a means of looking at *what can be*. Your answers are not an evaluative statement of your effectiveness. Some of your answers may make you feel proud. Some may make you feel sorry. These are not the intended results. The intended result is to *create awareness of what is* — no shame, no blame. The intended result is to *create awareness of your current reality*, much as you created awareness of your organization's current reality by using the Cycle of Change model in Chapter Two.

Now go back over the six questions and ask yourself what influence you would like to have in the areas they delineate. List your answers. As you look over your responses, ask yourself these questions and write down your answers.

- What is the gap between your current level of influence and that which you want to create?
- What supports and what thwarts your having the influence you wish to create? Ask yourself, "How do I hold myself back?"

Change is not easy. Even the smallest change is difficult. There are many ways to demonstrate this. Fold your arms. Now fold them the opposite way. Or write your name with the hand you normally use to write and time how long it takes. Now write your name with the opposite hand. Try to match as closely as possible the way your signature is written by your other hand and time your effort. What did you experience in doing these two tasks? Every time we ask ourselves or others to change, we go through this process. It is a process of unlearning and relearning, of moving from comfort to discomfort to a renewed sense of comfort. It is a process of letting go of *what is* to strive for and achieve *what might be.* It is a process of moving out of the structures we know—*form*—through a sense of loss and a simultaneous need for certainty—*fear*—to the achievement of total system enhancement—*renewal.* It is a process of going through our own change cycle, from *status quo* through *denial* to *confusion,* to *invention,* and on to *renewal.* It is a process that includes *holding on, letting go,* and *moving on.* Carol Pearson puts it this way: "Making a choice in a situation . . . helps me define what is important to me at the time and hence to know more about who I am. In that sense, I win whichever way I choose, if I choose honestly and not out of a sense of what I ought to do. The world outside mirrors our world inside. When I change my inner world, the outer one changes as well" (1986, pp. 109, 135). On a similar note, Joseph Campbell said: "[be not a] champion of things but of things becoming. The dragon to be slain is precisely the monster of status quo" (1970, p. 12).

Whenever you lead change in the processes of how you (as a system) produce, you lead change in the way the organization is run. Systemic patterns of behavior begin at an individual level—the level of leading and following—and are mirrored in the organizational level of system.

THE TRANSITION TO INVENTIVE ORGANIZATIONS: CRITICAL ASPECTS OF LEADING AND FOLLOWING

There is an old saying that if we do not know where we are going, any road will get us there. My paraphrase is that if we do not know where we are, how can we see where we might go? This book was written to help us see where we are and to help us use the six frameworks for invention to focus on our organization's current reality and desired future state.

The *transition* from fear (a focus on self) to form (a focus on structure) to invention (service and support to the entire system) begins with us. Transition begins with a pull toward opportunities that is stronger than an avoidance of what might be frightening to even imagine. Transition is anchored in our personal integrity—in living out the truth we know. Transition is nurtured by the value of partnership and honed by our courage to test and retest our underlying assumptions. Transition is ignited by our need to create *what can be*—a need that is more intense than the need to simply respond to *what is*. Transition is a passage that is undertaken because to do otherwise is to neglect our highest potential and our aspirations to contribute meaningfully in our lifetime.

In her book *The Hero Within*, Carol Pearson writes, "As we change, reality changes too. The more we have the courage to be ourselves, the more chance we have of living in communities that fit for us" (1986, p. 153). This quote speaks to the need to experiment—to create safe emergencies for ourselves to act in ways that live out the truth we know and to create an organization of our own choosing. To effect change, each of us has to commit to lead that change. To lead in an inventive organization is to guide the development of the system and lead change through participation and involvement. To follow in an inventive organization is to manage self and interactions with others in pursuit of common cause.

A Commitment Sheet is a tool that can help us identify the commitments we must make if we are to complete this transition from where we are to where we want to be. (See Exhibit 13.1.) Once completed, this sheet should be placed where you will see it every day to remind yourself of what you are working toward. When the commitments are met, look again at where you are and where you want to be. You have just driven another mile of road. To chart your course for the next mile, complete another Commitment Sheet.

Exhibit 13.1. Commitment Sheet.

My contribution to the current reality: _____
_____
_____
_____

My values—how I want to relate to my end users, internal customers, work associates, and the work itself:

Values   *Actions that live out the value*

_____   _____
_____   _____
_____   _____
_____   _____
_____   _____

Commitments I want to make (A commitment can be an experiment, a safe emergency.):

I will let go of _____
_____
_____

I will hold on to _____
_____
_____

I will move on to _____
_____
_____
_____

14

Looking to the Future:
Hope and Daring at Work

When I began to explore writing this book with my editor, Bill Hicks, he suggested that the last chapter contain my contemplations on the future of leading and following in inventive organizations and the value of my transition models. As I begin to write this last chapter, what strikes me is that there is no last chapter to write when it comes to leading and following. This book simply marks a milestone in the evolution of how we have thought about the acts of leading and following and how we might think about them. This book marks a mile of road built and driven. My hope is we will continue the process of building and driving a mile of road at a time—that we will continue to illuminate and test our entrenched assumptions about the acts of leading and following that create our organizations.

In thinking about the future, what stands out for me is that uncertainty is a permanent condition. It has always been so, even though it is human nature to diminish uncertainty when we view our experience in retrospect. Individually and collectively, we face uncertainty needing a sense of support and control. What is certain is that we are challenged to "weather" uncertainty just to survive. To prevail, we are challenged, in the face of uncertainty, to hope and to dare.

This chapter is divided into several sections, each of which contains what we can expect to happen in the last decade of this century, what we must dare if we do not want to be at risk, and what I hope will come true.

LEADING AND FOLLOWING

We can expect to continue to be challenged to view leading and following as actions rather than as specific roles. Formal roles as we know them will continue to change as we flatten our organizational hierarchies. This flattening will cause us to rethink a cherished organizational norm: to get ahead, we must climb the corporate ladder. The value on climbing a corporate ladder will be replaced with a value on building capacity and corporate community. To build both, we will be required to attend to a different kind of career development— one that zigs and zags through lateral moves to gain as much exposure as possible to the whole system. These zigs and zags will broaden our abilities to "see the big picture" and to "work the big picture."

A value on broadening will replace the old value on being a fast tracker—of climbing a steep hierarchy through a narrow technical expertise. When we climb fast through our narrow technical expertise, we serve no one in the long run, particularly ourselves. Our lack of exposure limits our vision and, thereby, our ability to achieve our highest potential. As fast trackers, we have to fall and little to fall back on because we do not have the time to develop ourselves in any one place in the organization or to hone our abilities to serve and support the entire system. When we climb too fast, we know that there is much we do not know and much that we cannot admit to not knowing. This leads us to be driven by fear and form, not service and support to the entire system.

Further, when we have narrow technical expertise, we

run the risk of having all of our eggs in the wrong basket. How many people in the last five years have had the ability to recover the positions they lost when their industries have been devastated? If we are to create long-term viability for ourselves and our organizations, we will have to acquire broad business skills, broad business knowledge, and a systems perspective. We will need to understand the dynamics of change and the linkages required to support the whole system—the dynamic series of relationships in action.

In the next decade, we will slowly replace steep organizational hierarchies with organizational clusters. These clusters will require leadership and followership as a set of values, traits, and skills that can be formally anointed or informally rotated among many. In essence, leading and following will be part of everyone's job. The models for leading and following in transition (Chapter Nine through Twelve) are an attempt to capture the essential skills we need to transition from our old roles of controlling and being controlled to self-regulation. I call these "transition models" because they are the next steps we must take if we wish to create inventive organizations.

These models are about mind-sets, not about formal roles. They illuminate what we need to do to create partnership and trust in every organizational interaction—internally with work associates and externally with customers and suppliers. These models require us to change our underlying assumptions about structure and roles, people and skills, and boundaries of all sorts. They force us to question our values about work. They begin to erode some beliefs about rewards—what they are and how they should be distributed. And they demand that we rethink information flows, decision-making processes, the division of tasks and allocation of resources—including technology—as well as the built environment. Leading and following do not occur in a vacuum. They create and are created by the systems in which they flourish or flounder.

If we *dare* to use these models, we risk making them things. They can become the next box, a prescription to cure our present ills or at least help us address our current dilemmas.

These models are only a snapshot. They may replace our existing models; however, they also require that we give up our old paradigm for all time.

My *hope* is that we seek out, acknowledge, and anoint every act of leading and following in every endeavor that requires our commitment to being and doing our best to serve self and others in our places of work. I hope that leading and following become so much a part of who we are, regardless of our "station" in life, that these acts are no longer associated with any particular title or formal role.

It is hard for us to let go of the power of titles—the intrinsic reward—we worked hard to achieve. If this were not so, we could live in a world that better honors the dignity and worth of each of us; we would no longer value people because of their titles nor would we believe that leaders are "one up" and followers are "one down." Not viewing our relationship as "one up, one down" allows us to act with greater awareness of, and responsibility for, creating new work and world communities—communities of respect, mutuality, interdependence, and partnership.

INVENTION

In the next decade, we can *expect* that, as customers, we will have more opportunities to serve ourselves through (1) technology, such as automated teller and ticketing machines, (2) information, such as that provided on over-the-counter medicine, which promotes self-prescription, and (3) products, such as personal blood pressure equipment, that enable us to monitor our own health. More "after sale" features will be available to consumers, such as twenty-four-hour 800 numbers for customer help desks. More personalized production and therefore greater choice in consumer goods and services will be possible.

At the same time, we can expect more smart products and user-friendly technology. In many ways, tomorrow's inventive technology will be based on a back-to-the-future mentality—using high-tech computer chips to create low-tech operating know-how, such as one-button remote programmers for video-cassette recorders, computerized writing pads that read hand-writing, or two-button radios that deliver "best sound" and volume control. There will be more invention around fewer conversion processes—voice-activated computers instead of ones that require types input and knowledge of software use.

There will be more and more demand for quality that creates greater product longevity and fewer service requirements over the product's life. The need for longevity, or re-pairability—as in the case of many small appliances—will be fueled by environmental realities that will force us to abandon our proclivity for disposable goods.

If we are to be inventive, we must dare to get out of the box of our current thinking and to keep on getting out of the successive boxes we create. One Japanese automaker's ad reads, "Forget everything you've heard about Acura Legend—our engineers did." When we make our existing advantages obsolete, we fuel invention. It is a mind-set the Japanese call *miryo kenteki kinshitsu*, which means "things gone right." It is beyond defect free. It means to delight and surprise customers.

To be inventive, we must change our notions about learning and failure. Learning requires experimentation. To achieve success, we must also risk failure. This means we have an obligation to make mistakes. We are at risk if we do not let go of doing only that which feels safe. We must risk testing new assumptions, trying new ways, testing our boundaries, and going beyond self-imposed limits. We are at risk if we do not recognize and reward efforts intended to create improvement as well as outcomes that were desired. And we are at risk if we do not redefine creativity and invention. Our current definitions are too narrow.

I hope that we will ask "why not" more often than we ask "why," and that we will act only in ways that add value to our products, our services, our processes, our lives, and our planet. We need to invest more than we reap so that we can continue to sow the seeds for new growth and betterment for everyone. We need to invest in our plants and equipment, in people and education, and in the infrastructure that support our abilities to continuously improve and invent. And to do all of this well, we need to fund ourselves out of our savings instead of our debt.

I also hope that we redefine creativity and invention so that these are not synonymous with Michelangelo and patents—that we will be able to see invention as the application of something intended for one use to another use. We need to see creativity in efforts to break the norms and rules associated with our current comfort zones, and we need to honor this creativity by making visible and rewarding the wisdom that is hidden when we avoid criticism by surreptitiously circumventing "barnacles" in our systems. To do otherwise is to ignore the invention, creativity, and wisdom that will ensure the viability of our enterprises.

CUSTOMER NEEDS AND WANTS

In the future, we can *expect* more research into how products fit into our lives and greater awareness of *kansei* engineering— consideration for the reason and emotions that create consumption—so that products and services will be engineered to meet both. Products made in one country will be more localized to the needs of the consuming country; for example, colors of cars made in Japan and colors of furniture fabrics made in Norway are not the colors of choice in the United States. As customers, we will expect more personalized products and services and we will desire products that enable us to be self-reliant. We also will expect flexible choices—different service levels for different pocketbooks and needs— regardless of whether our buying power is that of an individual consumer, a corporation, or an importing country.

We can also expect that direct attention to customer satisfaction will increase. More and more, we will be called by people from the company that provides the product or service. We can expect continuing attention to the customer after a sale is made because it is far more costly to obtain new customers than to retain old ones.

Simultaneously, we can expect companies to develop more awareness about which efforts provide service and which efforts wind up disturbing the customer. For example, as a frequent hotel guest, I often am disturbed by unexpected knocking on my hotel door when what I seek is the sanctuary of my room after a long day with a client. These interruptions are well intended. Do I want fresh linen, my bed turned down, mineral water, chocolates, a card announcing the next day's weather? Sometimes the room is simply being checked for a reason called "occupancy." Too much service is as bad as too little service. Customers will increasingly be asked to choose the level of service they would prefer and will increasingly be treated as individuals, as opposed to an undifferentiated mass.

To exceed customer requirements, we must *dare* to ensure that people who serve the customer have the support and control to do so. We are at risk if we do not find the balance in creating and offering different levels of service while making the knowledge and selection of choices easy. Customers should not have to learn our business to take advantage of what we offer. We are at risk if we do not find ways to develop more and different ways to learn and track customer preferences so that these preferences do not have to be restated. Catalog coding is a good example of information that helps the company to evaluate marketing strategies and inventory levels, but it does not provide enough retained information about a repeat customer that the customer need only to order and verify a product rather than provide detailed account information.

We also are at risk if we do not develop people and systems that are flexible and can handle the complexities of offering, tracking, and billing for different levels of service, without making choices complex and time-consuming for the customer. And we are at risk when we overuse technology, such as automated telephone ordering and call directing equipment, which delay rather than speed up the time it takes to reach the person called or complete the transaction.

I *hope* that customers will have broad access to goods and services without becoming pagans of consumption. Broad access does not have to mean we homogenize society. In the United States, we have sacrificed our regional differences by cloning shopping malls and franchising retail outlets for food and material goods. While people need to be free to produce and consume in a world economy, I hope the world retains and preserves its unique cultures so that we do not lose the richness of diversity. It is diversity that fuels invention and makes a better life possible for all.

CORE WORK

We can *expect* to see more turbulence inside organizations; efforts to achieve control over this turbulence will increase and will often add to it. The painful lessons of trying to adapt to external chaos are learned slowly. Peter Senge writes, "What we need to control is not outside events or others . . . we need to address chaos by focusing on integrating the system at all levels" (1990, p. 81). Before this is truly learned, we can expect more alphabet soup—a lack of systemic thinking in the implementation of programs and initiatives designed to streamline work and improve production and service—particularly as we continue to compound exponentially the seemingly unlimited possibilities for new technologies. This turbulence must ease if people and organizations are to thrive in a global economy. We will have to get smarter about what constitutes the essential work that meets or exceeds customer requirements, and we will have to challenge the status quo of policies, procedures, practices, and our underlying assumptions to sort out what we need to stop doing, start doing, and continue doing.

When it comes to technology, we can *expect* to feel both blessed and cursed. Technology will continue to impact managerial practices as people who are geographically and functionally dispersed are linked and integrated electronically. Electronic infrastructures create the possibilities for greater independence and a simultaneous yet less visible need for stronger interdependence. Machines and people are only one form of organizational relationship — a form that will never replace relationships between people. Technology also creates the potential and subsequent demands for faster response time, thereby exacerbating our preoccupation with speed and our need to pack as much as possible into the least amount of time.

Further, technology reduces the need for people who can be replaced by machines, while it increases the need for people skilled in monitoring and repairing machinery. We have yet to systemically address how to support the transition of people whose skills are replaced by machines to new means of gainful employment. If we do not meet this challenge, we will exacerbate the problems of homelessness, hopelessness, and all the ills attendant on being dependent on others for basic human needs.

Technology creates greater potential for lower costs and increased profits in the forms of speed to market and reduced cycle time, while it creates greater risk of more costs due to replacement of expensive worn-out parts and time consumed in complex repairs. Finally, technology can evolve so quickly as to make consumers feel robbed rather than rewarded when they purchase equipment that is obsolete and valueless before all of its features can be learned and used or when technical support is eliminated because such support is offered with only the newest models.

If we are to streamline our organizations, we must *dare* to think and act systemically. Systemic thinking about core work includes finding ways to add value to stakeholders, employees, suppliers, and customers as we address the duality of what is gained and what is lost in every organizational decision that is made and every action that is taken.

I *hope* that our definition of core work will expand to include a sense of responsibility for the whole—from the inception of the idea for the product or service to the use of that product or service. If we define core work as essential work, then what is essential is every aspect of the system that creates the whole—suppliers, customers, work associates, and stakeholders. To have responsibility for the whole, those who do the work must have contact with those who are served by the work in ways that enhance partnership and accountability for the whole. I also hope that everyone experiences the joy and satisfaction of knowing that what they do is meaningful and purposeful—for self and others—no matter the tasks to be performed or the technology employed. My hope is that our "activities and endeavors are so compelling, so gripping and absorbing, so satisfying, that [we undertake them] for the sheer pleasure of it"—to borrow a phrase from Mihaly Csikszentmihalyi.

SYSTEMS THINKING
AND INTERDEPENDENCE

We can *expect* to experience more turbulence at every level of system—individually, interpersonally, within groups, in our organizations and communities, and societally. As individuals, we will experience more stress and uncertainty if we continue to spend too many hours in workplaces we can no longer rely on to take care of us. We will experience more stress and turbulence in our simultaneous needs to balance our personal and professional lives, provide for our elders, our children, and ourselves, and to have more individual flexibility along with a stronger sense of community, which continues to erode as we become more mobile, engage more and more with technology, and create living conditions in which we can work at home and have the world brought to us electronically.

In our organizations, we can expect continued lack of

alignment between espoused and practiced values, between our efforts to improve quality throughout the entire operation and the simultaneous lack of quality in planning how these programs can be implemented to reduce rather than enhance the chaotic and out-of-control conditions they are designed to correct. Societally, we will experience continued repercussions from the 1980s and early 1990s, during which our economic future was bartered for immediate gain and image and packaging created a false sense of reality by helping us to cover up what is real.

This increased turbulence will result in an increased need to think systemically about how our individual realities are mirrored in society and vice versa. We will be challenged to see the connection between individual actions and collective outcomes and, thereby, we will be challenged to create more interdependence rather than more independence — to find our common cause and not just recognize and respect our diversity.

In our organizations, we will be challenged to use our strategies to develop our structures and reflect our values. Our structures, which must support our strategies, will inevitably include some form of hierarchy and be based on boundaries drawn to enhance service and support to the entire system rather than boundaries drawn to protect individuals and turf. Our structures will include strategic alliances that will create more interdependence and the possibilities for unbundling and reassembling current systems of production and service. And we will place greater emphasis on organizational values because shared values and goals are what hold increasingly dispersed operations together.

In terms of managing new structures and dispersed operations, we can expect successful CEOs will be those who focus on linkages, boundaries, and exchanges across boundaries that bring the right people together at the right time with the right resources to act in behalf of common cause. They will be aware of the need to operate globally and manage locally, sensitive to the values and underlying assumptions of different countries and cultures, and not lump countries and people into regions, such as Asia-Pacific, Europe, or Latin America, which are anything but homogeneous. They will ensure the development of electronic infrastructures to support exchanges across boundaries, without substituting technology for personal interactions that build the relationships we call organizations.

In terms of managing commitments and payoffs, we can expect to see more systemic views of reward mechanisms — gainsharing, in particular. Employees, regardless of their jobs, will have their pay aligned with the outcomes of the enterprise — so that they share in the gains and participate in the consequences of a loss. People cannot be divorced from corporate results and corporate results cannot continue to be divorced from the collective commitments and efforts that create the enterprise.

Individually, we must dare to use technology to work less, not more — to value home, community, and health along with work and financial well-being. We are at risk when the faster we go, the faster we go. Twelve-hour workdays and weekends at work do not create job stability anymore than making the "boss look good." When we sacrifice time with family and friends in pursuit of organizational fame, we often find the results to be temporal and the rewards hollow.

Organizationally, we must dare to create partnerships in all aspects of our operations if we are to enhance our ability to address the continuous uncertainty of our times. We must act on the recognition that everyone in the system creates the system; there is no hierarchy when it comes to problem solving, creating futures, and seeking continuous improvement. When we create strong linkages between product designers, machine operators, and parts suppliers, we enable ourselves to surpass customer requirements. And when we create equity in the enterprise for everyone involved in the enterprise, we create shared commitment and accountability for the results of our collective endeavors.

Societally, we must dare to think of others as ourselves. We are at risk if we do not give up our old notions about individuality, if we continue to believe that someone can win when everyone else loses or that anyone really gets ahead when to do so means others fall further and further behind. We risk bankrupting our communities when we do not understand that every closing of a plant, every liquidation of a business, every leveraged buyout that creates organizational debt and depletes organizational assets will ultimately debilitate individuals, towns, cities, states, and the entire infrastructure of society.

I *hope* that as individuals we come to understand that our preservation is in our interdependence. There are more demands on us individually than we can address individually; therefore, we cannot perpetuate our well-being until we simultaneously honor commonality, diversity, and pluralism—until we act in ways that simultaneously respect the "I," the "We," and the "Us."

Organizationally, I hope that production does not begin or end in manufacturing and distributing products—that there is support after the product is sold, that there is concern for the ecology out of which every product or service is born, and that there is value added to the planet in the use and disposition of goods and services. And I hope that technology is used to only support relationships that are forged outside of technology.

Societally, I hope that we become a true community of nations without forsaking the richness of our diversity, and that as a community of nations, we are linked through a set of values that ensure the preservation and enhancement of our world.

SELF-REGULATION

We can *expect* that the dismantling of hierarchies as we now know them will be painful and slow, and that the belief that information is power will be hard to abandon. We can also expect to see newer forms of organization, increased sharing of information within all levels of the system, better defined measurement criteria, fewer restrictions on creativity, and more minimum critical specifications that support people understanding, influencing, working within, and controlling the economic, technical, and human aspects of the system as well as its built environment.

We must *dare* to believe that our survival is in our own hands. We are at risk if we do not abandon our attraction to dependency. We are at risk if we do not let go of the false status of the old paradigm, control and caretaking of the many by the few. We are at risk if we do not abandon the illusion of control as anything other than self-control and caretaking as anything other than serving self and others. It may be comforting to believe that someone is in control of events and conditions, people and interactions; yet this is an illusion. The only real control is for everyone to exercise their own self-control—to be self-regulating based on the knowledge that we are all, ultimately, interdependent. We are at risk if we do not eliminate bureaucracy because bureaucracy is based on fear—fear that people cannot act in service to themselves and others. Bureaucracy not only stifles invention and creates a false sense of control, bureaucracy is actually the evidence that control does not exist.

I *hope* that we create support and control at every level of the system, and that we act interdependently to build individual strength, organizational unity, and worldwide community through interactions that accord dignity and worth to all.

VALUES

We can *expect* to experience enormous difficulties in walking our talk, in living out the values we espouse as we relate to our customers, our work associates, and our work itself. We can also expect that because we are able to articulate these values, that we will continue to strive to live out the truth we know. We can expect to see more person-centered, rather than authority-centered, institutions, more circles and clusters than steep hierarchies, less focus on immediate rewards and more focus on the long-term implications of our actions. We can also expect to see more focus on what we bring to our communities and less focus on taking care of ourselves at the expense of our communities.

We must *dare* to live our values because we believe in them, not because we can manipulate others into achieving a desired outcome. As I write this last chapter, I am saddened to see the Malcolm Baldrige National Award for Quality become an end in and of itself. This Award was designed to "recognize U.S. companies that excel in quality achievement and quality management." Today, many companies have a new goal: win the Baldrige Award—instead of provide service and products that meet or exceed customer requirements while we live out our organizational values. A CEO of a large high-tech company reorganized his corporation and replaced senior level executives because his company did not receive the 1990 award. His edict: "Win within the next five years." This is a very extreme example of valuing the "thing" and not valuing the value. The award should be an acknowledgement of things gone right. Things should not be designed to win the award.

My *hope* is that we will live out the truth we know and not what is expedient or self-serving in the moment. I hope we strengthen our moral fiber and our ethical foundations so that we nourish our souls, our institutions, our communities, and the whole of humankind. I hope we learn to value one another ahead of financial gain, strategic advantage, and technological excellence, and that we measure ourselves by the content of our deeds and not simply the outcomes of our efforts. Most important, I hope we find alternatives to an economy based on endless consumption and societies based on the worship of materialism because to do otherwise is to condemn ourselves to spiritual poverty.

Much of my hope is found in the operating guidelines developed by the Implementation Steering Committee for a consumer products company that makes household cleaning products. This committee, which includes the plant manager, some business unit coordinators, and many work associates (employees) who represent the entire system, is facilitating the implementation of the plant's work redesign. These are their guidelines:

1. Maintain or enhance self-esteem.
2. Listen and respond with empathy
3. Ask for help when solving the problem.
4. Use the foregoing three principles when calling each other on violations of our guidelines with the intent to do better.
5. Deal with ideas and not personalities.
6. One person speak at a time. Meeting facilitator to assure this.
7. Always have an inclusion check on all decisions.
8. Be on time.
9. Helicopter rule.
10. Challenge each other to be open-minded.
11. "I think we can" clause.
12. Prompt multimedia communication to plant about business conducted at our meetings.
13. Be honest, straightforward, and to the point.
14. Have a sense of humor.

Their "helicopter rule" requires a special note. During the design phase, the metaphor of being up in a helicopter was used to reinforce how to maintain a focus on the entire system and not just on the various parts of the system. Sometimes design team members would say, "Oops, I just fell out of the helicopter." This guideline was adopted by the Implementation Steering Committee and, *together with its other guidelines, the ISC is maintaining a focus on all levels of the system — the individual level, the group level, and the plant level.*

HOPE AND DARE:
A FINAL COMMENT

"Albert Camus once wrote, 'Do not stand before me for I may not wish to follow. And do not stand behind me for I may not wish to lead — but stand beside me and be my friend and let us go forward together.' There are not a sufficient number of extraordinary people to build great companies. Fine companies must be the construct of relatively ordinary folks. In the conventional world, people want to know whether the followers have faith in the leaders. I'd rather know whether the leaders have faith in the followers. That is because I believe, that if we are to optimize our potential, the faith must begin with us" (Federman, 1992, p. 60).

Epilogue

During the writing of this book, my mentor, Dr. Maurice Mann, died of a massive heart attack at age sixty-one. His unexpected and untimely death has resulted in a deep loss for many people.

I have often called Maury Mann the "father of my career." He selected me to head up Human Resources at The Federal Home Loan Bank in 1976 when I was thirty-three years old and, in my father's euphemism, "still wet behind the ears." Maury selected me over many more experienced and older male candidates for a job that was, at that time, five years ahead of my resumé. I became the first woman officer of the bank, I was a member of the senior management committee, and I met monthly with the Board of Directors. Suddenly, the last of the corporate doors had opened for me. And in the years I worked for Maury at the bank, and in later years when I consulted to him when he was Chairman and CEO of the Pacific Stock Exchange, I had the great fortune to be inspired by this man — a man of deep principles, vision, and values — one who acted in service and support of the entire system.

Maury Mann's achievements are impressive. His career spanned the public, quasi-private, and private sectors. His

Doctorate in Economics from Syracuse University led to his becoming Vice President and Chief Economist for the Federal Reserve Bank of Cleveland and later Assistant Director of the Office of Management and Budgets. After leaving the bank, he joined Warburg Paribus & Becker, which later became Merrill Lynch Capital Markets, where he served as Vice Chairman. Almost ten years later, with a longing to leave behind the world of sole operative and once again "run something," Maury became Chairman and CEO of the Pacific Stock Exchange.

It is not the titles of his positions that make him memorable. It is his values, dedication, and aspirations. They are his legacy. As a leader, Maury also knew how to follow. He led those of us who worked with him to discover our own abilities to lead as well as follow. And in partnership with others, he honed, coordinated, and followed the collective wisdom in the systems he led, and by so doing, he created continuously renewing organizations in which everyone acted in service and support of the whole.

As I end this book, I revisit my dedication:

For Ted
and the next generation—
for whom leading and following
are in everyone's domain

As I reflect on the experiences that led me to write, I remember and honor Maury Mann. Having known him, I can look back and see the future.

> *But such was the preponderance of this man,*
> *who had not so much ruled as weighed down*
> *on his people and stamped them with his massive*
> *imprint, that when we lowered him into the grave*
> *we seemed not to be burying our dead, but laying*
> *a foundation stone. Thus we did not inter him but*
> *sealed him in the earth, now that he had become*
> *what he was evermore to be . . . our bedrock.*

> *—Antoine de Saint-Exupéry,* The Wisdom of the Sands

Inspirations: A Bibliography of Sources

Ackerman Anderson, L. S. "Managing in the Flow State." *Being First,* 1990 (entire issue).

Autry, J. A. *Love and Profit: The Art of Caring Leadership.* New York: William Morrow, 1991.

Badaracco, J. L., Jr., and Ellsworth, R. R. *Leadership and the Quest for Integrity.* Boston, Mass.: Harvard Business School Press, 1989.

Bellman, G. M. *The Consultant's Calling: Bringing Who You Are to What You Do.* San Francisco: Jossey-Bass, 1990.

Bellman, G. M. *Getting Things Done When You Are Not in Charge.* San Francisco: Berrett-Koehler, 1992.

Berenson, D. "Spirituality." Address given at Family Networker Conference, Washington, D.C., Feb. 1989.

Block, P. *The Empowered Manager: Positive Political Skills at Work.* San Francisco: Jossey-Bass, 1987.

Block, P. *Stewardship.* San Francisco: Berrett-Koehler, 1993.

Bolman, L. G., and Deal, T. E. *Reframing Organizations: Artistry, Choice, and Leadership.* San Francisco: Jossey-Bass, 1991.

Bounton, A. C., and Victor, B. "Beyond Flexibility." *California Management Review,* Fall 1991, pp. 53–66.

377

Campbell, J. *Hero with a Thousand Faces.* New York: World, 1970.

Carlsen, M. B. *Meaning Making: Therapeutic Processes in Adult Development.* New York: Norton, 1988.

Carlzon, J. *Moments of Truth.* New York: Ballinger, 1987.

Cohen, A. R., and Bradford, D. L. *Influence Without Authority.* New York: Wiley, 1990.

Cole, R. E., Bacdavan, P., and White, J. B. "Quality Participation and Competitiveness." *California Management Review,* 1993, 35(3), 73.

Conger, J. "Inspiring Others: The Language of Leadership." *Academy of Management Executive,* 1991, 5(1), 31.

"Compete?" *Business Week,* Dec. 17, 1990, pp. 61–93.

Csikszentmihalyi, M. *Flow: The Psychology of Optimal Experience.* New York: HarperCollins, 1990.

Davis, S. M. *Future Perfect.* Reading, Mass.: Addison-Wesley, 1987.

DePree, M. *Leadership Is an Art.* New York: Doubleday, 1989.

Drath, W. H. *Why Managers Have Trouble Empowering: A Theoretical Perspective Based on Concepts of Adult Development.* Greensboro, N.C.: Center for Creative Leadership, 1993.

Dumaine, B. "The Bureaucracy Busters." *Fortune,* June 17, 1991, pp. 35–50.

Einstein, A. "The Technology Opportunity." *Labor Relations Today,* July/Aug. 1990, pp. 1–2.

Elsass, P. M. "The Paradox of Success: Too Much of a Good Thing." *Academy of Management Executive,* 1993, 7(3), 84–85.

Faithorn, L. "Three Ways of Seeing." *Vision/Action,* 1990, 9(4), 13–17.

Federman, I. "Can Turnaround Be This Simple?" *Journal of Management Inquiry,* Mar. 1992, pp. 57–60.

Freeman, J. "Making Sense of Abundance." *Burning Bright,* 1989, 2(6), 1–2.

Frey, D. "First Person—Learning the Ropes: My Life as a Product Champion." *Harvard Business Review,* Sept.–Oct. 1991, pp. 46, 52.

Fritz, R. *The Path of Least Resistance*. Salem, Mass.: Stillpoint, 1984.

Fritz, R. *Creating*. New York: Random House, 1991.

Galagan, P. A. "David T. Kearns: A CEO's View of Training." *Training & Development Journal*, May 1990, pp. 41–50.

Gibb, P. "The Joy of Community and Then Some." *Vision/Action*, Sept. 1989, pp. 1–3.

Gillette, J., and McCollom, M. *Groups in Context: A New Perspective on Group Dynamics*. Reading, Mass.: Addison-Wesley, 1990.

Goldratt, E. M. *Theory of Constraints*. Croton-on-Hudson, New York: North River Press, 1990.

Goldratt, E. M., and Cox, J. *The Goal*. Croton-on-Hudson, New York: North River Press, 1986.

Hamper, B. *Rivethead: Tales from the Assembly Line*. New York: Warner Books, 1986.

Harman, W. *Global Mind Change*. Indianapolis: Knowledge Systems Inc., 1988.

Harmon, R. L., and Peterson, L. D. *Reinventing the Factory*. New York: The Free Press, 1990.

Harvey, J. B. *The Abilene Paradox and Other Meditations on Management*. San Diego, Calif.: University Associates, 1988.

Heider, J. *The Tao of Leadership*. New York: Bantam Books, 1985.

Henkoff, R. "Make Your Office More Productive." *Fortune*, Feb. 25, 1991, pp. 72–84.

Hersey, P. *The Situational Leader*. New York: Warner Books, 1984.

Hill, R. C. "When the Going Gets Rough: A Baldrige Award Winner on the Line." *Academy of Management Executive*, 1993, 7(3), 75–79.

Kaplan, R. E. *Beyond Ambition: How Driven Managers Can Lead Better and Live Better*. San Francisco: Jossey-Bass, 1991.

Katz, D., and Kahn, R. L. *The Social Psychology of Organizations*. (2d ed.) New York: Wiley, 1978.

Kearns, D. T. "Kearns' View on Training." *Training & Development Journal*, May 1990, p. 42.

Kearns, D. T. "Leadership Through Quality." *Academy of Management Executive*, 1990, 4(2), 86–89.

Kelley, R. "In Praise of Followers." *Harvard Business Review*, Nov.-Dec. 1988, pp. 143–144.

Klingel, S., and Martin, A. *A Fighting Chance: New Strategies to Save Jobs and Reduce Costs*. New York: ILR Press, 1988.

Koestenbaum, P. *The Inner Side of Greatness*. San Francisco: Jossey-Bass, 1991.

Kolesar, P. "Vision, Values and Milestones: TQM at Alcoa." *California Management Review*, 1993, 35(3), 163–164.

Krantz, J. "Lessons from the Field." *Journal of Applied Behavioral Science*, 1990, 26(1), 52, 60, 61.

Langan, P. A. "How to Plan for 1995." *Fortune*, Dec. 31, 1990, pp. 70–78.

Levitt, T. *The Marketing Imagination*. New York: The Free Press, 1986.

McCall, M. W., Jr., and Lombardo, M. M. *Leadership: Where Else Can We Go?* Durham, N.C.: Duke University Press, 1978.

McClelland, D. C. *Power: The Inner Experience*. New York: Irvington, 1975.

McCollom, M. "Reevaluating Group Development: A Critique of the Familiar Models." In J. Gillette and M. McCollom (eds.), *Groups in Context: A New Perspective on Group Dynamics*. Reading, Mass.: Addison-Wesley, 1990.

McGrath, M. E., and Hoole, R. W. "Manufacturing's New Economies of Scale." *Harvard Business Review*, May-June 1992, pp. 94–97.

Mantz, C. C., and Sims, P., Jr. *Super-Leadership*. New York: Berkeley Books, 1990.

Mason, M. *Making Our Lives Our Own*. San Francisco: HarperCollins, 1991.

Milani, M. M., and Smith, B. R. *Beyond the Magic Circles: The Role of Intimacy in Business*. Unity, N.H.: Fainshaw, 1989.

Miller, S., Wackman, D., Nunnally, E., and Saline, C., *Straight Talk*. New York: Penguin, 1981.

Moffat, S. "Japan's New Personalized Production." *Fortune*, Oct. 22, 1990, pp. 132–135.

Moore, T. *Care of the Soul: A Guide for Cultivating Depth and Sacredness in Everyday Life.* New York: HarperCollins, 1992.

Morgan, G. *Images of Organizations.* Newbury Park, Calif.: Sage, 1986.

Morin, W. J. *Trust Me.* Orlando, Fla.: Harcourt Brace Jovanovich, 1990.

Morrison, A. M. *The New Leaders.* San Francisco: Jossey-Bass, 1992.

Myers, M. S. *Every Employee a Manager.* San Diego, Calif.: University Associates.

Nevis, E. C. *Organizational Consulting: A Gestalt Approach.* New York: Gardner Press, 1987.

Ohmae, K. *The Borderless World.* New York: Harper Business, 1990.

Overman, S. "Leader Helps Improve Competitiveness." *HR Magazine,* May 1990, pp. 58-60.

Palmer, P. *To Know as We Are Known: Spirituality of Education.* San Francisco: HarperCollins, 1983.

Patchen, K. *Hallelujah Anyway.* New York: New Directions, 1960.

Pearson, C. S. *The Hero Within: Six Archetypes We Live By.* San Francisco: HarperCollins, 1986.

Peters, T. *Thriving On Chaos.* New York: Knopf, 1987.

Peters, T., and Waterman, R. H. *In Search of Excellence.* HarperCollins, 1982.

Poole, P. P., Gioia, D. A., and Gray, B. "Influence Modes, Schema Change, and Organizational Transformation." *Journal of Applied Behavioral Science,* 1989, 25(3), 271-289.

Prahalad, C. K., and Hamel, G. "The Core Competence of the Corporation." *Harvard Business Review,* 1990, May-June, pp. 80-88.

Reid, P. C. *Well Made in America: Lessons from Harley-Davidson on Being the Best.* New York: McGraw-Hill, 1990.

Rummler, G. A., and Brache, A. P. *Improving Performance: How to Manage the White Space on the Organization Chart.* San Francisco: Jossey-Bass, 1991.

Saint-Exupéry, M.A.R. de. *The Wisdom of the Sands.* Orlando, Fla.: Harcourt Brace Jovanovich, 1950.

Savage, C. M. *Fifth Generation Management: Integrating Enterprises Through Human Networking.* New Bedford, Mass.: Digital Press, 1990.

Schmidt, W. H., and Finnegan, J. P. *The Race Without a Finish Line.* San Francisco: Jossey-Bass, 1992.

Seligman, M.E.P. *Learned Optimism.* New York: Pocket Books, 1990.

Senge, P. M. *The Fifth Discipline: The Art and Practice of the Learning Organization.* New York: Doubleday, 1990.

Shapiro, E. C. *How Corporate Truths Become Competitive Traps.* New York: Wiley, 1991.

Sherwood, J. J., and Glidewell, J. C. *Planned Negotiation: A Norm-Setting OD Intervention.* Alexandria, Va.: NTL Institute, 1972.

Sine, S. "Rethinking the Organization." *Enterprise,* Spring 1990, pp. 24–27.

Slater, P. *The Pursuit of Loneliness.* Boston, Mass.: Beacon Press, 1970.

Slater, P. *A Dream Deferred.* Boston, Mass.: Beacon Press, 1991.

Smith, B. R., and Milani, M. M. *Beyond the Magic Circle: The Role of Intimacy in Business.* Unity, N.H.: Fainshaw Press, 1989.

Stacey, R. D. *Managing the Unknowable: Strategic Boundaries Between Order and Chaos in Organizations.* San Francisco: Jossey-Bass, 1992.

Stata, R. "Organizational Learning: The Key to Management Innovation." *Sloan Management Review,* Spring 1989, pp. 63–74.

Steele, F. *The Role of the Internal Consultant.* Boston, Mass.: CBI Publishing, 1982.

Steele, S. *The Content of Our Character.* New York: St. Martin's Press, 1990.

Stewart, T. A. "New Ways to Exercise Power." *Fortune,* Nov. 6, 1989, pp. 52–64.

Stewart, T. A. "CEOs See Clout Shifting." *Fortune,* Nov. 6, 1989, p. 66.

Tichy, N., and Charan, R. "Speed, Simplicity, Self-Confidence: An Interview with Jack Welch." *Harvard Business Review,* Sept.–Oct. 1989, 111–120.

Toffler, A. "Powershift." *Newsweek,* Oct. 15, 1990, pp. 86–92.

Vaill, P. "Notes on Running an Organization." *Journal of Management Inquiry,* 1992, 1(2), 130–138.

van Wolferen, K. *The Enigma of Japanese Power.* New York: Knopf, 1989.

Vogel, T. "At Xerox, They're Shouting 'Once More into the Breach.'" *Business Week,* July 23, 1990, pp. 62–63.

von Hippel, E. *The Sources of Innovation.* New York: Oxford University Press, 1988.

Weaver, P. H. "Robert Reich's Fascinating Flip-Flop." *Fortune,* Mar. 25, 1991, p. 135.

Webber, A. M. "Consensus, Continuity, and Common Sense: An Interview with Compaq's Rod Canion." *Harvard Business Review,* July-Aug. 1990, pp. 115–123.

Weisbord, M. R. *Productive Workplaces: Organizing and Managing for Dignity, Meaning, and Community.* San Francisco: Jossey-Bass, 1987.

Weisbord, M. R. *Discovering Common Ground: Renewing Corporations and Communities Through Strategic Search Conferences.* San Francisco: Berrett-Koehler, 1992.

Welch, J., and others. "Today's Leaders Talk About Tomorrow." *Fortune,* Mar. 26, 1990 (entire issue).

Wheatley, M. J. *Leadership and the New Science.* San Francisco: Berrett-Koehler, 1992.

Wheeler, G. *Gestalt Reconsidered: A New Approach to Contact and Resistance.* New York: Gardner Press, 1991.

"Why Nobody Can Lead America." *Fortune,* Jan. 14, 1991, p. 44.

Zaleznik, A. "The Leadership Gap." *The Executive,* 1990, 4(1), 9, 12, 13.

Index